THE POLITICS OF EVALUATION

Participation and policy implementation

Edited by David Taylor and Susan Balloch

First published in Great Britain in January 2005 by

The Policy Press
University of Bristol
Fourth Floor
Beacon House
Queen's Road
Bristol BS8 1QU
UK

Tel +44 (0)117 331 4054
Fax +44 (0)117 331 4093
e-mail tpp-info@bristol.ac.uk
www.policypress.org.uk

British Library Cataloguing in Publication Data
A catalogue record for this book is available from the British Library.

Library of Congress Cataloging-in-Publication Data
A catalog record for this book has been requested.

ISBN 1 86134 605 0 paperback

A hardcover version of this book is also available

Cover design by Qube Design Associates, Bristol.
Printed and bound in Great Britain by MPG Books Ltd, Bodmin.

Contents

List of tables, figures and boxes

Tables

Figures

Boxes

Acknowledgements

We would like to express our appreciation to all who contributed to the Politics of Evaluation conference from which this book has been developed. In particular, we would like to thank our plenary speakers Paul Lawless, Jane Tunstill, Peter Beresford, Shulamit Ramon, Julia Warrener and John Gaventa, those who presented papers (of which a selection have been edited for this book) and our very responsive audience. We should also like to thank colleagues at the University of Brighton for their support, especially Visiting Professors Peter Ambrose and Michael Hill, conference administrator Sallie White, research officer Laura Banks and editorial assistant Caroline Hollingworth. This has been very much a collective endeavour, although the final responsibility rests with us as editors.

David Taylor and Susan Balloch
University of Brighton

Notes on contributors

Peter Ambrose read Geography at Kings College London and subsequently completed an MA at McGill University as a Commonwealth Scholar and a DPhil at the University of Sussex. He taught Geography, Urban Studies and Social Policy at the University of Sussex from 1965 until his retirement in 1998. He is now Visiting Professor in Housing Studies in the Health and Social Policy Research Centre at the University of Brighton. Peter has published seven books and over 150 other works. His recent research has focused on the relationship between poor housing and poor health.

Hilary Arksey joined the Social Policy Research Unit at the University of York as a research fellow in 1995. Her research interests are in the areas of informal care, employment and disability and qualitative research methods. Hilary has worked on a number of empirical studies looking at employment issues for carers and disabled people, and more recently has undertaken literature reviews of the effectiveness of services to support carers. She is the co-author of *Interviewing for social scientists: An introductory resource with examples* with Peter T. Knight (Sage Publications, 1999).

Susan Balloch is Professor of Health and Social Care at the University of Brighton. She is also Director of the Health and Social Policy Research Centre, which organised the Politics of Evaluation conference on which this book is based. Her main research interests include the social care workforce, partnership working, community profiling and social exclusion. She is the joint author of *Partnership working: Policy and practice* (2001) and *Social services: Working under pressure* (1999), both published by The Policy Press.

Peter Beresford is Professor of Social Policy and Director of the Centre for Citizen Participation at Brunel University. He is Chair of Shaping Our Lives, the national user-controlled organisation, a long-term user of mental health services, Visiting Fellow at the School of Social Work and Psycho-social Sciences, University of East Anglia and a Trustee of the Social Care Institute for Excellence.

Thilo Boeck started his career as a practitioner in Lima, Peru, in Youth and Community Development work. As a research fellow at the Centre for Social Action, De Montfort University, he has explored issues of social inclusion and participation, with a particular focus on the enhancement of social capital, within a national and international context. His current research uses social capital as a heuristic device for an exploration of community regeneration, health promotion and criminal justice with particular emphasis on the active participation of local people throughout the research process.

Helen Charnley is a Lecturer in Applied Social Studies at the University of Durham. Her research interests and publications cover a wide range of community-based interventions for users of health and social work services.

Glynis Cousin is a Senior Adviser at the Higher Education Academy where she works with a number of educational development projects in UK universities. She has taught and researched in schools, community and adult education as well as higher education. Her publications explore issues of diversity, managing change and action research.

Judith Cousin is a freelance consultant specialising in regeneration, building project and community capacity, project development and evaluations for the voluntary and statutory sectors. She is a tutor for Sussex University's Managing Voluntary and Community Organisations course delivering the social policy, strategic planning and monitoring and evaluation aspects of the course. Her current work is focused around implementing Project Cycle Management (PCM) within regeneration programmes and is currently supporting a large New Deal for Communities programme to set up PCM processes and procedures.

Frances Deepwell is Senior Lecturer in Educational Development in the Centre for Higher Education Development, Coventry University. Since 1998 she has worked extensively on the implementation of online learning across the university, including design and integration, administration, troubleshooting, staff development, evaluation and dissemination. She is currently involved in EU and national e-learning projects. Originally trained as a translator, Frances has over 10 years' experience in teaching using a wide range of evolving technologies, in community as well as university education.

Jennie Fleming is a Principal Lecturer in Research at DeMontfort University with considerable experience in youth and community work in both voluntary and statutory sectors. Since 1995, she has developed tools and methods of qualitative research and evaluation with community members and service users at the Centre for Social Action, De Montfort University. As lead researcher on a Health Development Agency-funded project, Jennie contributed to refining a social capital framework. She is currently using this framework in evaluating a Healthy Living Centre and an ESRC-funded research project, 'Young people, social capital and the negotiation of risk'.

Kay Graham completed a degree and PhD in Geography at the University of Sheffield. She has subsequently held a number of positions in the public sector. First, she worked for Surrey police in a research capacity, moving on to a similar role in the then Department for Education and Employment. Kay worked as Evaluation Manager at Nottingham New Deal for Communities programme until January 2003, when she moved back to the now Department for Education and Skills, working on policy for at-risk young people.

Lucy Grimshaw is a Research Associate in the Cities Research Centre at the University of the West of England, Bristol. Her research interests are urban regeneration, coordination of area-based initiatives, social inclusion and evaluation. She is currently working on the national evaluation of New Deal for Communities and the evaluation of Single Local Management Centres. She is also completing a PhD on Gender and Regeneration in the UK and Spain.

Amanda Harris completed a degree in European Social Policy at Anglia Polytechnic University and an MA degree in Social Science Research Methods at Nottingham Trent University. She first became involved in Nottingham's New Deal for Communities programme as a local resident, and has subsequently held a number of positions within the organisation. First, she worked as an outreach worker for a grants fund, then as a research assistant responsible for Health Impact Assessment, and more recently as Research and Evaluation Officer.

Karin Janzon trained as a social worker in Sweden and, following an MSc in Social Research, moved into research, policy development and planning, working for 20 years in local authorities in London and the South East. As an independent consultant, she undertakes research, performance assessment, policy development work and training for the Department of Health, local authorities, health agencies and voluntary organisations. She also works in partnership with the University of Brighton, where she recently contributed to a series of projects to support community planning.

Stella Law trained originally as a research scientist, working for many years in cutting-edge astrophysics research. She subsequently moved into operational research in the Civil Service, where she spent five years in the Economics and Operational Research Division of the Department of Health. As an independent consultant, she has undertaken a range of projects for the Department of Health, local and health authorities and voluntary organisations, particularly in the areas of needs assessment, evaluation and research and analysis, including a range of community development projects in partnership with the University of Brighton.

Audrey Leathard is a Visiting Professor of Interprofessional Studies at South Bank University. She has specialised in furthering partnership working between health and social services as a board member of both the UK Centre for Interprofessional Education (CAIPE) and, until 2002, of the *Journal of Interprofessional Care*, together with editing issues on discrimination, the spiritual and pastoral dimensions, as well as on ethics and inter-professional care. In

1994, her edited publication, *Going inter-professional: Working together for health and welfare*, was published by Routledge. A new edition has just been published by Brunner Routledge, entitled *Interprofessional collaboration: From policy to practice in health and social care* (2003). In 1990, her book, *Health care provision: Past, present and into the 21st century* (with Stanley Thornes), also presented a major update on the wider developments in this field.

Lynda Measor is a Reader in Applied Social Science in the School of Applied Social Sciences at the University of Brighton. After completing undergraduate and postgraduate work at the University of Sussex, she taught at the University of Zaria in northern Nigeria for two years and then was a Research Fellow at the Open University until taking up a post at the University of Brighton. She has research interests in criminology, education and gender, and has recently published books on juvenile nuisance and on young people's views of sex education.

Georgie Parry-Crooke is a Senior Lecturer in Social Sciences at London Metropolitan University, where she has been responsible for the design and delivery of postgraduate programmes in social research and evaluation. Georgie has conducted a variety of evaluation and research studies in the fields of health, mental health and homelessness, many of which have focused on the health of women. In 1999, she was elected to the Academy of Learned Societies in the Social Sciences and is a former member of the UK Evaluation Society Council.

Alison Penn is an independent researcher in health, social care and community development. This has included evaluation research into homelessness, health sector capacity planning, community health projects, master planning for New Deal in East Brighton, labour market research into homecare in Brighton and local and national research into the needs of young people. She graduated with a DPhil from Sussex University in social history on 'National-local relations in voluntary organisations in the post-war period'. Alison is currently researching social history into the St Michael's Fellowship, a provider of care for unmarried mothers since the early 1900s.

Hazel Platzer is an independent research consultant and a Visiting Lecturer at the University of Brighton. Prior to this she held teaching posts in nursing and health studies for over 10 years and has a background in general and psychiatric nursing. As an academic researcher and freelance consultant, she has conducted a number of studies investigating service users' experiences of health care and has evaluated several advocacy projects in the voluntary sector.

Debi Roker is one of two Assistant Directors at the Trust for the Study of Adolescence (TSA), an independent applied research and training organisation, where Debi manages the research programme. She has been involved in applied youth research since 1985. Debi is passionate about research and its potential to improve young people's lives. She is particularly interested in the use of research to inform policy and practice, and in collaborations between researchers and practitioners.

Mike Rowe was a civil servant in the Department of Social Security before taking up research at Nottingham Trent University and now at the University of Liverpool. His current work is on the changing nature of accountability and governance in the public sector, particularly in the context of regeneration partnerships.

Ian Smith is a Senior Research Fellow within the Cities Research Centre at the University of the West of England, Bristol. In particular, he has written on the contribution of cultural policy to urban competitiveness and social cohesion, on the construction of neighbourhood problems through discourse and on the experience and construction of social exclusion. He is currently working on a range of research projects including the National Evaluation of the New Deal for Communities.

Peter Squires is a Reader in Criminology at the University of Brighton. His chief publications include *Anti-social policy: Welfare, ideology and the disciplinary state* (Harvester, 1990); *Gun culture or gun control* (Routledge, 2000); and *Young people and community safety* (with Lynda Measor, Ashgate, 2000). Besides this, his recent work has focused on crime prevention and the management of anti-social behaviour, crime and disorder. This has included the evaluation of a range of youth justice projects, the evaluation of a number of CCTV crime prevention initiatives and Neighbourhood Warden schemes and, most recently, separate projects on young people stealing cars and joyriding and ASBO enforcement work.

Cathy Sullivan is a Senior Lecturer in Social Sciences at London Metropolitan University with extensive experience as an evaluator and applied researcher in education policy and other arenas. She has been actively engaged in curriculum development and teaching of evaluation and research methods at postgraduate and undergraduate levels, drawing on insights from both practitioner and academic perspectives. Cathy is an Associate of the University's Institute for Policy Studies in Education, and a member of the UK Evaluation Society London Network and SRA Training Committee.

David Taylor is Head of the School of Applied Social Science at the University of Brighton. He writes on citizenship, social identity and new forms of welfare governance. His most recent book is *Breaking down barriers: Reviewing partnership practice* (HSPRC, 2001). He has held visiting positions at the University of Sydney and City University New York and is a member of the editorial collective of the journal *Critical Social Policy*.

Marilyn Taylor is Professor of Urban Governance and Regeneration at the University of the West of England, Bristol. She has been involved for many years in research on community development, the voluntary and community sector, partnerships and neighbourhood renewal, and has recently published *Public policy in the community* (Palgrave, 2003). She is currently Chair of the Urban Forum, an umbrella body for voluntary and community organisations in regeneration in the UK, a member of the Advisory Group for the Active Community Unit at the Home Office and is on the Executive Board of the International Society for Third Sector Research.

Preface

This book has grown out of an established tradition of evaluation research undertaken by the Health and Social Policy Research Centre at the University of Brighton. Central to this tradition has been the recognition of evaluation as an inherently political activity. As our experience grew, we decided to bring together a range of academics and researchers to consider the wider aspects of the 'politics of evaluation'. As a result, a national conference on this theme was held at the University of Brighton in November 2002. All contributors to this collection presented papers at the conference and subsequently revised them for publication. Four themes consistently surfaced in discussions about the politics of evaluation: governance, participation, partnerships and learning from evaluation. The book is organised around these themes. This, we hope, has allowed us to present a structured analysis of the thinking that characterises theoretical approaches to evaluation and the methodologies employed.

The politics of evaluation: an overview

David Taylor and Susan Balloch

Evaluation: an inherently political activity

Evaluation research should be understood as inherently political. That is this book's starting point. While most commentators recognise that evaluation operates within political constraints, we go further and suggest that evaluation itself is socially constructed and politically articulated. As a practice aimed at producing scientific knowledge, we see evaluation as materially and discursively constituted. It is given meaning within wider social and political relations. We believe this approach avoids some of the deficiencies to be found in recent academic debates about the politics of evaluation research. It does not weaken our belief in the importance of evaluation or the role of evidence in reaching judgements about social policies and programmes. Rather, it suggests that these need to be set within a wider understanding of both the politics of evaluation practice and the political role attributed to evaluation.

A fierce controversy rages within academic evaluation theory between *scientific realists*, who argue for the possibility of an independent reality capable of objective description, and *social constructionists*, who argue that all knowledge is contextual, relative and subjective. The former view stresses the primacy of independent judgement by scientific evaluators while the latter sees evaluators as facilitators and negotiators between different viewpoints. Proponents of both positions, however, seem to agree on one thing: that evaluation is political. The scientific realists Pawson and Tilley (2000, p 11), who advocate what they call 'realistic evaluation', argue:

> the very act of engaging in evaluation constitutes a political statement.

They accept the objective reality of politics but go on to dismiss the social constructionist view of evaluators negotiating between a plurality of stakeholder perspectives as naive. We would agree with them when they argue (2000, p 20) that a simple pluralist perspective may fail "to appreciate the asymmetries of power which are assumed and left untouched by the vast majority of policy initiatives". Ironically, however, leading advocates of the social constructionist approach, such as Gubba and Lincoln (1989), also stress the political nature of evaluation. In a critique of scientific realism's quest for objective knowledge, they state (1989, p 7):

> to approach evaluation scientifically is to miss completely its fundamental social, political and value-oriented character.

Both of these views, then, see the *practice* of evaluation as political.

Our position goes further than either of these approaches, however. We suggest that evaluation operates within discursive systems and that its social meaning is pre-constituted within wider relations of power independently of any particular use. This approach differs from that taken by Pawson and Tilley in that it places a much stronger emphasis on the social and political *meaning* of evaluation as a socially constructed activity. It is not just a matter of what evaluators do or how results are used; rather, we must also consider the role of evaluation as a means of political legitimation. This need not lead to a simple political relativism. From our perspective, 'meaning' in evaluation research is not negotiated within a simple plurality of competing stakeholder interests. Different stakeholder views and interests are expressed from positions of more or less power and these relations of power are capable of being independently grasped.

Some commentators have criticised the particular historical focus of evaluation as 'reformist' and 'petty political'. While this dimension of evaluation certainly could be the basis for critique, we believe that evaluation has to be understood, not only as a project which can be turned to different political ends, but as a 'way of knowing' constitutive of broad social meaning. As such, evaluation can be approached via the intellectual traditions of scientific social research but is subject to the same 'paradigm wars' described by Oakley (2000).

Within these traditions, evaluation is highly contested and subject to the same arguments between realists, relativists and others that characterise scientific social research more generally. Oakley (2000) makes the point that paradigm wars (such as that between quantitative and qualitative methodologists, or between realists and constructivists) are of interest as much for what they hide as for what they reveal. They often serve to mask underlying relations of power, which produce institutionalised discriminatory ways of knowing. Oakley talks of 'gendered ways of knowing' and the legitimacy/illegitimacy bestowed on 'feminised' (qualitative) methods by the power of gender relations within the academy and beyond. We would extend her point to other social relations associated with 'race', sexuality, the body, or other markers of difference and inequality. In 1999, for example, John H. Stanfield launched a devastating critique of the racialisation of evaluation within the American academy. He pointed out that the way evaluation had evolved predisposed researchers not only to ask negative questions about black experiences but *not* to ask questions about the strengths of communities which might shed a more positive light on black people (Stanfield, 1999, p 421). He saw the racialised structures of white-dominated research as reinforcing negative stereotypes of poor black people. Just as Oakley sees knowledge as gendered, Stanfield sees it as racialised.

These claims illustrate the point that the practice of evaluation takes place within power structures. The purpose of our argument, therefore, is not simply to seek a more objective evaluation practice in order to *overcome political bias* but rather to understand evaluation as an *inherently* and *inescapably* political project imbued with issues of power at every level. We hope evaluators will reflect not only on differing methodologies but how their work relates to wider issues of power. As Shaw and Crompton (2003, p 202) wrote in a recent review:

> services and evaluations are constructed within legislative, policy and funding processes and are shaped by considerations of inequality.

They go on to quote Everitt:

> the political relationship between taken for granted understandings and dominant ways of seeing things in a society divided by gender, race, class, sexuality, disability and age should make us extremely wary of evaluations that focus only on the practice as though it existed uncontentiously within a policy and social vacuum. (Shaw and Crompton, 2003, p 202)

Evaluation and governance

This perspective allows us to see evaluation as contributing to political and policy discourses at several levels – from formal party politics to local practices; from policy formation to policy implementation. At the level of wider political relations in Britain in recent years, evaluation research has become a central legitimating device for evidence-based policy. New Labour's attempt to govern an increasingly "dispersed state at arm's length" (see Clarke, 2003) has brought a heavy reliance on 'undogmatic evidence' of 'what really works'. This search for the holy grail has given evaluation a privileged status in legitimating new approaches to social policy. As Janet Newman (2001, p 2) writes, "policies introduced in the first years of the (New Labour) government ... emphasised innovation, experimentation and *policy evaluation* to build sustainable long-term change in public services" (emphasis added). She goes on:

> Political statements couched in the language of the Third Way repeatedly emphasise the need to retreat from dogmatic, ideological politics ... to a focus on 'what counts is what works'.... The growth of interest in evidence-based policy is linked to a number of developments including the explosion of data, developments in IT, the growth of a well-informed public unwilling to rely on professional judgement and the growth in the size and capability of the research community. These developments have been complemented by

the expansion of managerial approaches to the collection and use of evidence
represented in programme evaluation. (2001, p 69)

This speaks not only to the political role of evaluation and evaluators but also
to the construction of a particular 'way of knowing' (the scientific constructions
of evidence of policy implementation) as a basis for changing forms of
governance.

Locating evaluation within a governance perspective, then, helps us set it in
a wider political context, for, as Mary Daly (2003, p 5) writes, governance is
about "the framing, orientation and implementation of policies".

In this way, we can see recent approaches to policy implementation based on
partnership, interagency working and user involvement as new forms of
'networked governance' (see Balloch and Taylor, 2001; Taylor, 2001). Partnerships
have been a key focus of evaluation in recent times as contributions to this
volume indicate. But as the various contributions show, evaluation of new
delivery forms throws up important questions about how to understand and
design appropriate evaluations.

Newman (2001) points out how this new governance agenda is based on a
rational scientific model of the policy process, and Pawson and Tilley (2000,
p xii) acknowledge that:

at its grandest [evaluation] faces[s] the task of keeping the flame of reason and
rational progress alive.

It is in this sense, they argue, thoroughly 'modernist'. It has become the "mantra
of modernity" (2000, p 2), a kind of rationalist scientific project for social
improvement and progress. But as Newman points out, within this rationalist
model "there is a clear separation between knowledge production (by experts)
and knowledge use (by practitioners)" (2001, p 71). Evaluation researchers
who provide much of the 'evidence base' for this 'knowledge' confront this
dilemma between expert knowledge and its use – not only by practitioners,
but also by politicians, policy makers and service users.

Politics in practice: participatory evaluation

One approach to the politics of evaluation that has gained ground is *participatory
evaluation*. This comes in different forms, reflecting some of the disagreements
we referred to earlier between scientific realists and social constructivists. Realists
tend towards a view of participation based on the inclusion of participant
perspectives by evaluators who still remain firmly in control, whereas
constructivists see the role of evaluation as giving participants the central voice
without privileging the views of the evaluator. Some recent approaches such as
that represented by Beresford (Chapter Four of this volume), argue that
evaluation research should give back control to service users in evaluation and
social research. These approaches, which consider the directly political nature

of evaluation strategies, are considered in more detail below. However, before understanding the politics of participation, we need to consider participation for 'what' and 'why'.

Jennifer Greene (1999, p 161) asks the question of evaluation, "what do meaningful representations of program quality contribute to the larger conversation about the public purposes of social investments?" Recast, this question could easily become, 'since so much of evaluation is commissioned by policy makers, how far does it confirm the framing of policy issues within dominant political discourse?' Evaluators have some opportunities for asking 'how?', but are more limited in their options for saying 'what' is to be evaluated and 'why'. A simple answer, of course, might be that it is the job of policy makers to make policy, practitioners and professionals to implement policy, and the job of evaluators to evaluate the outputs or outcomes. Evaluators should know their place and the limits of their role. However, this position runs counter to the well-developed argument that evaluation should not be just a post hoc adjunct but an integral part of the design of service delivery from the start. It should consider the needs of all stakeholders unless it is to passively and implicitly accept prevailing power relations. Indeed, unless evaluation is designed in this way it may quickly run up against the limitations described by Squires and Measor (Chapter One of this volume), and the methodological problems described by Fleming and Boeck (Chapter Fourteen).

The focus on 'evidence' as a basis for policy places a heavy duty on evaluators to deliver verdicts which are simple and authoritative, couched in politician-friendly performance measures. This approach to evidence has been widely criticised. As Glendinning et al (2002, p 11) argue:

> New Labour discourse ... advocates a pragmatism based on evidence of 'what works'. Promotion of evidence-based policy and practice is itself far from [un]problematic and sidesteps major epistemological issues such as what constitutes evidence.

It is not only a question of what constitutes evidence, we argue, but whose evidence and evidence of what and why. As Tilley (2000, p 4) writes, the question evaluators need to ask is, "what works, for whom in what circumstances". But who should be asked and about what? These are as much political as methodological issues. The questions and the answers they generate are likely to be influenced by an understanding of the purpose of social programmes and the values underlying them. From this perspective, evaluation is a value-driven activity that depends on an understanding of the power relationship between commissioners, policy makers, service providers, service users and evaluators.

Approaches to participation

Cousins and Whitmore (1998) distinguish between two different approaches to participatory evaluation: what they call, 'practical participatory evaluation' and 'transformative participatory evaluation'. Both approaches stress the central role of participant knowledge in evaluation. But transformative participatory evaluation has an explicitly political aim: to enhance participants' understanding of the "connections among knowledge, power and control" (1998, p 8). There are major similarities between this approach and what is sometimes called 'empowerment evaluation'. Fetterman (1998, p 2) writes that:

> empowerment evaluation has an unambiguous value-orientation – it is designed to help people help themselves and improve their programs using a form of self-evaluation and reflection.

A wide range of political adjectives has been used to describe the purposes of empowerment evaluation: self-determination, democratisation, advocacy and liberation. It is seen as a collective project that entails a very different role for the evaluator than in 'traditional' quasi-experimental evaluation. Realist evaluators like Pawson and Tilley (2000) advocate dialogue between participants and evaluator in a process of mutual learning and teaching. Participants, they argue, "know a lot but are not know-alls about their programs" (2000, p 200). Empowerment evaluators, however, lose their special status as expert and "their role becomes one of collaborator and facilitator rather than expert and counsellor" (Zimmerman, quoted in Fetterman, 1998, p 3). The central aim of this approach is, for Fetterman (1998, p 3), "self-determination, defined as the ability to chart one's own course in life".

Participatory evaluation with these ideals, however, faces a set of challenges. Cousins and Whitmore (1998) talk about stakeholder diversity and depth of participation. The logic of participation will inevitably throw up a diversity of stakeholder interests and there is a danger that, viewed from the naive pluralistic perspective we cautioned against earlier, this can lead to a relativistic stalemate where each stakeholder's view is seen as equally plausible. However, if stakeholders are understood as positioned in wider power relations, there is the possibility of a 'realist' approach employing a more conflict-oriented perspective. In this respect, we suggest that evaluators need to approach evaluation with a sociological understanding of the structured bases of inequality in society.

In relation to what Cousins and Whitmore call 'depth', there are important considerations about the representativeness of stakeholders to be borne in mind. Many social programmes and their evaluations can be captured by the established activists or those whose voice is dominant in associated discourses – often the most organised groups in the community. The way in which particularly disempowered service users are included is a complex one as Platzer, in Chapter Five of this volume, points out. She argues, for example, that the dominant model of instructed advocacy could actually exclude the voice of some mental health service users from evaluation research. The question then is on what terms can and should users participate in evaluations?

Participation also plays a central role in contemporary discourses around new forms of governance. Rather than delivering genuine change, there is, according to Newman (2001, p 137), a danger that the importance attached to participation is really more about legitimisation of new forms of governance "than about a genuine willingness to transform decision-making processes":

> On the one hand, participation processes [open] up new spaces which could
> be captured by user groups, voluntary organisations and community groups,
> claiming a stronger role in decision-making. (2001, p 138)

But at the same time there is a danger that the basis of participation may itself be exclusionary. This is especially so when participation is undertaken on what are seen as stigmatising terms; that is, the acceptance by participants of a disempowered identity or social location (the point made earlier by Stanfield in relation to 'race'). Newman cites an example of a programme participant/ service user who self-defines as lacking money, but who is reluctant to self-define as socially excluded. Their participation in an evaluation project may validate an outcome based around a focus on exclusion/inclusion and a subordinate status. Participatory evaluation, therefore, needs to avoid the danger of assigning some totalising identity (Taylor, 1998) – in this case 'socially excluded' – which further disempowers those in need. In certain circumstances, Newman (2001, p 139) claims:

> participation may worsen relationships between users and providers, between
> communities and public bodies between citizens and government ...
> communicating clearly about the aim and scope of consultation, and giving
> feedback about the outcomes, are clearly important. But the political tensions
> in the process, and the potential conflict these give rise to, cannot be massaged
> away: more effective management cannot solve problems in the political domain.

One might paraphrase and say that effective strategies for participatory evaluation cannot always change the fundamental situation in which service users find themselves. Evaluators, then, might wish to set their work with participants in this wider understanding.

Zimmerman (quoted in Fetterman, 1998, p 2) distinguishes between empowerment processes and empowerment outcomes:

> Empowerment processes are ones in which attempts to gain control, obtain
> needed resources, and critically understand one's social environment are
> fundamental. The process is empowering if it helps people develop skills so
> they can become independent problem solvers and decision makers ...
> empowering processes for individuals might include organisational or
> community involvement; empowering processes at the organisation level might

include shared leadership and decision making; and empowering processes at the community level might include accessible government, media and other community resources. Empowered outcomes refer to the operationalisation of empowerment.

Empowered outcomes, therefore, are demonstrable substantive gains for participants. In the dual role of facilitator and, in some cases, advocate, the empowerment evaluator is directly situated in a political milieu in which their value commitment to processes and outcomes may well be challenged.

A framework for analysis

Politics enters evaluation, then, at all levels. In terms of the evaluation process it may be possible, for analytical purposes, to represent this as a set of interrelated and interacting dynamics.

In the first instance we need to consider the *social construction of evaluation* itself as part of wider social and political relations. What role is accorded to evaluation in changing forms of governance? This immediately leads us to questions about the *framing* of the issue to be evaluated. This will depend on dominant policy orientations and the way in which social issues are politically constructed. As Pawson and Tilley (2000, p 12) illustrate:

> an interest in evaluating 'prison reform' will evaporate if criminality rather than rehabilitation is seen as the problem.

Defining what or if something is to be evaluated is itself an intensely political act and raises questions about the dominance of particular understandings of social problems, their anticipated solutions and power of 'agenda setting'.

It also raises questions about the *purpose* and *role* of evaluation. Is it, for example, concerned with legitimation of a programme based on a particular framing of the issue and policy orientation towards it? Feinstein (2002, p 434) claims:

> one key use of evaluations is to persuade the 'authorising environment' and the public at large that a program should continue [with a new phase] or be cancelled, 'legitimising' or 'delegitimising' it by providing information concerning its performance and results.

Its purpose can also be seen as either 'instrumental' or 'technical' – concerned with the collection of 'objective evidence', often in easily handled performance data for policy makers and/or managers – or it can be seen as empowering participants and service users to take control in the way Zimmerman or Beresford describe.

Related to this is the *balance of stakeholder interests* and the relative power between them, including funders, service providers and service users. This issue is felt particularly in the balance between what Squires and Measor call 'top-down' evaluation versus 'bottom-up' evaluation (Chapter One of this volume). However, whether evaluation is inspired by the 'top' or the 'bottom', some stakeholders may have more at stake than others and the balance of interests may shift as evaluations unfold. As Themessl-Huber and Grutsch (2003, p 93) write:

> some stakeholders will regard the evaluation as a chance to develop the organisational culture as well as their personal status quo. Others will have premonitions about resulting job losses and devastating budget cuts.

This point is clearly illustrated in practice by Roker in Chapter Eight of this volume. We might add, however, some might have concerns (as described by Newman earlier) that their involvement may further stigmatise or simply act as a legitimating device for advocates of consultative decision-making and inclusive policy making.

At the next level, we need to consider *methodology* and *evaluation design*. In what ways does the design of the evaluation accommodate different interests and allow for different voices to be heard? Can the design accommodate changes along the way as power dynamics shift, and in what specific ways does the design allow participation? Themessl-Huber and Grutsch (2003, p 94) argue that, for participatory evaluation:

> conscious and active participation of stakeholders is not a necessary pre-requisite for empowering and emancipating the participants ... stakeholders are not required to have a vital interest in the evaluation. They learn and acquire knowledge by being informed about the progress of the project.

Careful consideration, therefore, needs to be given to differential strategies for involving different stakeholders and the relative strength and depth of their involvement.

Related, of course, to methodology, are the *methods* employed for data collection and the type of *evidence* sought. Considerations here will include how different methods allow a voice to the disempowered and whether traditional social research methods or emerging non-traditional methods facilitate different voices; for example, as Graham and Harris argue (Chapter Six of this volume), more 'participatory methods' such as the use of the creative arts may function as means to allow expression and participation by those who might be hard to reach by traditional methods.

Two other aspects of the evaluation process around learning raise questions of politics and power. On the one hand, there is the consolidation of *learning from evaluation* evidence and experience, either in terms of organisational learning or community learning and the development of sustainable social capital. Fleming and Boeck (Chapter Fourteen of this volume) remind us that the notion of social capital (or, more correctly, the perceived lack of it) can be stigmatising. "The evaluation of social capital building" they write (p 210), "should not be used to stigmatise individuals, or make judgements about their lives, but should refer to the relationships between people, institutions, structures and organisations in communities". On the other hand there is *learning to evaluate*. Parry-Crooke and Sullivan (Chapter Fifteen of this book) consider how the learning environment itself should be considered a politicised arena.

Lastly, *dissemination* of evaluation results raises the question about the *use* of evaluation and its impact on policy and provision. Of course, no matter how good the dissemination in terms of its accessibility to its target audience and the force of its conclusions, it may have little impact if the prevailing political climate is at odds with its findings. Equally, it may simply be ignored having been commissioned in the first place as a token adjunct.

In this sense, one can pose the question how far evaluation outcomes contribute to the framing and reframing of the policy agenda; in other words, the extent to which and whose 'evidence' forms a basis for policy and is genuinely used to change and develop services. Fetterman (2001), a major proponent of 'empowerment evaluation', sees the internet as offering enhanced opportunities for wider dissemination of evaluation findings. He argues that its ability to disseminate information quickly on a global scale provides an invaluable communication tool for empowerment evaluation. The internet not only aids dissemination of ideas but resulting online discussions can lead to refinement of the evaluation process itself, he suggests. Allied to the use of non-traditional forms of data in evaluation this approach may increase accessibility to and participation in evaluation processes and findings. Despite attempts to improve dissemination, however, there is often a problem of the 'time lag' for evaluation results to feed through into programme delivery. This is highlighted by Leathard (Chapter Nine of this volume). The problem becomes, then, with the passing of time, whether subsequent change can be attributed to the outcome of evaluation findings or whether another set of variables has created an effect in the intervening period.

The structure of this book

The issues discussed above are placed in context in the contributions to this book. As explained in the Preface, the book comprises four broad parts to emphasise the theoretical perspectives and empirical data that relate the politics of evaluation to governance, participation, partnership and learning. Evidence from these four crucial areas of reflection reinforces the need for a more critical approach to evaluation than has generally been the case.

Part One: Governance and evaluation

The three chapters in Part One provide different perspectives on the relationship between centrally imposed evaluations and local autonomy and governance. In Chapter One, Squires and Measor consider some of the dangers of national, centrally-driven evaluations, arguing that the chief reason why evaluations cannot explain what works is their relative neglect of the perspectives and experiences of the central actors. They focus on the connection between 'the new and quasi-scientific language of programme evaluation' and the 'actuarial-interventionist logic of contemporary youth justice'. Examples are drawn from their evaluation of nine different projects for Youth Offending Teams (YOTs) in five different local authority areas. They illustrate the ways in which evaluation becomes more a part of a process by which compliance with programme goals can be assured than a scientific attempt to assess the effectiveness of different strategies.

Squires and Measor observe that, above all, the Youth Justice Board and the Home Office were seeking clear evidence of the crime reduction that the youth offending flagship was intended to deliver. In pursuit of this, 'central evaluators' were judged to have imposed their will on local evaluations, restricting severely their scope to work on the basis of local contracts or develop relationships with key local stakeholders. Substantial pressures were experienced to generate quantitative data without any meaningful assessment of what the data actually meant, excluding therefore the knowledge and experience of local evaluators. Because the evaluation audited against previously established criteria, thus avoiding difficult questions and defying development of a critical approach, it effectively did little more than mirror the policy process. This hard-hitting analysis is highly critical of the extent to which "technical and pragmatic evaluations aim at helping those in power put their ideas into practice". The authors see a real danger to intellectual freedom in the type of research such evaluations sponsor.

Ambrose's starting point in Chapter Two is the baseline study prepared for the East Brighton New Deal for Communities, known as 'eb4U'. Government guidance required the use of 67 indicators arranged in 12 thematic sections, prescribed in advance by an external agency and designed to apply to all Pathfinder areas. Their imposition on the evaluation, justified by the search for evidence in a standard format, parallels the process described in Chapter One. Concerned at the lack of local consultation, Ambrose worked with the East Brighton community to identify numerous other indicators suggestive of areas of concern untouched by the national framework. He proposes an alternative range of indicators reflective of residents' participation, partnership working and service quality and organised to provide relevant information on structure, process and outcome. He concludes, "The failure to challenge prescribed indicators serves to impede power-sharing since indicators specified 'from above' may not cover issues of great concern to residents" (p 33).

In a different style, but picking up on the audit trail mentioned by Squires and Measor, Law and Janzon (Chapter Three) chart the development of the performance assessment system for social care. They cover the period from the introduction of the Performance Assessment Framework in 1998 to the organisational changes of 2004, including discussion of the yearly star ratings for each council with social services responsibilities (CSSR) introduced in

2002. There has been much criticism of this target culture and fears for the erosion of local autonomy, even though those performing well are allowed a 'lighter touch' from central government. However, recent signs from government suggest a reduction in central targets and 'greater scope for locally determined outcomes and methods of delivery', although this does not mean that the overall system of performance assessment will be called into question nor sanctions from the centre removed. Interestingly, and in contrast to Chapters One and Two, Janzon and Law observe that CSSRs now protest less against this process because they believe it has gradually become more robust and based on a more holistic approach to performance. One council put its staff through the exercise of pretending that all central performance indicators had been scrapped; when asked what they would put in their place, staff retained two thirds of the original indicators. The authors consider the extent to which users have participated in setting the agenda for performance assessment and note that there are still no directly user-defined indicators. The effectiveness of user involvement in improving quality of service is also an area that needs to be better evaluated – a point that leads us towards the second part of the book on evaluation and participation.

Part Two: Participation and evaluation

Peter Beresford (Chapter Four) opens this second part of the book with an exploration of some of the key concerns emerging from service users and service-user organisations in relation to research and evaluation. He discusses the ideological basis of participation, the ownership of discourse, the purpose of research and evaluation and the nature of research values. He sees the future of participatory research as particularly dependent on non-service users being prepared to offer support without taking control, enable rather than lead and support service users to find space and resources rather than take control of these themselves. It has to be said that the multiple examples of evaluation illustrated in this book fall somewhat short of such an approach, even where the idealism is shared.

This is exemplified in Chapter Five by Platzer's study of the difficulties of representing the views of people using mental health services. Her two-year evaluation focused on the effectiveness of Patient Councils in acute psychiatric hospitals, facilitated by group advocates from an independent mental health advocacy organisation. She identifies major problems in accurately expressing the views of patients to hospital managers on key issues in the therapeutic environment such as restraint and over-medication. Service users sometimes tempered their own views through fear of reprisal and also were prevented from identifying changes they would like because their own expectations of change were so low. Patient Councils themselves were also caught within a 'Best Value' culture that did not encourage them to identify ways of genuinely empowering service users. Platzer concludes that, "Evaluation of these programmes needs to concentrate as much on process as outcomes and question the underlying mechanisms if it is to make a useful contribution to developing good practice".

A more positive note is struck by Graham and Harris (Chapter Six) who open positively with an analysis of some of the challenges for evaluation within the national regeneration programme, New Deal for Communities (NDC), which covers employment, crime, education, health and housing in each partnership area. Here evaluation's principal aim is to ensure effective delivery of the NDC programme during its life rather than learn lessons after the event. Since NDCs are meant to be led by local people, a participatory approach to evaluation is appropriate. This both challenges the notion of objective inquiry and embraces the knowledge of stakeholders that then adds depth and richness to the research. Graham and Harris provide a working definition of participatory evaluation that emphasises the importance of drawing on local resources and capacities and ensuring stakeholders are key in the decision-making process. While acknowledging that participatory evaluation is both time-consuming and often chaotic, they emphasise the opportunities it offers for local people to learn new skills and engage with local issues.

Creative participatory approaches to evaluation can draw on multiple resources, including photography, sculpture, textiles, story-telling, social mapping and drama. Illustrations of these are given within the context of the Nottingham NDC where people have proved receptive to 'fun ideas' and found them less burdensome than traditional approaches to evaluation.

Continued optimism characterises Cousin, Cousin and Deepwell's perspective in their analysis of the role of the evaluator working within inevitable external constraints (Chapter Seven). Drawing on ideas relating to realistic evaluation from Pawson and Tilley and appreciative inquiry from Ludema, they advocate a theory driven perspective that positions the evaluator and project members as teachers and learners within a shared project. An emphasis on what works, as opposed to the barriers to development, is strongly advocated. A range of techniques that can be effectively deployed in both community and classroom settings, including narrative inquiry, is identified, leading to the positive conclusion that participatory evaluation can benefit all involved if carried out in the spirit of a learning partnership.

In Chapter Eight, Roker shows how participative evaluation can develop over time. She starts off by discussing issues that arise in evaluating parenting projects and interventions designed to offer information and support to the parents of teenagers. Both process and outcome evaluation were found to be important, particularly in understanding what parents themselves had gained. Her graphic example of a parent who said she had learnt nothing new but then went on to reflect on what she had gained in friendship and support confirms this. Conflicting views among senior staff and funders on the aims and purposes of evaluation were identified, including looking for facts and figures to justify the project's funding, identifying how well the project has gone and what can be learnt from it and deciding if the project has met its objectives. However, in later projects, with greater awareness of the rights of young people to express their views, more emphasis was placed on what participants themselves thought of a project, both when it was being set up and on completion.

Part Three: Partnerships and evaluation

The third part of this book brings together three considerations of the politics involved in evaluating different types of partnerships. In Chapter Nine, Leathard identifies contrasting findings from partnership evaluations, including a more efficient use of staff resources, better service provision and a more satisfying working environment, although these are countered by frustration with the slowness of procedures and a lack of economies of scale. She sets out some of the political issues surrounding interagency evaluation, noting in particular the deep structural divide between health and social care, the place of private–public concordats, the problematic definition of boundaries and funding issues. These are then linked to the policy arena with its rapidly changing legislation and guidance and endless reorganisations. She concludes that the extent of evaluation in this context has been limited and that, where evaluations have been completed, little appears to have taken place in response to their findings.

Similar political issues are identified by Balloch, Penn and Charnley in their account of an evaluation of projects designed to ease 'winter pressures' (Chapter Ten). Their retrospective study was carried out on the cusp of change, as Primary Care Trusts were forming and central government was shifting the goalposts for 'capacity planning' in health and social care. Their evaluation was also hampered by a lack of consistently collected data, tensions between services, resentment of the evaluators at a time of pressured change and an almost total lack of information on users' views. They make the point that, whatever the methodological preferences of evaluators, it is probably only possible to engage in participatory evaluation to the extent that the project under scrutiny has attempted to involve users: "The more top-down a project, the more difficult it is to identify and communicate with any services users it may have affected".

In Chapter Eleven, Arksey evaluates a partnership approach in Sunderland to supporting People into Employment (PIE), and identifies ways to improve partnership working. Partner members from similar organisations found advantages in cooperating rather than competing and were motivated through sharing useful information and applying their new knowledge to their own organisations. However, both internal and external problems emerged. Internally, there was disagreement over whether what counted was getting specified numbers of people into work or instead progressing them closer to work. Externally, a very restricted budget limited development and discrepancies between investments and results caused concern. Arksey notes that it was easier to influence internal rather than external problems, suggesting that a 'realistic evaluation' understanding stakeholders' perceptions may be futile if the wider macro-context is not supportive, a contention endorsed in the previous chapters. Arksey uses her case study to extend Piachaud's framework of types of capital.

By trading on well-established social capital locally, PIE enhanced social capital through shared learning that went beyond merely placing people in jobs. Social capital and shared learning are among the key themes explored in Part Four of this volume.

Part Four: Learning from evaluation

Chapter Twelve returns to the NDC initiative with a reflective discussion of the utility of evaluation. Evaluation is seen as a process of knowledge generation that can inform policy development and policy implementation. Smith and Grimshaw (Chapter Twelve) consider the evaluation discourses for stakeholders in NDC evaluation in terms of the implementation structure of evaluation, preferred forms of knowledge, attitudes to institutional learning and change and geographic tactics for knowledge acquisition. While the evidence is still emerging, it seems clear that formal evaluation is only one part of a broader learning process. However, evaluation evidence does not necessarily become part of organisational knowledge and is often filtered through political ideology. As such, monitoring information may be used as a form of governance, especially with regards to spending targets. The authors conclude that if NDCs are to develop the capacity for institutional learning then the national evaluation must play a key role, addressing both the current crisis in utilising evidence from evaluation as well as disseminating findings effectively at all levels.

Rowe and Taylor think evaluation makes little sense unless understood as part of a learning process. In Chapter Thirteen, they reflect on the evidence-based policy discourse for assuming that there can be clear and uncontested outcomes from interventions, which can then be fed back into policy implementation. They explore the extent to which this rational process was achieved in two local regeneration initiatives established as part of the URBAN programme in Brighton and Nottingham. They conclude that the learning from the evaluations was limited to those directly involved and register the disappointment felt by participants that the learning from URBAN was not taken on board by the NDC. They attribute this to the determination of the NDC to start afresh without concern that they might be 'reinventing wheels' and see this failure to learn from past experiences as a characteristic of the last thirty years of regeneration programmes in the UK.

Chapter Fourteen explores how the concept of social capital can be adapted and used as a tool for participative evaluation of community-based work. Here, Fleming and Boeck consider social capital provides an excellent framework for evaluation and one which allows people to demonstrate the impact of their work with communities and inform their own practice and project development. A key feature of the framework is that learning must be shared. For those involved this imposes quite a heavy burden and project workers and community members may require substantial support. When evaluation comes to an end, findings must be produced in easily accessible forms so that learning can continue. To encourage sustainability the authors emphasise the need to offer training to local participants about social capital, employ local people or community members as workers, adopt a flexible and responsive management style, support the collection of both quantitative and qualitative data and provide long-term funding for initiatives.

In Chapter Fifteen, Parry-Crooke and Sullivan begin by endorsing the view that "every action is a political act, political in the sense that there is continuing competition for status among the clients of an evaluation" (Alkin, 1990). They then ask a leading question: if evaluation is agreed to be an inherently political activity, where do the politics find expression in a student's learning environment? Their answer is structured around a consideration of student expectations and a focus on political dimensions. They believe that strategies need to be devised which will help students to distil the essence of politics within evaluation while using their own practical experiences as a positive learning tool. Their discussion relates to many of the issues previously raised in the preceding chapters, emphasising that performance assessment (Part One) should be seen as a social construct and that shifting contexts demand sensitivity and negotiation in evaluation (Part Three). In exploring how students can be stimulated to consider the politics of evaluation before studying real life examples, they encourage those involved with student learning to consider how best a book like this may be used. As they rightly conclude, the politics of evaluation represents more than a single and tokenistic topic and underpins every aspect of evaluation from commissioning, design and delivery through to dissemination.

References

Balloch, S. and Taylor, M. (eds) (2001) *Partnership working: Policy and practice*, Bristol: The Policy Press.

Clarke, J. (2003) 'Performing for the public: Evaluation, evidence and evangelism in social policy', Paper presented to the Social Policy Association annual conference, Middlesbrough, July.

Cousins, J.B. and Whitmore, E. (1998) 'Framing participatory evaluation', in E. Whitmore (ed) *Understanding and practicing participatory evaluation: New directions for evaluation*, San Francisco, CA: Jossey-Bass.

Daly, M. (2003) 'Governance and social policy', *Journal of Social Policy*, vol 32, part 1, pp 113-28.

Feinstein, O. (2002) 'Use of evaluations and the evaluation of their use', *Evaluation*, vol 8, no 4, pp 433-9.

Fetterman, D. (1998) 'Empowerment evaluation and the Internet: a synergistic relationship', *Current Issues in Education* (www.cie.ed.asu.edu/volume1/number4).

Fetterman, D. (2001) *Foundations of empowerment evaluation*, Berkeley, CA: Sage Publications.

Glendinning, C., Powell, M. and Rummery, K. (2002) *Partnerships, New Labour and the governance of welfare*, Bristol: The Policy Press.

Greene, J. (1999) 'The inequality of performance measures', *Evaluation*, vol 5, no 2, pp 160-72.

Gubba, E.G. and Lincoln, Y. (1989) *Fourth generation evaluation*, Berkeley, CA: Sage Publications.

Newman, J. (2001) *Modernising government: New Labour, policy and society*, London: Sage Publications.

Oakley, A. (2000) *Experiments in knowing: Gender and method in the social sciences*, Cambridge: Polity Press.

Pawson, R. and Tilley, N. (2000) *Realistic evaluation*, London: Sage Publications.

Shaw, I. and Crompton, A. (2003) 'Theory, like mist on spectacles, obscures vision', *Evaluation*, vol 9, no 2, pp 192-204.

Stanfield, J.H. (1999) 'Slipping through the front door: relevant social scientific evaluation in the people of colour century', *American Journal of Evaluation*, vol 20, no 3, pp 415-31.

Taylor, D. (1998) 'Social identity and social policy: engagements with postmodern theory', *Journal of Social Policy*, vol 27, part 3, pp 329-50.

Taylor, D. (2001) *Breaking down barriers: Reviewing partnership practice*, Brighton: Health and Social Policy Research Centre, University of Brighton.

Themessl-Huber, M. and Grutsch, M. (2003) 'The shifting locus of control in participatory evaluations', *Evaluation*, vol 9, no 1, pp 92-111.

Tilley, N. (2000) 'Realistic evaluation: an overview', Paper presented at the founding conference of the Danish Evaluation Society.

Part One
Governance and evaluation

ONE

Below decks on the youth justice flagship: the politics of evaluation

Peter Squires and Lynda Measor

"Criminologists have ceased to play, or be allowed to play, a significant part in the public debates about crime and crime policy, and one consequence has been that these debates have become less sophisticated and more simplistic, relying upon slogans, soundbites and partisan populism." (Paul Wiles, Criminologist and former head of the Home Office Research Unit)

Introduction

Our interest in evaluation has been arrived at almost by accident. Perhaps it is the same for everyone. Driving our particular focus on this issue have been our recent experiences as local evaluators for a series of young offender projects. Reflecting upon those experiences has brought us to a recognition of the close (and mutually reinforcing) relationships between the government's strategy for young offenders and the process of evaluating the resulting 'interventions' within which we were implicated as evaluators. As we argue in this chapter, there is a clear and direct connection between the new and quasi-scientific language of 'programme evaluation' operating within a strict and supposedly 'evidence-based' discourse of 'what works' and the new 'actuarial–interventionist' logic of contemporary youth justice (Feeley and Simon, 1992, 1994). Here, we attempt to develop a critique of both, although never losing sight of their intimate connection.

Setting a context

Before developing our critical commentary upon the evaluation process that accompanied the rolling out of the Youth Justice Strategy, following the 1998 Crime and Disorder Act, it is important to describe something of this strategy and the central role of evaluation within it. The government was clearly committed to an 'evidence-based' approach to tackling youth crime, as elaborated by the Audit Commission Report of two years earlier (Audit Commission, 1996). In the same vein, the rigorous cataloguing of outputs and rapid dissemination of 'what works' findings regarding demonstrable 'good practice' which might be replicated in new settings were very much part of the overall strategy (Goldblatt and Lewis, 1998; Home Office, 1998; Hope, 2002). Accordingly, when the newly established Youth Offending Teams (YOTs) were presented with an opportunity to submit special project bids to the Youth Justice Board (YJB), an evaluation component (of around 5% of each project funding bid) had to be identified.

The types of projects for which new funding was available reflected the forms of interventions that evidence suggested could be successful with young people either 'at risk' or believed to be in the early stages of criminal careers (such as mentoring projects, restorative justice projects, cognitive and behavioural projects or education projects). Alternatively, funding went to projects implementing the new types of court orders becoming available after 1998. These included 'bail support' or 'remand management' projects, or programmes to evaluate the new Final Warnings, Parenting Orders or Detention and Training Orders. Later, a new round of projects involving the new Referral Orders or the Intensive Surveillance and Support Programmes was added although, interestingly, it appears that these were not to be *individually* locally evaluated.

Performance and evaluation

The types of projects being developed and the new orders and interventions being deployed are particularly important. This is so, not just in the narrow sense that they were, after all, the procedures being evaluated; rather, the point is more general, for there are, as we have suggested, important relationships between the aims and objectives of the youth justice strategy and the means by which these were to be attained, and the particular evaluation methodologies adopted to reinforce implementation of the projects and, finally, to assess their relative effectiveness. As Tilley has noted (2000, p 98) "evaluation research is particularly concerned with change, and with efforts to engineer it in a predictable and consistent way". There is a strong sense in which the evaluation of the new youth justice projects was central to the attempt to usher in new ways of working with young offenders, complete with new performance targets, prompt recording of outcomes, rapid aggregation and dissemination of results – not to mention the considerable political pressure to deliver. Evaluation became a key feature of performance management in a closed-loop process which was intended to feed back to the project managements and the YJB information about the achievement of key targets. This preoccupation with evaluation reflected, in part, the drive for efficiency in public services. Secondly, it embraced a new managerialist emphasis demanding that success (what works, for whom, when and where) be capable of replication, and finally, it marked an attempted rejection of the damaging old pessimism attributed to Martinson in 1974, that 'nothing works', or Brody in the UK two years later, that nothing made much difference (Martinson, 1974; Brody, 1976). In this sense, evaluation became part of a managerial process by which compliance with programme goals could be assured and performance against project targets assessed (Garland, 2001, p 119).

This emphasis on evaluation was new although the policy it was evaluating drew upon the substantial research findings of criminologists such as Farrington and his colleagues regarding the 'onset' of criminal careers (Farrington, 1996), and those of Graham and Bowling (1995) which were distilled within the 1996 Audit Commission Report. This research identified six key criminogenic 'risk factors' that, above all else, appeared to propel young people towards criminal and antisocial activities and criminalising encounters with the police. Although these large-scale, quantitative, cohort analyses were not especially concerned with particular intervention programmes, they did embody the key assumption of 'actuarial' criminology (Feeley and Simon, 1992): that delinquency could be relatively predictable and thereby manageable (Ulmer and Spencer, 1999). In turn, this placed an emphasis upon the appropriate targeting of policy interventions which lies at the heart of the 'what works' approach, which was adopted for evaluation of the youth justice strategy. As we attempt to show in the following discussion, there is a direct relationship between the emerging quasi-scientific language of 'programme evaluation', employing a new discourse demanding evidence regarding both 'performance' and 'compliance', and 'what works' within the youth justice system, and the ways in which young people themselves were targeted, processed and managed by the system. Indeed, we would go further to argue that both youth justice practitioners and ourselves as evaluators became ensnared in essentially similar, mutually interlocking, processes of performance and compliance. The purpose of this chapter, therefore, is to develop a critique of both the manner in which the YJB evaluation exercise was established and of the design and implementation of the policy it was set to evaluate, although never losing sight of the intimate connection between them.

For instance, in the YOT evaluations, neither national nor local evaluators were asked to develop any qualitative or critical commentary upon the youth justice strategy. In fact, in one telling exchange with central evaluators on one of the projects we were evaluating, we were told in no uncertain terms, "What we really want are the numbers. You can supply as much of the other stuff as you like. It might help us set a bit of a context for our own reports, but what we really want are the numbers".

With the emphasis on quantitative statistical data and cost–benefit analysis, and with the pressure to monitor performance and ensure project compliance against targets, there was certainly no encouragement to question or interrogate these issues. (We develop these points later in this chapter.) For the moment, our argument is that the role of the evaluations was not to assess whether the interventions 'worked' as such, but rather, principally, to assess how well they *performed* against targets and vis-à-vis one another. Thus, even when evaluators had signed contracts with local YOT managements and developed their own local evaluation strategy, these agreements were summarily cast aside as a new tier of central evaluators emerged insisting upon an evaluation process run according to their own quantitative templates.

We have tried to set the Youth Offending strategy in context and then briefly indicate some of the issues arising from the ways in which the Young Offender projects were developed and evaluated. The unequal relationship between the requirements of evaluation, the implementation of the policy and the needs and concerns of the young people experiencing youth justice 'interventions' was far from accidental. Indeed, as we have explained, not only did the emerging evaluation regime summarily cast aside the local agreements struck between local evaluators and their YOTs, it also tended to remove from the evaluation process those features which might have permitted the development of a genuinely informed picture of the ways in which the new policies were working. Worse still, the stultifying administrative rigour of quantitative evaluation which formed the mainstay of the national evaluation regime seemed, at times, likely to imperil the success of the very youth justice interventions themselves – either by driving practitioners to distraction by the weight of bureaucratic processing required in each case, or by the exposure of the young people themselves to a series of relatively crude, 'one-size-fits-all' interventions. Often, where projects succeeded in engaging effectively with young people, it could be almost entirely attributable to the commitment, experience, skill, personal charisma and hard work of the youth justice practitioners themselves. That is to say, factors that the national evaluation did not acknowledge and in which, apparently, it had no interest.

In this particular chapter, we are not so much attempting to explore the wider context in which an evaluation regime so unsuited to its task came to be adopted – or the shortcomings of the youth justice strategy itself (we consider this more fully in Squires and Measor, 2004: forthcoming). Rather, here we are more directly concerned with the particular practical 'politics of evaluation' as they manifested themselves in this case study. However, acknowledging, for the moment, our interim observations regarding the unequal relationships between policy, evaluation and, especially, the young people themselves, in the next section we proceed to develop a more analytical commentary. We seek to explain and understand our evaluation experience from our position as local evaluators, moving from there to some more critical observations on the politics of evaluation in contemporary criminal justice.

Evaluation hierarchies and political filters

An initial question must concern why the process was structured in the way we have described. For instance, what made the YJB, apparently at such a late stage in the proceedings, introduce a second tier of national evaluators with their own specific agenda and strategies. The answer, we believe, is related to a series of issues concerning political accountability, surveillance and discipline.

The quality and character of the relationships the national evaluators developed with the locals requires discussion and analysis. We have commented already on the authority structures that were established. Local evaluators were told precisely what information to collect and also how to both collect it and present it according to 'templates' handed down. There was, in these interactions and relationships, relatively little room for negotiation, and no recognition that local evaluators might have a real, professional contribution to make. In other words, 'normal' academic forms of interaction did not apply. Deadlines for the submission of reports were set in the same authoritative tone and accompanied by a statement of penalties if deadlines were exceeded (such as universities currently employ with students, or even that criminal justice agencies impose upon offenders). More directly, we would argue that the processes adopted for the management of the evaluation process bore an uncanny resemblance to the modes of working being adopted for monitoring and supervising the young offenders themselves.

It is important to reflect upon why this approach and such structures were adopted. We have little doubt that the answer that the YJB and the national evaluators would have given would have emphasised the need to secure easily comparable data across a nationwide scheme. Had local evaluators been allowed to go their own ways then widely differing kinds of data would have resulted and few quantitative comparisons would have been possible. What seemed to be required was a precise measuring of the implications of a new programme. A neat and tidy technical account of what worked and what failed was needed. Above all, the YJB and, closely behind them, the Home Office, wanted the unambiguous evidence of the 'crime reduction' that the youth offending flagship had been launched to deliver. Pitts has made the point in no uncertain terms:

> the primary target of New Labour's new youth justice strategy is not the criminal behaviour of a handful of young offenders but rather the voting habits of a much older constituency. (Pitts, 2000, p 3; see also Muncie, 2000)

Notwithstanding our critique of the implementation of this evaluation programme, the 'what-works' paradigm, from which it is directly derived, remains a beguiling and 'common-sense' approach to policy evaluation. Precisely because of this, its appeal to 'taken-for-granted' principles is difficult to challenge. As Hope (2002) has argued, this new 'realist approach' was an attempt to move on from the depressing 'nothing works' viewpoint that gained populist credence in the mid-1970s. That said, of course, he concluded, rather sceptically, that the 'Faustian bargain' that the social scientist policy evaluators had made with the politicians may not, ultimately, have been worth it. Accordingly, he argues, it is important to question the nature, characteristics and assumptions from which this evaluation paradigm is derived. For us, such questions suggest some serious flaws in the theoretical analysis on which both this 'flagship' youth justice strategy and its tightly drawn scheme of evaluation have been based. In turn, such flaws have significant implications for the findings and the knowledge which might be derived from the evaluation exercises undertaken, as well as for any policy lesson which might be drawn.

There are a number of serious problems that resulted from this choice of structure and approach. We have already drawn attention to some of these in the first section of this chapter and need to go on now to draw out some of the others, as well as the underlying issues which may be at stake.

The first point relates to the establishment of the two-tier structure of evaluation: the hierarchy of evaluators. It is easy to draw attention to the seeming de-professionalisation of local evaluators as researchers and easy to analyse the problem (and then perhaps to dismiss it) as lying in the offence given to the renowned shaky egos of academics. It is an easy attack to make and there may be some truth in it. Local evaluators who were academics simply found themselves in a more tightly drawn disciplinary structure than they are accustomed to, working in the sheltered employment workshops that universities often represent in popular mythology. Like the rest of the workforce, we simply needed to knuckle down and learn to do as we were told. The politics of this evaluation and the political lessons for unruly academe were therefore clear and unambiguous.

Outside looking in

When national evaluators largely ruled out local expertise and the opportunity for negotiation around the conduct of local evaluation contracts, they also ruled out the knowledge and experience that local evaluators may have had. Rather like the ways in which the skills and experiences of youth justice practitioners (crucial to the success of many projects) were disregarded, so, too, the experience of local evaluators was considered, at best, irrelevant and, at worst, an irritation. Yet many local evaluators had years of experience of researching young people and, for example, coaxing them to talk openly. A political stance which ruled knowledge from 'below' as suspect and useless meant that much experience and expertise from professionals was lost – and both the data gathered and the quality of the evaluation suffered as a result. The grand irony here was that, not only did the evaluation process effectively rule out dissenting voices regarding the very nature of evaluation but that, what was overlooked as a consequence, were precisely the very contextual and experiential factors that might have allowed more meaningful conclusions to be drawn regarding the effectiveness of many projects. Thus, the views and experiences of the youth justice practitioners themselves were omitted and, equally crucially, so too were the views and experiences of the young people.

As Pawson and Tilley (1997) have argued, programmes cannot be considered as some external impinging 'force' to which subjects 'respond'. Rather, programmes 'work' if subjects choose to make them work and are placed in the right conditions to enable them to do so:

> This process of constrained choice is at the heart of social and individual change
> to which all programmes aspire. (1997, p 294)

We would simply argue that what is true for the project is also true for the evaluation. If evaluation remains oblivious to contextual factors and fails to draw upon practical and experiential insights we will never discover why any given project 'works' or not, why it may be successful for some and not others and which features of it might successfully be transplanted elsewhere.

We would also argue, however, that there are other more significant issues at work and these relate back to what we earlier referred to as the 'overlapping layers of scrutiny and leverage' which formed part of the evaluation arrangements. The YJB extended its scrutiny arrangements into academic hierarchies themselves, drawing some layers of academe into the process. Hierarchies of knowledge and of status were drawn into these webs of surveillance and discipline, which were applied to the lower-order evaluators. Patterns of relationships within the academic world, where a spirit of controversy and independent questioning were valued and encouraged, clearly did not apply. At the same time as local evaluators were caught within the 'overlapping layers of scrutiny and leverage' at the project level, they were also exposed to similar processes further up the evaluation hierarchy. There is an interesting symmetry here as all became enmeshed within networks of surveillance and monitoring that were new and unusual in their rigour. For us, this also raises enormous implications for the ways in which the young people who had offended were also treated by the agencies.

Evaluation and technical issues

The YOT evaluations are a good example of the types of evaluation schemes now proliferating in the UK under the banner of 'evidence-based policy making'. Their stated aim is to develop a body of knowledge that is in essence technical and pragmatic and which can directly inform policy development. Pratt (1989) has discussed the fundamental shift that has happened in youth justice agencies – from welfare/justice paradigms to a more pragmatic and managerialist model of corporatism. Such changes, he argues, are intimately related to shifts in socioeconomic context. Corporatist strategies, in his view, are distanced from wider philosophical and moral arguments about welfare, justice or punishment and instead simply promote cost-effective and efficient ways of managing the delinquent populations (Pratt, 1989). The YJB evaluations were motivated with the same breezy spirit of 'can do' and the same energetic pragmatism as the programmes themselves. The problem is that both had theoretical and (we would argue) practical weaknesses that would haunt and flaw their ability to achieve what they sought in the long run.

However, programmes that advertise themselves as pragmatic and technical tend to be popular despite the problems they throw up. We have already addressed five practical difficulties encountered during our evaluation work. We now turn to critically consider some wider themes and issues arising from this work, both for evaluation practice and for the youth justice policies themselves.

Statistics, performance and cost–benefit analysis: questions of accountability and surveillance?

We referred earlier in this chapter to the emphasis that was placed on quantitative data and the 'lower status' given to qualitative and interpretative findings ('other stuff'). We related this to managerial issues of performance and compliance and to the cost–benefit performance orientation of the evaluation. How can we explain this emphasis and the effort that was put into its enforcement by the national evaluators? At a basic level, it appears that this relates closely to a blinkered, modernist preoccupation with 'performance management'. Even the old adage, 'what counts is what can be measured', no longer applies. Instead, what counts is what can be compared against targets, while (to paraphrase Pawson and Tilley, 1994) the evaluation gazes past the real questions while effectively obscuring the local, contextual, human interactive and experiential factors that give us the greatest purchase upon why interventions succeed.

By contrast, where technical considerations predominate, we can suggest some simple explanations for the types of evaluation problems alluded to in the first section of this chapter. There has been a good deal of auditing and evaluation in different areas of public sector services that seems to have the major ambition of allowing for the creation of comparisons. Perhaps the most familiar are educational league tables or hospital waiting lists. We have suggested that arrangements for similar mechanisms are now extending into the youth justice field; yet league tables have also been used to 'name and shame' and to audit and control. We are back again to our core themes of surveillance and discipline, and to the 'overlapping layers of scrutiny and leverage' which form part of the policy.

This perspective opens a window on another issue concerning the role, responsibility and even complicity of the evaluator in such processes of surveillance, monitoring and (eventually) resource allocation. It is an issue which begins to raise significant questions about the role of the social sciences.

Policy and the evaluator

One critique of the technical and pragmatic approaches selected by this style of evaluation is that they relate in an apparently clear and non-critical way to policy, but more importantly to power. Technical and pragmatic evaluations aim at helping those in power to put their ideas into practice through technical evaluations. In the first place, they do not seek to question the project or the programme but simply to assess it to the best of their technical abilities. They do not seek to object or offer a critical perspective on what is being done. Rod Morgan (2000, p 85), one of the UK's leading criminal justice policy researchers and now head of the National Probation Inspectorate, makes the point most tellingly:

Criminology is often called upon to assist the process by which felons are identified or individually targeted, risk-assessed or treated but there is much less encouragement for projects that consider crime in terms of broader social or economic policy, or which examine closely the quality of justice distributed by criminal justice decision-makers. Thus though New Labour appears committed to an evidential approach to 'what works' ... the question 'what works?' is nevertheless asked and required to be answered in individualistic and narrowly conceived terms. That is, the question is posed within the parameters of prevailing government policy.

Implicit here is recognition that evaluations do not seek to interrogate the assumptions behind policies or trace the questions which have not been addressed or which have been excluded. It was clear that in the YOT evaluations neither national nor local evaluators were asked to seek to identify or shed light on some important 'silences' regarding youth justice strategy. With the emphasis on statistical data, cost–benefit analysis and numbers, and with the pressure to monitor performance, project compliance and the simple collection of data, there was certainly no encouragement either to interrogate or to offer critical insights.

Voices in branches of the social sciences other than criminology have been critical of evaluations which do not seek to ask awkward questions. Those involved in educational policy making have pointed out that there has been "a decline in government interest in investing in independent questioning and self-criticism" (Hargreaves, 1986, p 131). We would argue that such trends are clearly in evidence in criminal justice policy research too. Understanding the politics of evaluation implies we need to look at the wider funding context. In the last 20 years in Britain, the levels of funding available for research have shifted significantly. In 1980, the budget that the then Social Science Research Council (SSRC) had for research was cut by around 75%. This is but one example of the trend. Funding diminished for what one might want to call 'pure research'. Funding for research which had critical investigation and what Hargreaves called 'independent questioning' was reduced considerably. Funding for research was shifted increasingly into funding for programme evaluation. However, evaluation does not have the free pursuit of knowledge as its central focus and, by virtue of the fact that it is tied into a particular funder, some of its independence and space to develop criticism is diminished. There is a more general argument made by commentators in a wide range of policy fields that the decline of 'research' itself represents an erosion of democratic rights (Jones and Novak, 1999).

The argument, however, goes deeper if we follow contemporary sociological thinking. Technical evaluations of the kind we are examining can be considered examples of what Foucault (1977) called 'knowledge–power practices'. Foucault observed the complex interweaving of knowledge and power within political discourses that developed with the modern state and the emergence of the social sciences in the 19th century. The emerging academic disciplines assumed a key role in the regulation of human populations in modern societies (Rose, 1985, 1989; Squires, 1990). Equally, for Hughes (1998, p 4), the concept of 'discourse' captures "the complex interconnections between forms of knowledge, power relations and institutionalised practices at specific times and in specific places". This suggests the need for a critical perspective on the role of 'the expert' – or discourse practitioners – and, in our context, suggests the need for a clearer understanding of the role of the criminological evaluator. If Hughes is right, the 'expert acting as evaluator' has important implications for the governance of social problems.

Developing this line of argument, Poster (1990) draws out the connections between discipline, discourse and surveillance which featured at the heart of Foucault's historical analysis of the origins of modern penal treatment of offenders, but updates them for a more contemporary context. He could be describing the activities of the youth justice practitioner or, at one step removed, those of the ever-attentive project evaluators:

> In modern society, power is imposed not by personal presence and brute force … but by the systematic scribblings in discourses, by the continual monitoring of daily life, adjusting and readjusting ad infinitum the norm of individuality…. There must be a detailed regimen to effectuate appropriate changes [and] a method or system of keeping track of the change in each [offender]…. Without a systematic record of the subject's behaviour surveillance is incomplete. For the programme of reform to have its effect, the individual must become a case with a meticulously kept dossier that reflects the history of his deviation from the norm. (Poster, 1990, pp 90-1)

Most tellingly of all, Poster concludes:

> the emerging science of criminology [first] supplied prison administrations with the impetus and knowledge of record keeping and its evaluation. (1990, p 91)

And so, we would argue, it has continued.

But does this matter? What is the practical significance of this critique for contemporary criminology? The question goes to the heart of the place of the social sciences in contemporary society and raises fundamental issues about our role and obligations as social scientists. What should social science be doing in the world? Should it simply be there as an adjunct to policy as an administrative handyperson to enable new policy implementation to avoid blockages and difficulties? Should social science have a wider role of independent questioning and a leaning towards self-criticism? Arguably, the question goes back to the foundations of sociology as a discipline. Some theoretical stances within the field would be happy to line up with government and governance but not all. Garland (1994) has discussed the way that some criminologists have been happy to participate in such power-related exercises and become a part of the 'governmental' project in criminology that is concerned with "enhancing efficient, equitable administrations of justice through charting crime patterns and monitoring the practices of CJ agencies" (p 49).

Others are less than happy with such a role, which they see as avoiding critical issues of social justice. We need to take note of what Taylor et al (1975) argued regarding the relatively unquestioning relationship of orthodox criminology with the extant social order, which took part of its task to be the evaluation of effective intervention and behaviour management within the penal system on behalf of existing social relationships. In their view, "scholarship must go beyond mere description to find ways of challenging the exercise of power and authority while investigating it" (Taylor et al, 1975, p 279). Other criminologists have also argued that social scientists need to be aware of an incorporation process occurring among social scientists, whereby research becomes involved with the formation of policy and therefore with forms of governance (Garland, 1994; Hope, 2002).

The questions are significant, and at one level require clear personal commitments on the part of social scientists. There are styles of sociological research which ask the researcher to go further – to take a Stoic line. The Stoics believed that all activity had to be 'moral' if it was to be worth anything. Strong (1988) likewise suggests not only that sociology should take an ethical line but that it should, in the C. Wright Mills tradition, take on a political commitment.

Politics and method

In the first section of this chapter, we also drew attention to the methodological approaches selected by the national evaluators and the YJB. The methodologies selected for these evaluations now require examination on the political and ethical grounds we have alluded to earlier in this chapter. We need to scrutinise the technicist and pragmatic YJB evaluation programmes, for they prioritise the asking of certain kinds of questions and the collection of certain kinds of data. We first consider the kinds of questions which are asked and, by contrast, the silences which also exist.

Questions asked – and not asked

The YOT project and the evaluations of them operate on a pragmatic and technical level – they are interested in 'what works' when dealing with those who have been caught offending. There is no space for Hargreaves's 'independent questioning'; but the process goes deeper than that for it is here that we can discern certain important 'silences'. There is no mention within the boundaries of such evaluations of the contexts in which youth offending occurs. There is therefore no space for social action directed at poverty, deprivation or social exclusion – just technical solutions for dealing with those who have been caught offending. Issues of social solidarity are avoided as are those of collective social control over the wider environment. The political implications are clear: such programmes and their evaluations specify what is important, what deserves consideration in such a context – and it rules out what is not. Valier (2002) points out the importance of criminologists' analyses of the way that crime has been an increasingly politicised issue:

> In Great Britain we saw the emergence of law and order campaigns as a response to a [broader] sense of social crisis. (p 122)

Yet all of these processes of problem identification and targeting and of causes and solutions are hidden from view by the measures adopted to evaluate youth justice programmes. Evaluators, by agreeing to remain within the technical boundaries set – of collecting statistics, auditing the achievements of certain programme inputs (costs and benefits) and monitoring compliance – accept the political sleight of hand which has been accomplished. They accept the 'silences' and are in turn silenced.

One implication – and it is a fundamentally political one – is that certain kinds of solutions are never entertained; they never get on to the agenda, they are excluded. Garland (2001), for example, discusses the profound difficulties in contemporary society caused by significant economic and social changes over the past two decades. He describes these as vital shifts in society which are undeniably associated with the onset of late modernity. He contrasts the scale and severity of these changes which directly connect with the criminal and disorderly activities of young people but then contrasts these with the narrow and 'numbing mundanity' of the managerially driven strategies of crime management and social control that societies have attempted to graft onto the transitions of adolescence. These social control strategies are fundamentally intertwined with methodological choices made regarding their evaluation.

We have already drawn attention to the inadequacies of some of the methodological strategies employed. Evaluation studies tend to be dominated by what might be called the quasi-experimental model of research. In this model, measurements are taken before and after the implementation of a measure and any observed difference is usually ascribed to the new initiative. It is part of a cult of scientific measurement which persists in policy circles as well as reflecting what Maguire (1994, p 236) has called "the power of numbers". In a pseudo-scientific way, statistical sophistication passes for sophisticated analysis. The problem can be that the wrong questions have been asked in the first place, based on a flawed analysis of the issue to be researched. This is hidden by complex numerical calculations that conceal unresolved analytical and social science problems.

Some criminologists have addressed the problem directly. Pat Carlen (1992) exposes the specific difficulties of technical evaluations in the context of crime – they lie with our grasp of what crime is and with our understandings of what might lead an individual to begin or desist activities defined as criminal. She points out:

The assumption that common sense understandings of crime are non-problematic implies that an 'easily recognisable reality' exists that is accessible through empirical research. (1992, p 59)

Walklate (1996) takes the analysis further, arguing that evaluations are frequently based on an assumption "that we can all identify the causes of crime and that we all agree on what is likely to prevent it". Cohen (1996) likewise commented:

I am uneasy about the triumphalist narrative of realism – with its important dismissal of sceptical questions as a romantic hangover from the past – or a distraction from the demands of confronting crime. (p 102)

Furthermore, writing over 30 years ago, Schur (1973) insisted upon recognition being given to the value choices lying behind criminal justice policy strategies and objectives – and the processes by which these were evaluated:

Value choices, similarly, are a prerequisite for meaningful evaluation research – an area in which we might, at first glance, assume we confront a straightforward and merely technical question. Actually, asking whether a given programme is effective involves more than simply asking a technical question. The criteria of effectiveness depend upon what the programme goals are, and these goals are not nearly as self-evident as is supposed. The 'effectiveness' of a programme for gang members will depend on whether the primary goal is keeping them out of court, reducing their anti-social behaviour, or pushing them into socially constructive activities. (Schur, 1973, p 143)

Without these questions having a place in evaluations, we will only achieve technically accurate, beautifully configured accounts which reproduce the lack of an agreed analysis of the problem in the first place. In turn, as Pawson and Tilley (1997) have added, the lack of a precise conception of the problem and uncertainty about the very contexts and mechanisms which result in projects succeeding (or not) are precisely the factors which tended to reinforce the pessimistic 'nothing works' cycle in the first place. If we could not specify why a given intervention worked where it did, we might be unlikely to reproduce it properly elsewhere and, in turn, we ought not to be surprised by its failure to deliver the anticipated outcomes. The argument, from nearly 30 years of criminology, is for effective theorising and a persistence in asking critical questions in order to maintain the process of reflective self-criticism that Hargreaves demanded. Such an approach is not only required for good quality social science, but it is also likely to result in more effective policy.

So there are specific problems associated with evaluations of criminologically oriented programmes and interventions that reach to the heart of what we think crime might be. The problem is wider than that, however, and affects evaluations more generally. It is involved with the problem of the 'realist gaze' in evaluation work. The assumptions reach to the heart of critical research methodology and ask questions promoted by social action approaches about the nature of society and its interactions which reproduce that reality on a daily basis. Interactionist approaches and phenomenological work raise questions about what research is doing, highlighting its role in the certification of 'taken-for-granted' and hegemonic reality. Such approaches ruthlessly expose any naivety about research and render doubtful any notion that the researcher is simply gathering material, as opposed to a more complex process of creating both it and social reality through the act of research. However willing we are to follow these philosophical byways, the principle is clear: that we need to be more sceptical about what the pseudo-science of evaluation can achieve.

Acknowledging this also alerts us to a further issue regarding the intensely political position in which evaluation places the researcher. It is to this issue that we now turn.

The politics of evaluating

Our starting point here is that undertaking evaluations is an inevitably politically positioned activity. Such statements are not without problems, for, as with the rest of this chapter, they ask that we interrogate 'taken-for-granted' assumptions. In this case, we seek to problematise and interrogate the concept of evaluation and remove it from its common-sense place. This discussion is allied to our identification of a particular 'discourse' of evaluation described earlier, within which young offenders are encouraged or induced (expected) to modify their behaviours by exposure to criminologically validated intervention programmes and practices and all under the gaze of an evaluator.

We especially need a clear recognition of the difficulties that are likely to arise in that process of evaluation for, as Becker (1970) commented, "To take on that task is not necessarily to make oneself popular" (p 126). In part this is because as social scientists we challenge what he called the:

> Hierarchy of credibility regarding those to whom we tend to listen. In any system of ranked groups, participants take it as given that members of the highest group have the right to define the way things really are. (Becker, 1970, p 127)

In a very obvious and yet paradoxical sense, this means that the young offender participating in a youth justice programme – already a stigmatised and excluded status – is the very last person to whom it is thought necessary to listen. There is a monumental irony in this, insofar as the intervention programme itself is to impact upon the motivation of the young person. Yet, paradoxically, this is the very person whose views and experiences are considered the least worthy of recording. Little wonder then that 'nothing works': the motivation of the central character has been deemed irrelevant and often remains unknown.

As Becker has noted, 'accounts from below' are seldom welcome. Basic grade 'hands-on' project practitioners are the next least likely to have their views and perspectives considered. Becker's explanation for this relates closely to our legacy of project failure in delinquency management:

> Officials usually have to lie. This is a gross way of putting it but not inaccurate. Officials must lie because things are seldom as they ought to be. Since they are supposed to – officials develop ways of denying the failure of those institutions to perform as they should and explaining those failures which cannot be hidden. (Becker, 1970, p 126)

For such reasons, Becker thinks we normally accept the 'hierarchy' of credibility. One of the major implications of this process is that because we, as citizens, do not always realise that there are sides to be taken we are, almost invariably, taking one of them. As Goodson (1992) has pointed out, for social scientists this creates particular difficulty for the academic researcher. The 'hierarchy of credibility' is a feature of society whose existence we cannot deny even if we disagree and seek to resist. When we acquire sufficient sympathy with subordinates to see things from their perspective we know we are frequently flying in the face of what, apparently, 'everyone knows'.

A number of difficulties can arise if we challenge 'taken-for-granted' assumptions, in this case about the nature of evaluations and the processes of definition and exclusion of which they form part. There are issues for researchers who do this about simply not being believed, or of being perceived as an 'awkward squad' or as outsiders who look too deeply and make a fuss. As today's apparently increasingly elastic field of youth disorder and Anti-Social Behaviour (ASB) would suggest, society has real power in sanctioning transgression against what is taken for granted. When evaluators working on 'performance and compliance' in youth programmes attempt to include the perspectives of young people in order to try to understand not 'what works' – but *why* things work, *who* they work for, *what* features of programmes have the most impact and *how* the process of programme implementation has an effect – then this too becomes transgression. It can cast unwanted critical light on the values of the programme itself or, beyond that, upon the policy from which particular interventions are derived. In contrast to this, we would insist, instead, that this is simply social science doing its job – and a better, more creative, accountable and democratic job than the blinkered vision encapsulated in much contemporary programme evaluation. Two final themes, to which we have already alluded, complete this argument.

Social problems and accountability

Throughout this discussion, and above all else, we have attempted to demonstrate two main arguments. The first concerned the ways in which the evaluation process has mirrored the policy process. The evaluations were very much part of the youth justice strategy, but they formed part of the YJB compliance and performance process rather than some reflective, arm's length consideration of it. Where the youth justice interventions were, to a large extent, top-down, managerially driven, intervention-focused and largely preoccupied with individual youth behaviour, compliance with court orders and administrative procedures, then so too were the evaluations. What was audited was performance against criteria (ASSET forms completed, Final Warning projects run, mediation encounters facilitated, mentors trained and 'paired up', time delays prior to court appearances, integrity of bail support packages, participation rates and so on) rather than whether any of these actually contributed to reducing offending, reassuring the public or enhancing community safety, let alone addressing the needs presented by the young offenders themselves, in their communities.

In other words, striking a crude parallel with the ubiquitous operating theatre analogy, it was possible to say that the operating theatre was clean and fully equipped, the staff well-trained and on time, the patient delivered in good order for the operation whereupon the surgeons, anaesthetists and nursing staff performed their duties with consummate skill and precision. While the operation itself was a demonstrable success, unfortunately no-one was any clearer whether the patient needed his appendix removed, whether he felt any better as a result or even whether he survived.

As Pawson and Tilley argue in the conclusions to their 1994 article (p 305), an evaluation study should examine whether the problem addressed has diminished during the currency of the policy. In other words, has the policy impacted upon the problem. In the case of the youth offending project evaluations we were largely unable to tell because the evaluation criteria were defined in almost entirely bureaucratic terms. A great deal of activity was apparent: there were many new forms to complete, more young offenders to meet, new agencies to liaise with, targets to chase and so on. However, it is difficult to tell whether crime and disorder rates have fallen – although more young people are receiving custodial sentences and high-crime communities still feel beleaguered even as the Home Office is extending its Anti-Social Behaviour and intensive surveillance programmes. Nationally, a reconviction study was being coordinated across the various project types but the results are not yet available. Different types of projects in different parts of the country will inevitably prove more or less effective, but despite the extensive programme of individual evaluations or, rather, as we hope to have demonstrated, *because* of the form these have taken, we have failed to put the 'why' into 'what works'.

And so, to turn finally to the other major theme of this chapter, the chief reason for this failure relates to the nature of the evaluation processes themselves and the relative neglect of the perspectives and experiences of the central actors – primarily the young people themselves and the youth justice practitioners who worked with them. In this sense, we argue that both the youth justice strategy and the evaluations of it contained significant accountability deficits. In turn, we regard these deficits as serious flaws in the conception of the youth justice strategy as a whole and the policies flowing from it – and potentially fatal errors in any attempt to secure a meaningful evaluation of it. Things could have been very different.

This analysis leaves us with a more complex picture of the place of evaluation and knowledge-based expertise in contemporary political life, and a more uncomfortable awareness of our own contribution to those processes of governance. What then should we as academic researchers do? There may be a temptation to leave the field and its complexities and, as Hope (2002) has implied, simply avoid the polluting 'Faustian' contract. Implicit in what we have been arguing is a case for social scientists remaining engaged in the policy debate – but not uncritically. Despite all the difficulties involved, it is important that social scientists continue to undertake evaluation activities. If social scientists do not undertake this work and, in doing so, continue to challenge the ways in which research processes are conceived, on grounds of ethics as well as a broader democratic accountability, then there may well be others, such as management consultants, systems analysts and 'customer satisfaction' evaluators, who are neither so well trained nor so discriminating keen to step in – and that could be much worse.

At the heart of these questions, there lie some fundamental issues which have to do with the integrity of policy development. The notion of 'evidence-based policy making', while often incompletely or rather selectively realised, expresses a laudable and creative aim. By contrast, the subordination of informed local evaluation to national and managerialist imperatives, the enforced silences and the denial of dialogue and discussion renders the process less like creativity and openness and more akin to closure: a form of policy-driven evidence seeking, we might add, validation and legitimation (a kind of spin-doctoring) rather than an informed critical analysis which might actually help in the resolution of social problems. And as we have insisted throughout, critical analysis is an indispensable requirement of effective and informed evaluation. Above all, those closest to the issues, the YP and those who work with them, should not be effectively excluded from the examination of what is going on.

Overview

- Evaluators of new youth justice projects were required to gather clearly defined quantitative data (in order to assess how well the interventions performed against targets) and not to develop any critical commentary on the youth justice strategy.
- There were problems with the approach employed, particularly because it neglected the central actors: that is, the young people themselves as well as the local expertise of practitioners and evaluators.
- It also did not allow for any analysis beyond a simplistic conception of 'what works'. For example, it did not give opportunity to explore why things work, who they work for and which features of a programme may have had the most impact.
- Social scientists must continue to undertake evaluation activities and to find ways to challenge research processes that subordinate informed local evaluation and silence issues situated outside of defined technical boundaries.

• Evaluation is an inherently 'political' activity both in a localised and a more general sense. At the local level, those whose work is being evaluated can often feel very much under scrutiny and this can create a variety of difficulties. More generally, evaluation is about policy outcomes and, especially when these are politically sensitive, there may well be political pressure to contain 'findings' potentially critical of the effect of new policies. Messengers still get kicked.

References

Audit Commission (1996) *Misspent youth*, London: The Stationery Office.

Becker, H. (1970) *Sociological work. Method and substance*, Chicago, IL: Aldine, pp 126, 128-9.

Brody, S.R. (1976) *The effectiveness of sentencing*, Home Office Research Study no 35, London: HMSO.

Carlen, P. (1992) 'Criminal women and criminal justice: the limits to and potential of feminist and left realist perspectives', in R. Matthews and J. Young (eds) *Issues in realist criminology*, London: Sage Publications, pp 51-69.

Cohen, S. (1996) 'Crime and politics – spot the difference', *British Journal of Sociology*, vol 47, no 1, pp 220-32.

Farrington, D. (1996) *Understanding and preventing youth crime: Social policy findings*, York: Joseph Rowntree Foundation.

Feeley, M. and Simon, J. (1992) 'The new penology: notes on the emerging strategy of corrections and its implications', *Criminology*, vol 30, pp 449-74.

Feeley, M. and Simon, J. (1994) 'Actuarial justice: the emerging new criminal law', in D. Nelken (ed) *The futures of criminology*, London: Sage Publications, pp 173-201.

Foucault, M. (1977) *Discipline and punish*, Harmondsworth: Penguin.

Garland, D. (1994) 'Of crimes and criminals: the development of criminology in Britain', in M. Maguire, R. Morgan and R. Reiner (eds) *The Oxford handbook of criminology*, Oxford: Clarendon, pp 11-56.

Garland, D. (2001) *The culture of control: Crime and social order in contemporary society*, Oxford: Oxford University Press.

Goldblatt, P. and Lewis, C. (eds) (1998) *Reducing offending: An assessment of research evidence on ways of dealing with offending behaviour*, HORS 187, London: Home Office.

Goodson, I. (ed) (1992) *Studying teachers' lives*, London: Routledge.

Graham, J. and Bowling, B. (1995) *Young people and crime*, HORS 145, London: The Stationery Office.

Hargreaves, A. (1986) 'Research policy and practice in education – some observations on SSRC funded education projects', *Journal of Education Policy*, vol 1, no 2, pp 115-32.

Home Office (1998) *Guidance on crime and disorder reduction partnerships*, London: The Stationery Office.

Hope, T. (2002) 'The road taken, evaluation, replication and crime reduction', in G. Hughes, E. McLoughlin and J. Muncie (eds) *Crime prevention and community safety*, London: Sage Publications, pp 37-57.

Hughes, G. (1998) *Understanding crime prevention*, Buckingham: Open University Press.

Jones, C. and Novak, T. (1999) *Poverty, welfare and the disciplinary state*, London: Routledge.

Maguire, M. (1994) 'Crime statistics, patterns and trends: patterns and their implications', in M. Maguire, R. Morgan and R. Reiner (eds) *The Oxford handbook of criminology*, Oxford: Oxford University Press.

Martinson, R. (1974) 'What works? Questions and answers about prison reform', *Public Interest*, vol 35, pp 22-54.

Morgan Report (1991) *Safer communities: Home Office standing conference on crime prevention*, London: The Stationery Office.

Morgan, R. (2000) 'The politics of criminological research', in R.D. King and E. Wincup (eds) *Doing research on crime and justice*, Oxford: Oxford University Press, pp 61-87.

Muncie, J. (2000) 'Pragmatic realism: searching for criminology in the new youth justice', in V. Goldson (ed) *The new youth justice*, Lyme Regis: Russell House Publishing, pp 14-34.

Newburn, T. (2002) 'The politics of youth crime prevention', in J. Muncie , G. Hughes and E. McLoughlin (ed) *Youth crime: Critical readings*, London and Buckingham: Sage Publications/Open University Press, pp 452-63.

Nicolaus, M. (1972) 'The professional organisation of sociology', in R. Blackburn (ed) *Ideology in social science*, London: Collins.

Pawson, R. and Tilley, N. (1994) 'What works in evaluation research', *British Journal of Criminology*, vol 34, pp 291-306.

Pawson, R. and Tilley, N. (1997) *Realistic evaluation*, London: Sage Publications.

Pitts, J. (2000) 'The new youth justice', *Criminal Justice Matters, No 38*, Winter, pp 24-6.

Poster, M. (1990) *The mode of information: Poststructuralism and social context*, Cambridge: Polity Press.

Pratt, J. (1989) 'Corporatism: the third model of Juvenile justice', *British Journal of Criminology*, vol 29, no 3, pp 236-54.

Rose, N. (1985) *The psychological complex: Psychology, politics and society in England, 1869-1939*, London: Routledge.

Rose, N. (1989) *Governing the soul: The shaping of the private self*, London: Routledge.

Schur, E.M. (1973) *Radical non-intervention*, Englewood Cliffs, NJ: Prentice-Hall.

Squires, P. (1990) *Anti-social policy: Welfare, ideology and the disciplinary state*, Hemel Hempstead: Harvester-Wheatsheaf.

Squires, P. and Measor, L. (2003) 'Criminology by moonlight: working for the YJP', Paper presented to BSG Conference, Bangor, July.

Strong, P. (1988) 'Means and ends in sociological research', Paper presented at the 'Politics of Field Research' conference, Institute of Education, London.

Taylor, I., Walton, P. and Young, J. (1975) *The new criminology*, London: Routledge.

Tilley, N. (2000) 'Doing realistic evaluation of criminal justice', in P. Jupp, P. Davies and P. Francis (eds) *Doing criminological research*, London: Sage Publications.

Tilley, N. (2001) 'Evaluation and evidence-led crime reduction policy and practice', in R.M. Matthews and J. Pitts (eds) *Crime, disorder and community safety*, London: Routledge, pp 81-97.

Ulmer, J.T. and Spencer, J.W. (1999) 'The contributions of an interactionist approach to research and theory on criminal careers', *Theoretical Criminology*, vol 3, no 1, pp 95-124.

Valier, C. (2002) *Theories of crime and punishment*, Harlow: Longman.

Walklate, S. (1996) 'Community and crime prevention', in E. McLoughlin and J. Muncie (eds) *Controlling crime*, London: Sage Publications.

TWO

Urban regeneration: who defines the indicators?

Peter Ambrose

Introduction

This chapter focuses on *who chooses* and *who defines* the indicators to be used in assessing the success of urban regeneration programmes, including the measurement of resident 'participation'.

It is universally acknowledged that 'progress' should be measured over the life of any urban regeneration programme. This is significant to all investors in managing the process, from public, private and voluntary sectors, to the local authority, to the government departments responsible for maximising the cost-effectiveness of interventions of this kind and most significantly to those living in the area. Relevant and practicable indicators of progress must therefore be identified at the outset and their values monitored as the programme unfolds.

But at this point, the universality evaporates, or is at least undermined. What is 'progress' in this or any other context? Even more important, who or which interests are to define it? This question is key because it is a short and almost automatic step from claiming the power to define progress to specifying the indicators to be used to measure this particular version of 'progress'.

It follows that indicators, far from being boring, self-evident things, are in fact highly contestable in that they are implicit statements of political preferences. Those who specify them 'from above', and expect no challenge, act disingenuously. Those involved in regeneration who allow them to pass unchallenged miss the opportunity to take part in any debate about what constitutes 'progress'. This is potentially disabling – especially for resident participants in the process.

This point is exemplified by the use of rising property prices and rents as indicators of 'progress' in a regeneration area. Such trends suit particular interests – notably those of existing owner-occupiers in or near the area and development companies who may wish to invest in the area as a speculation on rising future property and land prices. But there is a conflict of interest. Rising property prices and rents do not suit the interests of those currently in the area who may aspire to home ownership. It may 'price them out'. To adopt this variable as an indicator of 'progress' implicitly prioritises the interests of one group over the other.

Criteria for urban regeneration indicators

These reflections were first prompted by a commission to carry out the 1999 'baseline' or 'benchmark' study for the East Brighton New Deal for Communities (NDC) regeneration programme (the East Brighton NDC now has the title 'eb4U'). The departmental guidance documents issued in advance specified 67 Mandatory Indicators and the task was to gather baseline information on all these so that change could be measured as the ten-year programme unfolded.

A cursory glance prompted the thought that this was not a good set of indicators. This led logically to the identification of a number of criteria that indicators of progress in regeneration programmes might reasonably be expected to comply with. The list included the criteria in Table 2.1 opposite.

The East Brighton NDC 'benchmarking' project

The prescribed set of 67 NDC indicators in the government guidance was arranged in 12 thematic sections. As a means of measuring progress in the NDC Pathfinder areas, the set as a whole had a number of serious shortcomings and individually nearly half of them failed to meet the criteria set out earlier in one or more ways.

Shortcomings in the set as a whole

The set was prescribed in advance by an external agency and was apparently designed to apply to all the Pathfinder areas. There was no sign of any input from residents of any of the Pathfinder areas in the selection of the indicators (see Table 2.1: criteria **1, 2, 3** and **8**). The indicators appeared to concentrate on comparisons with other areas rather than on progress made through time in any particular area (see **10**). Many of them were insufficiently specified (see **4**). There was no discussion of sensitivities that might arise in the selection and management of information (see **8** and **12**). Nor was there any discussion of the circumstances in which various categories of indicators might be applicable (see **11**) or that different sets of indicators might be applicable to different areas (see **9**).

Shortcomings in individual indicators

It would be wearisome to specify and offer further comment on all the mandatories that failed to meet one or more of the criteria set out (see Ambrose and MacDonald, 2000, for a fuller discussion). But a selection of the 67 is listed below under the 12 thematic subdivisions together with an indication of which of the criteria they failed to meet. These are numbered in column 3 of Table 2.2 (p 44).

Table 2.1: Criteria list identified

Number	Criteria
1	Indicators should measure changes in specifically those social and economic conditions that the NDC programme is attempting to improve – bearing in mind that, according to the explicit intentions of the Government, the regeneration should be as 'community-led' as possible.
2	The measurement of progress in any endeavour must relate closely to the aims agreed upon. It follows that the indicators to measure progress in the NDC programme can be determined only *as the main aims emerge* and not in advance.
3	It follows from 1 and 2 that the process of selecting indicators should be a participatory one in which local residents are fully involved. The indicators of progress should not be laid down in advance by some external agency.
4	All indicators selected should be precisely specified and capable of accurate measurement in either quantitative or some acceptable qualitative form.
5	Data relating to them must be available, or capable of being produced, for the specific NDC area identified, whether a 'standard' data collection area or not.
6	Movement up or down in the value on any indicator should have an unambiguous positive or negative meaning in terms of the programme's intentions.
7	The movement observed should, so far as is possible, reflect changes brought about by the activities initiated under the NDC programme rather than changes stemming from other policy interventions or from non-policy related factors.
8	The information produced on some indicators may have a 'downside risk' in the sense that it may feed negative perceptions and prejudices about the area. In this case the information must be carefully managed.
9	The NDC Pathfinder areas vary considerably - some are outer Local Authority estates, some inner urban mixed tenure areas of older housing, etc. Consequently the sets of problems differ between areas. It is therefore unlikely that the set of aims decided upon in all these areas will be identical. It follows that some local variation in the set of indicators selected will be necessary since no one set of indicators will be applicable to all situations.
10	It should be made clear whether the main aim of any selected indicator is to demonstrate differences from some local or national 'norm' or to demonstrate 'progress' within the area over time without reference to comparator areas. This clear distinction is often blurred in practice.
11	In the selection process there should be some understanding of the difference between 'structure', 'process' and 'outcome' indicators and of the usefulness of proxy indicators in some circumstances.
12	There should be clear justification in terms of programme objectives if indicators that are clearly intrusive on residents' privacy are selected.

Table 2.2: A selection of indicators that failed to meet criteria

Indicators	Comments	Criteria reference numbers
1. Demographic	All these indicators laid down are Census variables. The information on them as at the 1999 'benchmarking' date stemmed from the 1991 Census and further information would not have been available until 2001 or some time thereafter. The changes over the post-census period might reflect any number of factors other than the activities of the NDC programme. It was also difficult to judge whether changes in several of them ('% of working age' etc) should be seen as positive or negative outcomes.	1, 2, 5, 6, 7
2. Economic activity % registered unemployed	No distinction was made between short-term and long-term unemployed.	4
% caring for young or old		4, 5, 6
3. Incomes % of incomes by range (if known)	Unjustifiably intrusive.	5, 12
% of current debts by range (if known)	Unjustifiably intrusive, how is 'debt' defined? Does it include mortgages?	4, 5, 12
4. Housing management Housing management	Precise meaning?	4, 9
Tenant associations/ memberships	Active or passive membership?	4, 9
5. Education % of school leavers unemployed	At what point after leaving?	4
6. Health Standardised mortality rates	Not a sensitive indicator for small areas.	4, 5
Access to health service outlets	Distances or other measures?	4
7. Recreation and leisure Accessibility to sports facilities, libraries, post offices, pubs	Which ones? Distances or other measures? From which part of the area?	4 7

continued overleaf

Table 2.2: contd.../

8. Crime		
Number of recorded crimes and offences per 1,000 people	An especially incompetent indicator – form and pattern of crime? Under-reporting and reasons for? By location of crime or of perpetrator? NB If under-reporting is known to be a special problem then an increase in recorded crime might be a positive short-term outcome (see 6).	4, 6, 7, 10
9. Shopping		
Quality and choice in local shops	Under-specified? How to be assessed?	4, 9
% of residents who shop in the neighbourhood	Under-specified, dedicated survey required.	4. 5, 6, 9
10. Other commercial/ enterprise		
Number of self-employed		4, 5, 6, 13
Remaining variables		5, 6, 9
11.Transport		
% of residents using buses five or more times a week	Usage rate better measured in other ways.	4, 6, 9
12. Community		
Local institutional strengths and weaknesses in private, public and community organisations	Which ones? Obviously a highly complex issue.	4, 5

Local consultations about the indicator set

When confronted with the shortcomings of the set of Mandatory Indicators in the guidance document, the research team decided that all feasible steps to collect the information required on the Mandatory Indicators should be taken, including the carrying out of a household survey to gather data on certain of the variables. However, it was also decided to undertake an intensive round of consultations with all those with an interest in the NDC process in East Brighton to seek opinions on the usefulness of the Mandatory Indicators, to identify areas of residents' concerns that were not covered by these indicators and to ascertain from relevant agencies the feasibility of gathering information both on the mandatories and on the further indicators suggested in the course of the consultations.

Discussions were therefore held with the NDC Community Partnership, the three steering groups responsible for broad thematic areas of the regeneration process, subgroups of these steering groups, a large number of individual residents (both steering group members and others), many of the agencies providing services in the area and finally with representatives of other Area-Based Initiatives (ABIs) operating in overlapping parts of Brighton and Hove, some of whom had similar data needs.

Community-specified indicators as identifiers of priority needs

This round of consultation was extremely fruitful both in terms of identifying other important areas of residents' concern and in terms of gaining a fuller view from a number of sources about what it is sensible and feasible to measure. It became apparent from the consultations that often the suggestion of an indicator was, in effect, the identification of an important area of resident concern. In other words, *what we want to see measured is what we need*. In this sense the process of seeking suggestions about indicators feeds immediately into the process of identifying priorities for action, and thus for inclusion in the delivery plan.

Additional indicators identified in the consultations

It was clear that the Mandatory Indicators were in many cases poorly related to what residents, in particular, wished to see happening under the NDC programme and that vitally important areas of concern were simply not referred to in the guidance.

Some of the more important issues identified by means of the rounds of community and service provider consultation are listed below. This list of 40 or so indicators is by no means exhaustive. In all, over 100 additional indicators were identified. Many of these seemed likely to provide more sensitive and reliable information on issues already covered by the Mandatory Indicators. Others related to issues that the consultations show to be very important to residents but which were simply not covered at all by the mandatory indicators, for example substance misuse, bullying and harassment, childcare difficulties and problems encountered dealing with benefits agencies. (Some of the more important indicator areas suggested by respondents in the community and service provider consultation are cited in Appendix 1 at the end of this chapter.)

It was evident that this set of indicators, taken collectively and with the many others suggested by consultation, reflected far more sensitively the 'quality of life' concerns of residents. Most of these indicators are, in addition, relatively easy to measure from management databases, surveys and by other means. Although the list of new indicators, and the process by which they had been identified, was reported to the NDC managers, very few of these indicators were included in the delivery plan.

Indicators for 'participation', 'partnership working' and 'service quality'

Two of the key aims of government in regeneration situations are to increase 'community participation', or the extent to which residents are able, should they wish, to play some kind of part in the planning, provision and delivery of services and to improve 'partnership working', or to ensure that statutory agencies and voluntary bodies work more effectively together in delivering services. This is sometimes described as 'synergy'.

The implicit belief is that both community participation and better partnership working will produce gains in cost-effectiveness. In other words, it will be possible to deliver either the same standard of service at lower cost or a better standard of service at the same cost. Because 'community participation' and 'partnership working' are often elided both in the literature and in ongoing discussion, and because both are closely related to 'service quality', this section of the chapter deals with indicators concerning all three.

Evaluation of all three qualities is complicated by a number of factors. These include the looseness of the concepts themselves, the complex nature of modern administrative systems, the high rate of change and staff turnover *within* many individual service delivery agencies (which may inhibit the translation of knowledge gains into improved delivery) and the general presumption that participation, partnership working and better service quality are all positive developments. There is thus a risk, especially if formal Performance Indicators are involved, that impressionistic judgements about the changing levels of all three made from *within* agencies will tend to veer towards the positive.

These problems and dangers can be reduced, but perhaps not eliminated, in a number of ways. These could include the rigorous selection of indicators, reliance on quantitative and factual information rather than impressionistic judgements and the giving of equal weight to both service providers and users in the evaluation. Finally, given the variety of phenomena relevant to the evaluation process, there is a strong case for using an eclectic diversity of methods and indicators (Greene et al, 2001; Roche, 2001).

Previous discussions of performance indicators

Several summaries of performance indicator use are helpfully clear in categorising the approaches but offer little in the way of specific indicators that might be used to operationalise the approaches advocated. Foot (2001) for example covers seven different approaches and identifies a limited number of indicators from the literature covered. Similar useful general guidance on indicator selection is offered by Jones (2001). He stresses the need to ensure that the indicators are widely 'owned', especially by those doing the information collection, that one has to be aware that indicators have the effect of skewing resources towards problems that are measurable rather than those that are not, that coverage has to be balanced against the need to keep the number of indicators to a reasonable level and that a variety of indicator types will be required. Above all, he advocates, "measure what you value, don't just value what you can measure". This could well be adopted as a golden rule.

A literature review carried out for the Audit Commission highlights five publications (Chanan, 1999; Barr and Hashagen, 2000; Burns and Taylor, 2000; COGS, 2000; New Economics Foundation and Barclays plc, 2000) and discusses a number of others. Several of these are clearly designed for community use and include valuable checklists of matters to be covered. But many of the questions raised are of the type 'what is the range of ...' and 'how effective is ...' – in other words, the problem of quantification for comparison of changes over time remains to be solved. There is clear identification of *what* is to be measured but less help on the question of *how* to measure it. Nevertheless some specific indicators listed in these publications have been included below.

What exactly is to be measured?

There are three separable qualities requiring time series measurement:

1. *Resident participation in service delivery (RP)* – this is the extent to which service users are involved in the planning, management, delivery and evaluation of services and regeneration programmes.
2. *Partnership working (PW)* – this can be defined as the extent to which statutory and voluntary service providing agencies work together in the service delivery process, especially in dealing with user problems which, by their nature, call for a 'cross-agency' response.
3. *Service quality (SQ)* – this is the judgement made both by service providers and users about the quality of services actually delivered.

Note: It is likely that the indicators selected to measure these three qualities will tend to move in the same direction. *But this is not automatic.* For example, while a gain in PW should, other things remaining equal, produce a gain in SQ it does not follow that this will necessarily happen or, if it does, that the sole reason is the increase in partnership working. Any service quality gain might arise for quite unrelated reasons.

Types of indicators: 'structure', 'process' and 'outcome'

The indicators to measure change in the three qualities RP, PW and SQ need to be chosen in the light of the criteria for indicator selection set out at the beginning of this chapter, or some similar set. Other criteria might also be regarded as significant (see Jones, 2001).

There is the further complication (evidently lost in the NDC Mandatory guidance) that almost all indicators can be categorised under three broad headings:

- **Structure Indicators (S)** that reflect formal, written or legal structures.
- **Process Indicators (P)** that reflect working practices and norms.
- **Outcome Indicators (O)** that measure outcomes.

It is important to keep **S**, **P** and **O** indicators distinct from each other because it may well be that, although the 'rules' **(S)** specify, for example, increased resident participation or interagency working, the 'process' **(P)** may not actually implement the rules very well, nor may the 'outcome' **(O)** reflect their apparent intention.

The three types of indicator can be understood by analogy with making a pudding. The **S** is the recipe, the **P** is the making of the pudding and the **O** is the eating. Proverbially, the proof of the matter lies in the **O**, not in the other two.

But equally, as stressed by Leeuw (2001), **P** is vitally important. It is the people carrying out the process who exchange ideas, react with instinctive trust or distrust to each other, use each other's networks, form and destroy friendships, store grievances and constitute the changing relationships within and between agencies. It is people who frequently pay lip service to 'partnership working' and then act differently. Proverbially again, 'God proposes **(S)**, Man disposes **(P)**'.

Given the three qualities we are seeking to measure, indicators may be required in the following nine categories:

RP(S) Resident participation (structure)
RP(P) Resident participation (process)
RP(O) Resident participation (outcomes according to both agencies and residents)

PW(S) Partnership working (structure)
PW(P) Partnership working (process)
PW(O) Partnership working (outcomes according to both agencies and residents)

SQ(S) Service quality (structure)
SQ(P) Service quality (process)
SQ(O) Service quality (outcomes according to both agencies and residents)

In particular, it will be important to compare movements on the three sets of outcome indicators, **RP(O)**, **PW(O)** and **SQ(O)**, as views about changes taking place in resident participation, partnership working and service quality may vary between service providing agencies and resident users. If this is the case it is a serious matter because such a divergence may well be an impediment to the mutual trust and goodwill that is crucial to effective partnership working and resident participation.

Both the **S** and the **P** indicators may well be common across different service providing agencies. The **O** indicators vary depending on the service area under consideration. Clearly different indicators would apply to measuring progress towards 'a safer environment' than would apply to measuring 'better health', and so on. Nevertheless the imaginative use of 'cross-agency' indicators may well stimulate very productive 'cross-agency' thinking.

One such example was the inclusion of 'fewer low birth weight babies' into the Performance Indicators of a Director of Education. This forces one to think of the interconnections. Low birth weight babies (if allowances are made for culturally specific genetic factors) are a reliable indicator of poverty and prenatal care. These in turn are reflections of earning capacity in the area. This in turn relates to the educational achievement of school leavers. It would obviously not be fair to make career judgements about the director in the light of movements on this indicator. The point of introducing such indicators is to stimulate discussion of cross-sectoral effects and linkages.

There is an inherent danger, given the complexity of the processes to be measured, that the number of indicators selected will become too large to be manageable. But equally, many local authorities are reporting that too many indicators are externally imposed and therefore have little meaning either to them or to residents (both points made in Ambrose and MacDonald, 2000, and Tichelar, 1998). Some fully consultative process is therefore required to narrow down the list of proposed indicators to some manageable list of 'headline indicators'. It is then vital to ensure that those finally selected meet the criteria set out in Table 2.1 and that they include a substantial proportion that have been proposed by residents themselves. Examples of Resident Participation (RP) Indicators may be found at the end of the chapter in Appendix 2.

Operationalising the indicators

As has been argued, the process of arriving at an agreed set of indicators needs to be a fully participative one involving all stakeholders including residents and service users. This process is likely both to add to and subtract from the list suggested. Following this, there needs to be a more technical consideration of all the indicators selected from the point of view of measurability and availability of data at the required area scale. Some kind of arithmetic value for each one is desirable, even if it is just a binary 0/1 (for 'absent' or 'present'). This calibration is necessary so that changes in responses over time can be compared in as objective a manner as possible.

Most of the indicators suggested in the appendices can be expressed as some sort of arithmetic count or, in the case of the more attitudinal indicators, as values on a scale of possible responses (1-4 is often useful in that it does not allow a 'midpoint' response). The values can therefore be compared through time following successive iterations of the information gathering process. It is important that, as far as possible, the same respondents and agency staff are approached in successive rounds of information gathering so that the effects observed do not arise from changes in the sample.

Agency staff opinion on the various matters will need to be gained by periodic survey. It is vital that all surveys of agency staff use a structured sample with representation from a number of levels including senior management, junior management and 'frontline workers'. Much of the value of the work would lie in identifying the differences in attitude and perception about partnership working that might exist at these differing levels.

In terms of measuring the volume of interagency interaction, most forms of 'traffic' between agencies leave a 'footprint' of some kind. Phone calls and emails can be logged and the changing interagency pattern analysed. At a lower level of technology, staff diaries of interactions with other agencies can be kept for short sample periods. Even internal mail envelopes often carry a record of their circulation around an organisation and this may provide evidence of patterns of interagency contact.

Residents' opinions, whether about levels of participation, partnership working or service quality, might well be gathered in two different ways. One would be by using a standing Survey Panel of randomly selected residents who agree, for a consideration, to serve on the panel for a fixed period (perhaps two to three years). The views of this panel on selected issues could be canvassed periodically, perhaps using teams of trained residents to do the work as a part-time job.

A second approach would be an assessment in terms of how well 'the system' served individual residents when specific events requiring cross-agency working cropped up – for example instances of home adaptations, bullying at school or rehousing on health grounds. Improvements in joint working should show as reductions in the time taken to solve such 'cross-sectoral' problems, fewer phone calls that have to be made or fewer doors that have to be knocked on. By working from case histories and actual episodes that have required responses, rather than from impressionistic judgements, the evaluation can be made more factual.

Overview

- The definition of 'progress' is not a self-evident one in complex situations (such as urban regeneration), although managers of the process may act, thinkingly or unthinkingly, as if it were.
- The failure to challenge prescribed indicators serves to impede power sharing, since indicators specified 'from above' may not cover many issues of great concern to residents.
- The set of indicators prescribed for the measurement of progress in the East Brighton NDC programme was seriously flawed in the light of a set of reasonable criteria.
- In the case of the East Brighton NDC, consultation with the local community and service providers led to the identification of other indicators that were both more relevant to the situation and more practical and useable.

- Consideration of measurement needs in relation to three key aspects of regeneration requires that structure, process and outcome indicators be separately identified.
- All sets of indicators relating to urban regeneration should emerge from a fully participative process and concurrent with, and not before, the participative definition of regeneration priorities.

References

Ambrose, P. and MacDonald, D. (2000) 'The New Deal mandatory indicators – a critique', *The East Brighton New Deal for Communities Benchmarking and Monitoring Project: Final Report*, (Appendix), Report to Brighton and Hove Council, Brighton: Health and Social Policy Research Centre, University of Brighton.

Barr, A. and Hashagen, S. (2000) *Achieving better community development: ABCD handbook*, London: Community Development Foundation.

Burns, D. and Taylor, M. (2000) *Auditing community participation*, Bristol/York: The Policy Press/Joseph Rowntree Foundation.

Chanan, G. (1999) *Local community involvement: A handbook for good practice*, European Foundation for the Improvement of Living and Working Conditions and the Community Development Foundation.

COGS (2000) *Active partners: Benchmarking community participation in regeneration*, Yorkshire Forward.

DETR (Department of the Environment, Transport and the Regions) (1999) 'Achieving best value through partnership: Evaluating the contribution of partnership to best value' (www.local.dtlr.gov.uk/research/bestval/paper7/09.htm).

Foot, J. (2001) *Summary of existing approaches and issues re Performance Indicators to measure Community Involvement*, Background Paper, London: Audit Commission Seminar, December.

Greene, J. et al (2001) 'The merits of mixing methods in evaluation', *Evaluation*, London: Sage Publications.

Jones, D. (2001) *Using performance indicators*, London: Audit Commission.

Leeuw, F. (2001) 'Some methodological and substantive issues associated with the evaluation of partnerships', Department of Sociology: Utrecht University (President of the European Evaluation Society), Paper for the 4th World Bank Evaluation Conference, Washington, 23-24 July.

New Economics Foundation and Barclays plc (2000) *Prove it! Measuring the effect of neighbourhood renewal on local people*, London: NEF and Barclays.

Roche, C. (2001) *Evaluating partnerships for community development: Discussant notes*, Oxford: Oxfam GB.

Tichelar, M. (1998) 'Evaluating performance indicators: current trends in local government', *Local Government Studies*, vol 24, no 3, Autumn, pp 29-35.

World Bank (2001) *The World Bank's experience with local participation and partnerships: Lessons from an OECD evaluation*, World Bank, 23 July.

Appendix 1

Some of the more important indicator areas suggested by respondents in the community and service provider consultation:

- number of households where no one is working or has worked
- barriers to work, the benefits system and lack of knowledge of the labour market
- the level of need for training and other forms of support
- % of households receiving Council Tax Benefit
- % of people receiving Job Seekers Allowance
- access to Credit Union loans rather than dependence on high interest loans
- repairs response targets and % achieved
- incidence of neighbour disputes, racial harassment and domestic violence
- number of households with contents insurance problems
- rate of take-up of Council's contents insurance scheme
- standard of caretaker provision in flats (full time or floating)
- difficulties and delays regarding Housing Benefit
- conditions of roads and public places
- incidence of bullying
- incidence of racial harassment in schools
- incidence of school exclusions and the consequences
- Key Stage Two (KS2) data
- number of children with Special Educational Needs (SEN)
- number of adults taking further education and training courses
- childcare availability and cost
- access to screening (breast, cervical, etc) and take-up rates
- % taking routine dental checks
- accidents (broken down by most common categories)
- the incidence and forms of substance misuse
- % breastfeeding at key time points and by age
- % of children receiving 'enhanced service' from Health Visitors
- rate of referrals for speech therapy
- attendance at parentcraft classes and antenatal care
- levels of use of recreational facilities on offer and access cost of these
- incidence of non-accidental fires
- incidence of child abuse
- insurance industry rating by postcode area
- level of willingness to report criminal and antisocial behaviour
- access to pharmacy
- access to Post Office
- advice, information and support services available for business start-ups
- trends in public transport travel costs availability of early and late bus services
- profile of length of residence in the area
- strength of intentions to remain in the area

- number of social contacts in previous week
- number with inhibitions about going out
- strength of informal help and support networks

Appendix 2

Examples of Resident Participation (RP) Indicators:

RP(S) – Structure
- What is formally laid down about resident participation in service delivery and programme management; in other words what do 'the rules' specify?
- What level of participation in decision-making does this represent (using one of the well known schemes detailing hierarchies of participation).
- How much consultation took place, and with whom, in defining this set of rules?

RP(P) – Process
- Agency opinion about the degree to which these formal arrangements for participation work out in reality.
- Attendance/participation rate of residents at meetings, steering groups, etc.
- Agency opinion about how power is distributed between providers and residents.
- The range of methods used to record levels of consumer satisfaction and which interests were consulted in setting up these arrangements (Tichelar, 1998).
- Residents' opinions about how power is distributed between providers and residents.
- Assessment of the ways in which meeting agendas are drawn up and meetings chaired.

RP(O) – Outcomes
- Agency opinion about the extent to which residents' views have effect on specific outcomes at defined levels of agency operation (on a scale from strategic budgetary allocations at one end to the detail of service delivery at the other).
- Participating residents' opinions about the extent to which their views have effect on specific outcomes at defined levels of agency operation (on the same scale as above).
- % of residents who know about the laid down participation arrangements.
- % of residents who can name community representatives/councillors.
- % of residents who vote in local/special body elections.
- Number of visits to community websites.
- Total membership of local community organisations as % of population.
- Participating residents' views on the positive/negative effects for them of being active participants.

• The analysis of specific key decisions made in a formally participatory context to see the extent to which the voice of community representatives was decisive.

Examples of PW (Partnership Working) Indicators:

PW(S) – Structure
• What is laid down about interagency working in legislation/guidance/funding regimes?
• How much consultation took place, and with whom, when these rules were drawn up?
• How many formal service agreement 'contracts' exist between agencies?
• What % of the local authority spend goes into pooled budgets?
• In what % of job descriptions is interagency working an explicit requirement (as a % of time spent or in some other way)?
• For what % of jobs do Performance Indicators explicitly specify interagency activity?
• What % of staff development programmes and training resources are clearly related to improving partnership working?

PW(P) – Process
• Staff opinions about the changing closeness of working with other agencies. (Note – recorded at three levels, chief officer, middle management and 'frontline'.)
• Staff opinions about the power and 'pecking order' of various other agencies.
• How many training and staff development schemes include material on interagency working (World Bank, 2001)? (Note: this training should cover both previous attempts to reach the same ends in recent decades and the history of attempts in the local area – the 'collective memory' should be carefully fostered.)
• Level of staff understanding of other agencies' aims, responsibilities and procedures, etc.
• Designation/not of 'focal people' or 'lead persons' (first ports of call) for partnership working and knowledge of these in other agencies (World Bank, 2001).
• Presence/absence of new working partnerships that have arisen *organically* (that is, have not been officially prescribed) and how they arose (Leeuw, 2001).
• Staff opinions on how supportive/unsupportive their agency is/was to these new arrangements and how easy/difficult it was to integrate them into official practice.
• Do partnership working schemes have clear and agreed aims, terms of reference, priorities and lines of accountability and are conflicts openly addressed (DETR, 1999)?

- What is the volume of post/telephonic/electronic communication between agencies?
- Number of people known by name (or more closely) in other agencies.
- % of staff who have had short secondments to other agencies.
- Staff opinion of the impediments to better partnership working.
- Staff opinion on the additional burdens, if any, imposed by more partnership working (Leeuw, 2001).

PW(O) – Outcomes

- Agency staff opinion (at all levels) about whether or not they are working more closely together with other agencies and with which agencies.
- Staff assessment of the changes in the organisation, culture and practices of their particular agency as a result of more partnership working (World Bank, 2001).
- Staff assessment of whether they have derived personal gains from more partnership working (for example more job satisfaction, ability to work more creatively around problems, etc).
- Residents' assessments of changes in the degree of partnership working (in the light of experience with specified 'cross-agency' problems that have arisen for them).
- Assessments made by 'third parties' including frontline helping bodies such as CAB, councillors, housing/legal advice agencies, etc, about whether or not there is better partnership working.

Examples of SQ (Service Quality) Indicators:

SQ(S) – Structure

- What is formally laid down about service quality (government PSA targets, etc)?
- How much consultation took place, and with whom, in defining these standards?

SQ(P) – Process

- Agency views about whether the delivery process actually works to these standards.
- Residents' knowledge and understanding of these standards.

SQ(O) – Outcomes

- Agency staff opinion about the changing quality of their particular service.
- Residents' opinions about the changing quality of services and whether they are meeting the standards laid down.

THREE

Reaching for the stars: the performance assessment framework for social services

Stella Law and Karin Janzon

Introduction

In November 1998, the government issued a White Paper entitled *Modernising social services: Promoting independence, improving protection, raising standards* (DH, 1998). It contained a raft of new structures and processes for regulating standards of social services provision at both an individual and a corporate level. It also introduced the concept of a Performance Assessment Framework (PAF) to "provide a basis for a common understanding between central and local government on performance, value for money and resourcing issues in social services" (p 116). This heralded the inception of a sophisticated social services performance assessment system to monitor and compare the performance of social services provision on a local authority basis, building on the established inspection functions of the Social Services Inspectorate (SSI) and the then recently established system of Joint (SSI/Audit Commission) Reviews, and including a framework of statistical performance indicator information and twice-yearly self-auditing by councils with social services responsibilities (CSSR) to reflect the state of play in key national priority areas.

By 2002, this system had grown rapidly in sophistication, in response to the increasing requirements on it to provide a comprehensive and objective audit trail through all the available performance evidence on social care, culminating in the allocation of a yearly star rating for each CSSR, and (subsequently) the introduction of sanctions and rewards for failing and high performing councils respectively.

The main part of this chapter charts the development of the performance assessment system through those formative years. It gives an overview of the component parts of the system and of the methodology by which the star rating is determined. We explore and discuss some of the logistical challenges encountered in arriving at a single overall view of a council's performance; and present some contemporary views of practitioners in local authorities on the pros and cons of the performance assessment process and its potential for impact on services. We also discuss the extent to which the voice of service users is heard in this process.

This chapter also outlines the more recent organisational changes for social care inspection and discusses their implications for evaluation of social care services. In particular, major changes to the organisational structures for social care inspection were announced in the Health and Social Care (2003 Community Health and Standards Act), leading to the launch of the Commission for Social Care Inspection (CSCI) in April 2004, a new independent body bringing together the functions of the National Care Standards Commission, the Social Services Inspectorate and the Joint Review strand of the Audit Commission. These more recent developments herald an increased emphasis on the crucial voice of the service user in assessing and influencing the quality of the services they receive.

Political background

Modernising local government

Following the election of the Labour Government in 1997, the modernisation agenda of New Labour brought with it a raft of new policies and targets for social care, accompanied by an unprecedented level of centrally driven monitoring of local councils' performance in delivering this agenda. These developments were, and remain, part and parcel of a much wider agenda embracing the whole of local government. In March 1998, the Department for the Environment, Transport and the Regions (DETR) put out the consultation paper, *Modernising local government: Improving local services through best value* (DETR, 1998a), which introduced the concept of 'Best Value' across all aspects of local government. This would replace the previous imperative under Compulsory Competitive Tendering (CCT) for public services to be put out to open tender, establishing instead the principle of Best Value to provide the best that can be achieved within the resources available in the commissioning of services. The intention was to bring considerations of quality and economy back into more of an equal balance, with Best Value Reviews based on the 'four Cs' – challenge, compare, consult, compete – driving service improvements. This consultation also delivered the message that, while Best Value (including the setting of local service targets) was to be *locally* pursued, it would operate within the context of a *centrally* established service framework that would include a number of national standards and targets. It was closely followed in July 1998 by the White Paper, *Modern local government: In touch with the people* (DETR, 1998b), duly confirming the planned abolition – through the Local Government Bill – of CCT, and the formal introduction of Best Value.

Modernising social services

In November 1998, the Department of Health issued the White Paper, *Modernising social services: Promoting independence, improving protection, raising standards* (DH, 1998) – a sort of companion volume to the NHS modernisation agenda contained in *The new NHS* (Secretary of State for Health, 1997) produced in December of the previous year. This gave notice of the intended legislative change, through the Health Act Flexibilities, to enable social services to work more closely together with their health partners unfettered by limitations on the pooling of resources and responsibilities. It described a set of key principles for social services delivery – based, for adult services, on promoting independence, improving consistency of service provision and providing user-centred services, and, for children, on protection, quality of care and improved life chances. Underpinning all of this was a raft of proposals for monitoring and regulating standards of social services provision at both an individual and a corporate level, including the establishment of a General Social Care Council to set practice and ethical standards for individual social care practitioners, and a National Care Standards Commission to carry out the regulation of care standards at an institutional level. And it encompassed the introduction of the first National Service Frameworks (NSFs) – setting principles and standards of service delivery in specific areas of health and social care (starting with Mental Health, Coronary Heart Disease and Older People), established the Fair Access to Care agenda (setting out principles for eligibility for, and access to, services) and the Long-Term Care Charter and introduced Quality Protects as the basis for children's services development.

Social care inspections were in themselves nothing new. Social services departments were already subject to central formal inspection, partly through the Social Services Inspectorate (SSI) and also, since the mid-1990s, through five-yearly joint reviews by combined SSI and Audit Commission teams. The inspections gathered a variety of evidence on the performance of specific services and whole departments, based on observation and interviews, including feedback from service users. *Modernising social services* now introduced, as an additional monitoring and reviewing mechanism, the concept of a Performance Assessment Framework (PAF) for social services – providing the link with the Best Value agenda – to "provide a basis for a common understanding between central and local government on performance, value for money and resourcing issues in social services". The development of these PAFs represented a significant increase in the degree of control and intervention in the relationship between central and local government. They embodied the concept of local government functions being directly evaluated by central government against centrally set targets and expectations, and with explicit rewards and penalties attached. For social services they constituted a strong mechanism for standardising service delivery.

The performance framework for social services would be underpinned at national level by (Box 3.1):

Box 3.1: Supporting the infrastructure for Performance Assessment Framework

- the establishment of a standard set of objectives for social services;
- the publication of National Priorities Guidance, setting out key targets for medium-term achievements in health, social care and across the interface;
- the increased targeting of resources (through special grants) to support achievement of demonstrable change; and
- the establishment of mechanisms to monitor and manage performance.

Source: DH (1998)

The emerging framework for social services performance

These preparatory elements in the proposed modernisation, regulation and monitoring of social services delivery came together in February 1999 in the Department of Health consultation document, *A new approach to social services performance* (DH, 1999). Best Value was expected to be fully implemented across local authority functions from April 2000. The social services PAF would be designed to "provide local authorities, Central Government and others with the means to assess performance" (p 8, para 1.7). It would incorporate the measurement of social services performance against an eventual total of around 50 indicators, including the centrally determined Best Value indicators for social services and the targets contained in the National Priorities Guidance.

But the performance system would incorporate more than just statistical comparisons at national level: CSSRs would also be encouraged to develop local targets reflecting local concerns and priorities as well as keying in with the national agenda; they would be encouraged to work increasingly closely with other relevant local authority services such as education and housing, as well as in partnership with the NHS. Under Best Value, local authorities would be required to produce annual Local Performance Plans (LPPs) which would be subjected to external scrutiny. For the social services element, this scrutiny would come from the local auditor working together with the Regional Office of the SSI. The Department of Health were in the process of redefining and strengthening the role of these Regional Offices "to allow them to engage individual authorities more proactively on performance issues ... building a better understanding of the performance of social services than has been possible in the past"(p 22, para 1.37). A major feature of this overall programme would be an Annual Review Meeting (ARM) between social services and the regional SSI, also involving regional NHS as appropriate, and focusing on all manifestations of social services performance – including following up on any Inspections or Joint Reviews which had taken place during the year and considering all aspects of progress in pursuit of specific government priorities and objectives.

Development of the social services PAF

Collation of evidence and the Annual Review Meeting

As indicated in *A new approach to social services performance*, there were designed from the outset to be three essential components to the performance evidence system.

Box 3.2: The essential components to the performance evidence system

a) the performance *data*, supplied through the selected set of PAF Performance Indicators (see later in this chapter);

b) *evaluation* information. This would be derived from SSI inspections on particular service areas and from the five-yearly cycle of SSI/Audit Commission Joint Reviews; and

c) *monitoring* information – collected through Position Statements (later renamed Delivery and Improvement Statements) submitted by councils twice-yearly to furnish progress reports on current national priority areas and to outline future planning intentions.

Under the overall Best Value umbrella, it was also a requirement that the measurement of performance be structured according to (an appropriate modification of) the five Best Value domains (Box 3.3).

Box 3.3: Five Best Value domains

- meeting national priorities;
- cost and efficiency;
- effectiveness of service delivery and outcomes;
- quality of services for users and carers; and
- fair access.

The development of the PAF system was therefore designed (for each local authority) to capture the three evidence streams (data, evaluation and monitoring), extract the key messages from the evaluation and monitoring sources and structure the totality of the evidence according to the five Best Value domains together with an additional domain focusing on prospects for improvement. It also contained relevant contextual evidence about each council. The evidence was further divided according to whether it concerned Adult Services, Children's Services or crosscutting issues of Management and Resources.

Over the following years, the PAF information system grew into a sophisticated database known as the PADI (Performance Assessment Data and Information), enabling all of the component performance elements to be entered and identified to appropriate performance domains, alongside the contextual evidence. It supports the structuring of the information by the six domains and allows for accessing it at different levels of detail or summarisation. As such it represents a highly technical approach to collating evidence about performance and a helpful tool, both 'laterally' for inspectors in enabling them to assemble all of the available performance information for a particular council, set it in context and 'dig down' into the detail as necessary, and also 'longitudinally' in enabling overviews of performance evidence to be aggregated nationally or by region or local authority type in particular topic areas[1].

The combined evidence from the PAF system would be presented and discussed at the ARM, designed to be the culmination and focus of the annual performance assessment process. While the performance dialogue between inspectors and their councils would be ongoing throughout the year, the ARM would be the point at which the inspectors engaged formally with the council social services functions and their health partners, to review together the full range of performance evidence over the previous year, the background and circumstances of that performance and the authority's plans for future development. Local accountability would be served by the content and outcomes of the ARM being made public through a performance letter directed from the Regional Social Services Inspector to the council's Director of Social Services (or equivalent), outlining the key evidence and conclusions of the performance review (Box 3.4).

Box 3.4: The performance indicators

The choice and ongoing development of an appropriate set of quantitative indicators is an essential element of the performance system. The original set of social services indicators as set out in *A new approach to social services performance* was chosen to:

- provide some measure of performance against each of the five PAF/Best Value domains;
- enable progress against the national objectives for social services to be monitored;
- provide local authorities with a means of comparing their performance against that of others;
- support the process of improving performance by identifying areas both of possible good practice and concern, prompting questions and suggesting possible follow-up; and
- contribute to a shared understanding of performance across the social care–health interface through the inclusion of common indicators in the sets for assessing both health and social services performance.

In addition, the indicators were chosen with an eye to being:

- *attributable:* reflecting outcomes directly attributable to social services activity;
- *important:* reflecting issues important both to policy makers and to social services professionals and managers, as well as resonating with public concerns;
- *avoiding perverse incentives:* as far as possible introducing counterbalancing indicators where perverse incentives could threaten to distort behaviour;
- *robust:* measurement of the indicator should be reliable and coverage high;
- *responsive:* ensuring that change that matters can be observed and monitored; and
- *usable and timely:* data should be readily available and within a reasonable timescale.

An effect of this last requirement was that the first set of indicators would need to be based on data collections which already existed or were planned.

The collection of social services performance indicators per se was not a new development. For many years, the Department of Health has collected large volumes of returns from local authorities and used these to construct a range of indicators. The new development was to identify a limited set which would satisfy the above criteria and serve as a robust basis for the identification and exploration of performance issues and for comparisons, both between authorities and over time. The original draft set of PAF indicators was put out for consultation in *A new approach to social services performance*, and changes were made as a result of feedback from that consultation. It was recognised in the consultation document that there were inevitable shortcomings in these early indicators, based as they were on existing or planned data collections – not least that they were likely at this stage to be weighted towards process rather than outcome. The indicators would therefore need to be improved and refined over time, but remaining stable enough to enable the measurement of change. They would also need to develop in line with changes in government targets and priorities, including those expressed through the national service frameworks.

The star ratings

A key development in the social services performance system was the move, for the first time in 2002, to summarise the assessment of a council's overall social services performance in a single published 'star' rating – ranging from zero stars for the worst performing councils to a maximum of three. This was predicated by the move to introduce a single-rated Comprehensive Performance Assessment (CPA) across all local authority functions, as set out in the Department of Transport, Local Government and the Regions (DTLR) White Paper, *Strong local leadership – Quality public services* (DTLR, 2001) starting with the upper tier authorities at the end of 2002 and progressing to district councils in 2003. The introduction of CPA expresses the most recent, and again radical, development in the relationship between central and local government, in which both the detail of the financing freedoms and flexibilities and the level of monitoring and control are dependent on the CPA rating which a council receives. The social services star rating was to constitute the social services element of the CPA.

The assignment of the star rating is a structured process, which takes into account all of the available social services performance information and leading to a judgement against a set of standards, criteria and descriptors. The standards are high-level statements describing the quality of service expected, and reflecting the government's strategic priorities for modernisation; criteria are given to define each standard in more detail, and each criterion is graded with descriptors designed to help refine judgements across four bands (SSI, 2004). The overall judgement is based on separate ratings for adult and children's services in each of two dimensions – an assessment of current services (four choices ranging from not serving people well to serving all people well) and an assessment of prospects for improvement (also four choices, ranging from poor to excellent). The sophisticated structuring of the PADI database is now crucial in enabling the identification of a clear audit trail through all the available evidence in arriving at the four ratings, which are then combined according to a precise set of rules to give a single end result; the assessment of current services is weighted more heavily than the prospects for improvement. Councils (and the public) are informed of the contributory adult and children's services ratings, as well as the final number of stars.

The diagram opposite illustrates the main processes of the SSI/CSCI annual review and social care performance ratings system, set in the context of comprehensive performance assessment (CPA) of councils.

Sanctions and rewards

The *Strong local leadership* White Paper set out the intentions to directly tie in levels of local council autonomy with overall performance ratings, from strong central control and monitoring over those with no stars to the 'light touch' for those considered to be performing well.

From 2003, all zero star-rated social services departments are subject to special measures by the SSI/CSCI and will normally be expected to produce a Performance Improvement Plan, the achievement of which is closely monitored. The central control exercised by the SSI/CSCI is explicit in the description of its role as "to ensure that the council understands its failings and is committed to addressing them, has a realistic improvement plan and sufficient capacity to deliver it" (SSI, 2004, p 23, para 8.1). Based on an assessment of the council's capacity for change, external consultants (Performance Action Teams) may be imposed on the council to ensure improved performance.

At the other end of the performance spectrum, the best performing authorities are awarded by an increased level of freedom in the use of some resources, a reduced programme of inspection and monitoring and reduced requirements for planning information.

Figure 3.1: The social services Performance Assessment Framework

Performance data
PSS Performance Assessment
Framework indicators and other
national data

**Annual review and
performance ratings**

Collation of evidence
and initial assessment

Evaluation
SSI/CSCI Inspections and Joint
Reviews
Relevant inspections by NCSC

Annual review meeting
with council

Monitoring
SSI/CSCI monitoring of progress
towards national and local objectives
and improvement targets through
Delivery and Improvement statements

Performance report
summarising performance
and improvement priorities

**Corporate assessment and
audit evidence**
Corporate assessment reports, auditor's
management letters and other Audit
Commission published reports

Performance judgements
validated, determined and
published

Social care performance ratings included in the council comprehensive
performance assessment ratings

Improvement and inspection planning
Meetings between Inspectorates and the council to agree improvement priorities
Inspectorates agree coordinated, proportinate inspection provisions

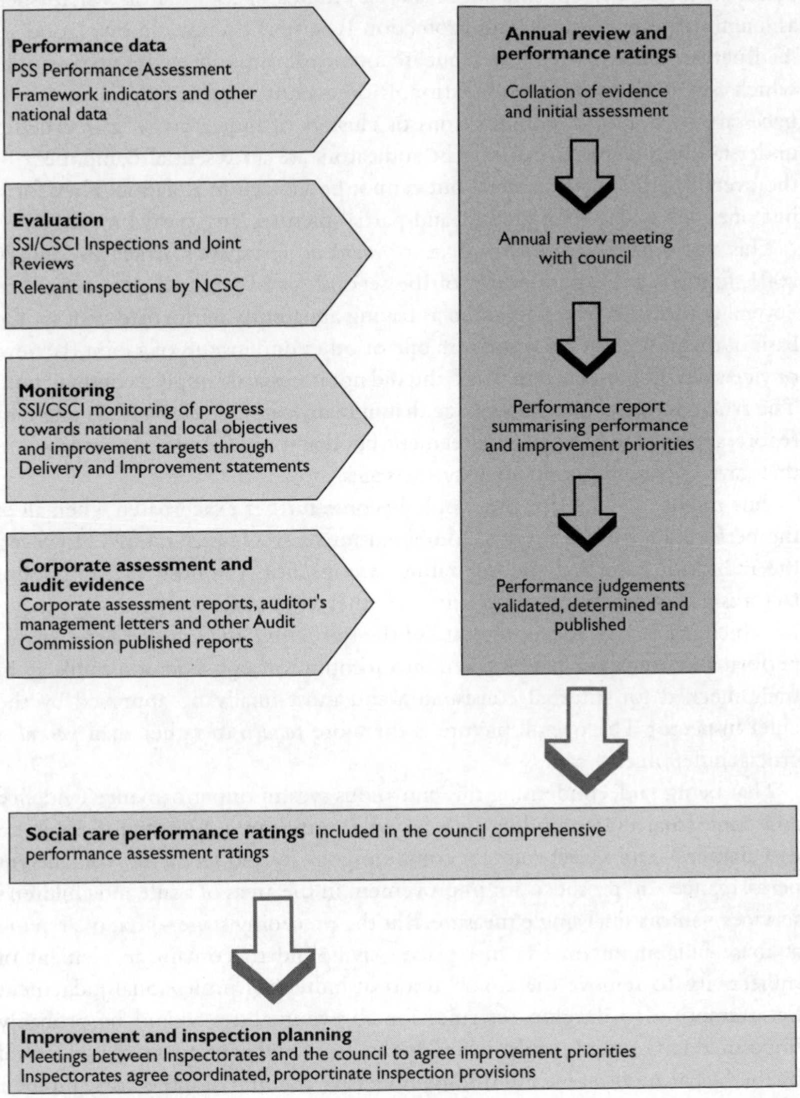

Source: SSI (2004)

Practicalities and challenges

The process for social services performance rating is complex and still developing. The system has been bedevilled by perceptions that it is purely about the quantitative indicators, as these have tended to occupy the centre stage, overshadowing the contribution of qualitative and more in-depth evidence from more detailed inspections and reviews. There are inherent dangers of using the performance indicator publications to draw up 'league tables' of performance against specific social services indicators, several of which (such as length of time on the Child Protection Register) do not indicate 'good' or 'bad' performance in themselves, but are intended primarily to flag up situations which *may* need further investigation. Moreover, it is often helpful – or even necessary – to look at combinations or clusters of indicators to gain a better understanding of performance. The indicators are an essential component of the overall performance system, but cannot be viewed in isolation. They form just one part of the total picture, and partial pictures give partial messages.

This was amply demonstrated in a *Guardian* newspaper article in January 2001, following the publication of the second set of performance indicators. Several authorities were identified as having apparently performed well on the basis of the indicators but poorly on one or other dimensions of a Joint Review, or vice versa. In most cases of detail, this did not necessarily imply a contradiction. The article went on to acknowledge that in many cases the *detail* of the different reports appeared to be in good agreement, but that it was the *summary* impressions that gave apparently contradictory messages.

One might imagine that this would become further exacerbated when all of the performance evidence was combined into a single 'star rating'. However, the indications are that the star ratings are essentially robust. The important factor is not so much the complexity (or otherwise) of the rating, as the process by which it is arrived at. In the case of the star rating, the whole of the formal performance evidence base is taken into account through a demonstrable audit trail, checked for internal consistency, and must finally be approved by the chief inspector. The overall picture is therefore *condensed* rather than *partial*, a crucial difference.

That being said, condensing this enormous wealth of performance evidence and contextual understanding into a single rating on a consistent basis is no easy matter. There are set rules for combining the four judgements – on current performance and prospects for improvement in the areas of adult and children's services – into a final single measure. But the preceding stage – that of arriving at these judgements in the first place – is bound to contain an element of subjectivity. To remove the contribution of individual professional judgement by attempting to develop set rules for all eventualities would be probably impossible and certainly undesirable. This has been, and continues to be, addressed by the Department of Health through intensive training of inspectors and their teams in the art of assimilating all the range of evidence presented through the PADI system, drawing from it the key messages in terms of performance on a local and national basis and ensuring that their judgements are supported by a robust and defensible audit trail through the available evidence.

Finally the choice and development of the performance indicator set is itself a challenge. While not the whole picture, they certainly constitute an important part. The basis on which the indicators were chosen is generally accepted as sound; the question tends to be the degree to which they are actually seen as *being* attributable, important, and so on (see the second section of this chapter:

'Development of the Social Services PAF'). It was recognised at the outset that, given the restriction of using existing or already planned data collections, these indicators would need to develop over time with the introduction of new data streams, especially as more and better data became available directed towards measuring outcomes. In a paper presented to the Social Services Research Group (SSRG) annual conference 2002, Miller (2002) expands on a number of drawbacks and potential for misuse in the then current indicator set. Perhaps the main message from this – apart from the acknowledged need for the indicator set to continue to be critically assessed, revised and developed – is that, as for evidence as a whole, indicators too have to be viewed as part of a complete and balanced picture. It can never be appropriate to base any form of judgement on a single indicator, or even on an entire set of indicators viewed in isolation from each other. Five years down the line from the framework first being introduced, the Department of Health has now started a fundamental review of all the PAF performance indicators.

Over the whole of this evaluation structure hangs the essentially political question/challenge of central directivity versus local autonomy. This is one to which there is no universally acceptable answer. The pendulum swings, and wherever it is there will be those who feel it has gone too far one way or the other. The Local Government Association (LGA) has been strongly critical of the 'target culture', pointing to the erosion of local autonomy. The most recent signs from central government are that the pendulum may be swinging back towards more local control. The Devolving Decision-Making review (HM Treasury and Cabinet Office, 2004) – the first parts of which were reported in the budget speech in March 2004 – signalled a reduction in central targets and greater scope for locally determined outcomes and methods of delivery, a move welcomed by the LGA (*Community Care*, 2004). But, while there may be a change in direction from central to local performance standards, the overall system of performance assessment is not called into question, nor is the possibility of sanctions from the centre:

> local communities should have the freedom to agree for each service their own local performance standards – choosing their own performance indicators and monitoring both national and local performance indicators with *national powers as a back stop*. (HM Treasury and Cabinet Office, 2004, p ii) (emphasis added)

At the same time, there are signs that the performance assessment framework in social services is gaining more acceptance. When the third round of social services star ratings were announced in 2003, criticism by social services directors was more muted than in the previous years. Directors acknowledged that the system was now more robust than when it was first introduced and based on a more holistic approach to performance. External review was felt to be valuable in preventing complacency, but concerns remained about public league tables and the damage they can do to staff morale (Andalo, 2003).

Views from the operational end

So, what does it feel like from the point of view of the local authority social services functions whose service delivery task this whole edifice is designed to support? In researching this chapter, we informally consulted the views of a number of social services officers from a range of councils. The responses were mixed, but similar in several respects. Respondents in general appreciated the assessment system and would not like to see it disappear. Responses included the comments that measuring performance is right, that everyone actually *wants* to provide a good service and that it is helpful in providing a focus on central government priorities. The general feeling was that the principle was right but that the 'how' – both of content and delivery – needed increased clarity and further development.

For instance, it was felt that the individual relationship between inspectors and their councils needed to be made more use of, supporting evaluations with a more explicit recognition of local context and circumstances which might affect some aspects of performance. Concerns included small councils struggling with economies of scale (for example, less able to employ dedicated quality and performance staff), councils situated outside of London but close enough to be subject to London pricing levels, non-city-centre councils with city-centre levels of deprivation and councils whose boundaries embraced multiple PCTs and/or more than one Strategic Health Authority.

Inevitably, there were perceptions of shortcomings and limited usefulness among some of the present set of performance indicators. Suggestions for development are set out in Box 3.5.

Box 3.5: Suggestions for development of performance indicators

- development of more precise definitions to ensure consistency of measurement;
- 'slimming down' of the indicator set to ensure that all add demonstrable benefit to service delivery;
- avoidance of 'mixed' indicators (for example, combination of unit costs for fostering and children's home placements, or residential and intensive home care for adults); and
- avoidance of 'satisfaction' indicators which make no distinction on who has delivered the service.

To this must be added the observation of Miller (2002) that the set of indicators need to be viewed together as part of an integrated picture, rather than in isolation, and that most councils would need help with developing the analytic capacity and mechanisms to enable them to do this. Interestingly, one council had put its staff through the exercise of pretending that all central performance indicators had been scrapped, and tasked them to come up with what they would put in their place; two thirds of the original performance indicators were retained.

Several respondents commented that resolving recruitment and retention issues was the lynchpin to everything else. They needed to feel that there was understanding and support for decisions to give this top priority in order to be able effectively to address the rest. More generally, there was a suggestion that there were just too many central government priorities to be able to handle them all at the same time, and that allowance needed to be made – in consultation with inspectors – for decisions to prioritise action on these locally within the context of local requirements.

Finally, there was real concern over the vulnerability of staff morale. This was coupled with a recognition that, if the performance system was to achieve its fundamental objective of delivering better quality services, then it was essential that its overall effect was to improve the morale of the workforce rather than further to endanger it. This meant that it was crucial that the system gave *all* councils every opportunity of recognising and receiving tangible credit for those areas where they were developing good practice, investing effort in difficult circumstances and/or performing well.

The user voice

A main purpose of performance assessment is to "promote improvement in the quality of care to service users" (SSI, 2004, p 4). Key questions are therefore the extent to which users have participated in setting the agenda for performance assessment, and whether the evidence collected and the processes used allow the service user's voice to be heard effectively.

There is no doubt that the national priorities agenda has been informed by concerns raised by both service users and practitioners over a long time. More difficult to pinpoint is the extent to which user involvement has succeeded in improving effectiveness and quality of services, and whether the elaborate system for performance assessment provides a channel for this. This in itself is an area that needs to be better evaluated. Research reviews produced by the Social Care Institute for Excellence (SCIE) in 2004 (Carr, 2004) showed that, generally, there was very little monitoring or evaluation of the difference service-user participation is making, although there is quite a lot of information about ways to involve service users and much consultation going on.

Within the performance assessment system, the inspection process in particular has actively sought the views of users through interviews and satisfaction questionnaires. An important addition was made to the PAF performance indicators in 2002, when two new indicators were introduced measuring user satisfaction with social services and user satisfaction with the council's response to their requests for change(s) to their services. However there are still no directly user-defined indicators among the PAF performance indicators, even though there is a growing body of evidence of what users see as important in service provision which could form a basis for quality indicators (for example, Qureshi and Henwood, 2000).

Strengthening inspection, regulation and performance assessment: recent organisational changes

April 2004 saw the launch of the Commission for Social Care Inspection (CSCI), a new independent body bringing together the functions of the National Care Standards Commission, the Social Services Inspectorate and the Joint Review strand of the Audit Commission. The commission has a much wider remit then its predecessor organisations and, for the first time, one single organisation has a total overview of the whole social care industry. By integrating inspection and assessment across the whole sector, it will be possible to track the services provided for individual users from assessment to delivery of services. There will also be close links with other audit and inspection bodies, including the Commission for Healthcare Audit and Inspection (CHAI), Ofsted and the Audit Commission.

The CSCI pledges to promote improvements in social care by putting the users firmly at the centre of its work (CSCI, 2004). In taking over the responsibility for inspecting and regulating social care providers, the new chief inspector has emphasised his wish to introduce inspections that are closer and more relevant to service users. There are also indications that the CSCI may put the user experience more at the forefront when assessing whether councils deploy their resources effectively when providing social services. One measure of effectiveness will be whether the services delivered actually meet the needs of the people using them (Gillen, 2004).

All indications are that the CSCI will continue the now well-established performance assessment regime. Indeed, the function to report annually to parliament on the state of social care in England has now been written into legislation. There are also enhanced enforcement powers, including power to issue notices to local councils when services are not improving as they should. Potentially, the evaluation function has been strengthened by giving the commission the power to carry out its own research, including studies into any aspect of social care services, for example, into whether particular models of care are effective.

The seemingly constantly changing local organisational structures through which social services are delivered will no doubt continue to pose challenges for performance assessment systems. 'Interface indicators' may patrol the borders between health and social care, but accountability for poor performance may still be an issue. The move of children's services from the Department of Health to the Department for Education and Skills, and integration of these services locally under Children's Trusts, will inevitably have further repercussions on the performance assessment agenda.

Conclusion

The social services Performance Assessment Framework constitutes an integral part of the national modernisation agenda. It has introduced a high level of central government scrutiny of local council activity coupled with published ratings of performance and a system of sanctions for failing authorities and rewards for those that perform well. There is no doubt that the developments in social services performance assessment have given politicians and managers more, and mostly better, information about the services they are accountable for, even though all the evidence needs to be interpreted with caution – although the jury may be out on whether this is leading to improved services and outcomes for service users.

The chapter reflects the incremental developments of policies and systems for performance assessments from 1998 to 2003, noting also the new organisational changes that will impact on future developments from April 2004. The signs are that the Performance Assessment Framework is here to stay but that it will also continue to change and adapt to new organisational relationships and political aspirations.

Overview

- The modernisation agenda of New Labour brought with it a raft of new policies and targets for social care, accompanied by an increased level of centrally driven monitoring of local councils' performance in delivering this agenda. The development was part of a wider corporate agenda linked to the introduction of the Best Value regime across all local authority services.
- The White Paper, *Modernising social services*, and the consultation document, *A new approach to social services performance*, introduced a new Performance Assessment Framework (PAF) underpinned by national objectives, priorities and targets, and mechanisms to monitor and manage performance. The framework would incorporate the measurement of performance against an eventual total of around 50 performance indicators, along with collation of evaluation evidence from inspections and from twice-yearly self-monitoring by local councils.
- The PAF system was designed (for each local authority) to capture the three evidence streams (data, evaluation and monitoring), extract key messages and structure the totality of the evidence according to the five Best Value domains together with an additional domain focusing on prospects for improvement.
- The evidence has been brought together in a single database, representing a highly technical approach to collating evidence about performance and arguably an invaluable tool for inspectors in helping them to assemble all of the available performance information for a particular council.
- For the first time in 2002, each council's overall social services performance was summarised in a single published 'star' rating, to be repeated annually. To arrive at a star rating, the whole of the formal performance evidence base is taken into

account through a demonstrable audit trail, checked for internal consistency and finally approved by the chief inspector. Since 2003, the star ratings are linked to a system of sanctions for 'failing' councils and rewards for high-performing councils.

- The performance assessment system has been bedevilled by perceptions that it is purely about the quantitative indicators. Single performance indicators have at times been inappropriately used to draw up 'league tables', and discrepancies between interpretations and judgements based on partial evidence have been highlighted by those critical of the systems.
- Consultation with social services officers have indicated that in spite of some misgivings the performance assessment system is generally appreciated. The general feeling was that the principle is right but that the 'how' – both of content and delivery – needed increased clarity and further development.
- While the national priorities for social services reflect user aspirations and concerns in the broadest sense, it is difficult to assess the extent to which users have influenced the agenda for performance assessment, and whether the evidence collected and the processes used allow the service user's voice to be heard effectively.
- The new Commission for Social Care Inspection (CSCI) will continue the now well-established performance assessment regime and the function to report annually to parliament on the state of social care in England has now been written into legislation. Potentially, the evaluation function has been strengthened by giving the commission the power to carry out its own research and by the CSCI pledge to put users firmly at the centre of its work.
- In 2004, the government signalled a reduction in central targets in favour of more locally determined outcomes and performance indicators. However, the overall system of performance assessment is not called into question, nor is the possibility of sanctions from the centre, with national powers retained as a 'backstop'.

Note

[1] For the reader interested in exploring the Performance Assessment System in more detail, we recommend the Department of Health website (www.dh.gov.uk/ PolicyAndGuidance/OrganisationPolicy/SocialServicesPerformanceAssessment/fs/en).

References

Andalo, D. (2003) 'Criticisms of star ratings muted as assessment becomes more refined', *Community Care*, 20 November, p 18.

Carr, S. (2004) *Has service user participation made a difference to social care services?*, London: Social Care Institute for Excellence.

CSCI (Commission for Social Care Inspection) (2004) 'About CSCI' (www.csci.org.uk).

Community Care (2004) 'Government plans reduction in targets', *Community Care*, 25 March, p 11.

DETR (Department for the Environment, Transport and the Regions) (1998a) *Modernising local government: Improving local services through best value*, London: The Stationery Office.

DETR (1998b) *Modern local government: In touch with the people*, London: The Stationery Office.

DETR (2001) *Strong local leadership: Quality public services*, London: The Stationery Office.

DH (1998) *Modernising social services: Promoting independence, improving protection, raising standards*, London: The Stationery Office

DH (1999) *A new approach to social services performance*, London: The Stationery Office.

DTLR (Department of the Environment, Transport and the Regions) (2001) *Strong local leadership: Quality public services*, London: The Stationery Office.

Gillen, S. (2004) 'Low-key start to new commission heralds a big inspection shake-up', *Community Care*, 1 April, p 20.

HM Treasury and Cabinet Office (2004) 'Devolving decision making: 1-Delivering better public services: refining targets and performance management' (www.hm-treasury.gov.uk/budget/budget_04).

Miller, N. (2002) 'The weakest link: priorities for improvement in Personal Social Services performance indicators', SSRG 2002 Annual Conference, Leicester.

Qureshi, H. and Henwood, M. (2000) *Older people's definition of quality services*, York: Joseph Rowntree Foundation.

Secretary of State for Health (1997) *The new NHS: Modern, dependable*, London: The Stationery Office.

SSI (Social Services Inspectorate) (2004) 'SSI Performance Assessment 2004 operating policies' (www.dh.gov.uk).

Part Two
Participation and evaluation

Service-user involvement in evaluation and research: issues, dilemmas and destinations

Peter Beresford

Introduction

Is user involvement in research and evaluation necessarily an empowering and liberatory activity? This has been a growing question for service users, service-user organisations and service-user researchers. There has been a tendency traditionally to approach benign sounding ideas like 'participation', 'user involvement' and 'empowerment' relatively uncritically. More recently, they have been subjected to more critical consideration. Their complexity and ambiguity have begun to be explored (see Baistow, 1995; Beresford and Croft, 1996; Cooke and Kothari, 2001). Increasingly, service users and service-user researchers are now concluding that the potential of user involvement in research and evaluation depends on the nature, process, purpose and methods of such research and evaluation.

At the same time, movements of disabled people, mental health service users/ survivors, people with learning difficulties, older people, people living with HIV/AIDS and so on, have developed their own research approaches, as well as undertaking their own research. The disabled people's movement was a pioneer in taking this forward. It identified a range of principles and values for research and evaluation. These included that research and evaluation should:

- be based on more equal relationships between researchers and research participants;
- work to support the empowerment of service users; challenging their disempowerment; and
- be committed to making broader political, social and economic change in line with the rights of service users (Oliver, 1996; Mercer, 2002).

Such an approach places question marks for some service users and service-user researchers over getting involved in research, which is not explicitly committed to these goals.

This questioning of whether user involvement in research may have regressive and regulatory implications as well as liberatory and empowering ones comes at a significant time. It is happening when there is increasing endorsement and support for greater user involvement in research from many quarters: from government, statutory and non-statutory research funders and commissioners; and from a growing number of researchers, research institutions, policy makers and practitioners, as well as from many service users and their organisations.

Some key concerns

There is thus a tension in current developments in user involvement in research. At once, there are increasing requirements and provisions for it and a growing questioning (particularly by service users) of its purpose and merits. This increasing questioning of user involvement in research by service users and their organisations; worries about what it is for, what it may mean for individuals and where it is leading, is now featuring in both informal and published discussions (for example, Lindow, 2001; Faulkner, 2003). Such doubts about user involvement may help explain why research approaches from service users tend to be framed in terms of emancipation and liberation, rather than participation, with participation seen as a necessary, but not sufficient, condition for liberatory or emancipatory research (Swain, 2001).

A range of concerns are now emerging from service users and service-user organisations. It may be helpful to focus on four of these:

1. the ideological basis of involvement;
2. whose discourse?
3. the purpose of research and evaluation; and
4. the nature of research values.

The ideological basis of involvement

Interest in user involvement in research and evaluation from government, service system and funders, has highlighted the importance of involving the perspectives of service users to inform research (by including their knowledge and viewpoints) and as a basis for informing policy making and the service system for improved efficiency and decision-making. In this, it echoes managerialist/ consumerist approaches to user involvement in policy and planning more generally. Service-user interest has been in the democratisation of research and its use as part of a broader strategy of liberation and change making. In this it reflects the democratic model of involvement developed by these service-user movements which prioritises improving people's lives and the circumstances in which they live.

These two approaches to user involvement have very different origins and commitments. The first, the managerialist/consumerist approach, developed in the last quarter of the 20th century out of the commitment of the emergent political New Right to more market-driven approaches in both political ideology and public policy, with a devaluing of state intervention and provision. It placed a new emphasis on purchase of services and individualised arrangements and responsibility for health and welfare. The recipient of welfare was reframed as a consumer (albeit sometimes an involuntary one) and rhetoric of individual 'choice, voice and exit' developed. With the emphasis on improving the 'three Es' (economy, efficiency and effectiveness), user involvement was framed in market research terms of 'improving the product' through market testing and customer feedback.

The managerialist/consumerist approach to user involvement has so far mainly been based on consultative and data collection methods of involvement. It has served both self-consciously and implicitly as a means of user 'intelligence gathering'. Its role has never been framed in terms of altering the distribution of power or the locus of decision making – although sometimes the rhetoric of involvement has hidden this. With the advent of New Labour administrations in the UK from 1997, accompanied by the terminology of the 'third way', there has been an increasing emphasis on the managerialist role of user involvement and provisions for user involvement in audit and inspection have been strengthened alongside existing arrangements for involvement in service planning, individual assessment, comment and complaints procedures and (in a consultative sense) in service management.

The democratic approach to user involvement is particularly linked with organisations and movements of disabled people and social care service users. It is primarily concerned with people having more say in agencies, organisations and institutions which impact upon them and being able to exert more control over their own lives. Service users' interest in participation has been part of broader political and social philosophies that prioritise people's inclusion, autonomy, independence and achievement of their human and civil rights. Participation has been one expression of a commitment to 'self-advocacy': of people being able to speak and act on their own behalf. It has also been conceived of primarily in terms of people's involvement through collective action in independent disabled people's and service users' groups and organisations. This democratic approach to involvement is explicitly political. It is centrally concerned with ensuring that service users as participants have the direct capacity and opportunity to make changes, and to effect influence on their lives and broader environments. It highlights issues of power and is clearly committed to the (progressive) redistribution of power (Campbell, 1996; Campbell and Oliver, 1996; Oliver, 1996; Newnes et al, 2001).

These two approaches to participation – the managerialist/consumerist and democratic approaches – are not necessarily consistent with each other. One is essentially a tool for information gathering, for executives to inform policy and provision without any commitment to the redistribution of power or control, while the other is liberatory in purpose, with a commitment to personal and political change and empowerment. The latter's concern is with bringing about direct change in people's lives through collective as well as individual action. While the logic of the democratic approach is for 'user-led' and 'user-controlled' services, a managerialist/consumerist approach is compatible with the retention of a provider-led approach to policy and services. The democratic approach is explicitly political (and can expect to come in for criticism for this reason), but the managerialist/consumerist approach tends to be abstracted and treated as if it were unrelated to any broader ideology or philosophy. The differences between the two approaches, however, are frequently not made explicit; so thus far, the managerialist/consumerist approach has predominated in public policy. Service users and their organisations frequently report that they experience initiatives for involvement as tokenistic. The gains from managerialist/consumerist approaches to user involvement are so far seen by many service users as limited.

There are signs that user-controlled research approaches reflect a democratic approach to participation, whereas the more numerous initiatives offering user involvement in research come closer to a managerialist/consumerist approach to participation. If this is the case (as it seems it might be), then, underpinning ideological differences may give rise to increasing concerns about tokenism which mainstream initiatives for user involvement in research and evaluation will need to examine and address (Faulkner, 2003).

Whose discourse?

Questions are now also being raised by service users and service-user researchers about whose discourse and whose knowledge; whose agendas, issues, concerns and interests user involvement in research and evaluation is seeking to advance. This is an important issue, bearing in mind that for many members of the disabled people's movement, which was a pioneer in developing its own research approaches, traditional research was seen as "a greater source of exploitation than liberation" (Barnes and Mercer, 1997, p 5). They emphasised the destructive effects of traditional research, arguing that it had formed part of a broader system of oppression manifest in the subordination of disabled people in western societies and the (discriminatory) responses that were made to their impairments (Oliver, 1990, 1996). Similarly, some mental health service users/survivors see much mainstream mental health research as having powerful and potentially damaging effects. They highlight the disproportionate influence the pharmaceutical industry has exerted, both on the nature and focus of research and on the 'treatments' which have generally been adopted.

Thus, for many active service users and service-user researchers, merely contributing to existing research approaches and focuses would not necessarily be seen as a progressive activity or one to prioritise. Major questions are raised for them. Will their involvement just be an 'add-on' which will serve to advance the service system and/or dominant government discourse and knowledge base? If so, is that necessarily consistent with service users' interests and empowerment? Service users and their organisations have learned that the interests and objectives of state and service system are not necessarily the same as theirs. How helpful is such involvement likely to be to the development and advancement of service users' own body of knowledge and cannon of work, analysis and discourse – or might it actually conflict with them? Is it enough to be involved merely to advance the dominant discourse and debate, in the process providing more knowledge for the state and service system, which may have oppressive potential? If service users and service-user researchers get involved in 'other people's research', then on what terms and conditions and what set of values and principles might ensure that this was ultimately a positive and progressive rather than a disempowering activity? These are large questions and, at the moment, we are at the beginning of recognising their significance. Much work still needs to be undertaken to address them.

The purpose of research and evaluation

Service users, particularly within the disabled people's movement, have identified a third and related concern. What is the purpose of research and evaluation? Is it primarily to extend the body of knowledge – that is to say, is it concerned fundamentally with a process of inquiry and knowledge formation (essentially for its own sake) – or is it, as Mike Oliver, the disabled theoretician and activist, has asked, to change and improve the lives of people as service users? Is its concern investigation *or* production? Oliver (1992, p 111) identified three key priorities for the 'emancipatory' research paradigm which the disabled people's movement pioneered: reciprocity, gain and empowerment:

> [D]isillusion with existing research paradigms has raised the issue of developing an alternative, emancipatory approach in order to make disability research both more relevant to the lives of disabled people and more influential in improving their material circumstances. (Oliver, 1996, p 141)

Oliver (1997), like other commentators has, however, emphasised that 'emancipation' is the goal, not necessarily the achievement, of such research. The degree to which such research may actually be able to support disabled people to emancipate themselves may often be limited and difficult to estimate. The point is that it is the primary aim and goal of the research which predetermines how and why it is undertaken.

People and groups experiencing high levels of exclusion, discrimination, disempowerment and impoverishment (such as health and social care service users), are much more likely to be concerned with research committed to change than research prioritising knowledge production.

The nature of research values

Finally, the question arises for service users and service-user organisations as to whether the value base of traditional/conventional dominant research paradigms can be reconciled with new paradigm and emancipatory research approaches of researchers associated with the health and social care service-user movements. The first set of approaches have stressed their scientific base and values of 'neutrality', 'distance' and 'objectivity'. The second set have been open about the value bias of all research and evaluation and about their own explicit commitment to and acknowledgement of subjectivity; the inherently political nature of research; its need to recognise where its affiliations lie; and their own determined commitment to empowerment and emancipation.

One of the consequences of more service-user involvement in research and evaluation is likely to be a shift in research from commitment to positivist methodology, towards increased interest in new paradigm research approaches. We need to ask if the two – that is, positivist and new paradigm research – can coexist or whether they are inherently incompatible and in conflict. If we conclude that the latter is the case, what are the implications likely to be? This is a matter of fundamental significance that cannot be glossed over because service-user and political enthusiasm for user involvement are pressing research projects and structures towards more participatory approaches. It demands to be addressed seriously and systematically.

There is also now an increasing interest among service users, their organisations and user researchers in *user-controlled* or *user* research. This closely connects with ongoing debates and emerging views about the four issues that have just been identified:

- the ideological basis of involvement;
- whose discourse?
- the purpose of research and evaluation; and
- the nature of research values.

Ambiguous responses to involvement

As yet, there is no agreed definition of user-controlled research; there is no consensus about its component parts or even what is meant by 'control'. What we can say is that it highlights research that:

- originates from service users (including research participants);
- involves them in (some or all of) its different stages;
- may include service users as researcher(s); and
- aims to advance the rights, needs and interests of service users.

An increasing number of service users are now becoming trained to undertake user-controlled research; a small but growing number of service users are embarking on PhDs and undertaking user-controlled research projects. Initiatives to undertake user-controlled research are being established in university research departments, as well as forming links from outside with such departments.

However, while there is now considerable and growing interest in and support for user involvement in research and evaluation, so far relatively little user-controlled research has been supported or commissioned. It continues to be the most difficult to get funding for and, as service users, its advocates tend to have the least conventional credibility. They are likely to be seen as being able to make the weakest knowledge claims.

These tensions and contradictions are reflected in the growing number of service users who are struggling on their own to become engaged in research, as well as the increasing efforts of service-user organisations struggling to get more user-controlled research and evaluation commissioned.

Ways forward

There is now a broad spectrum of research which addresses the issue of user involvement. It is important that the most comprehensive approaches to user involvement in research, emancipatory and user-controlled research approaches, come to be included in this spectrum on equal terms. So far, this does not seem to be happening. It is important to ask how the research community and research organisations, as well as the research funders and research commissioners, can support service users, service-user researchers and their organisations in order to take forward the development of user-controlled research systematically, and on more equal terms, so that its particular contribution, strengths and weaknesses may be subjected to systematic and thorough scrutiny and review. This is likely to raise practical and philosophical issues, as well as issues about supporting diversity and inclusion in a wide range of senses (for example, to ensure that the research contribution of people with learning difficulties, black and minority ethnic service users and service users who communicate differently (for example non-verbally) can be included on equal terms).

Supporting user-controlled research approaches so that they can develop effectively, is likely to require a joint initiative between non-service users and service users, with the former offering support, without taking control, enabling rather than leading; supporting service users to find space and resources, rather than taking hold of these themselves. This needs to be a focus for much more discussion between services users and other researchers. Only in this way is the full range of approaches to service-user involvement in research likely to develop – from very limited and specific involvement, to research developed and controlled by service users themselves. Only then will it be possible for user involvement to be systematically evaluated and reasonable judgements applied.

Overview

- There have been increasing requirements and provision for user involvement in research under New Labour.
- The extent of the empowering potential of user involvement depends on the nature, process, purpose and methods of the research/evaluation.

- Dominant discourses and practice in research user involvement tend to be rooted in the managerialist/consumerist model rather than the democratic one. Thus service users are often led to feel their contribution is tokenistic.
- There is a growing questioning among service users and service-user researchers as to the purpose and merits of user involvement. Is it to create change and improvements in the lives of service users or to merely add to a body of knowledge (and even perhaps be used in a way that may be found oppressive or disempowering)?
- There may be a conflict of methodologies between those associated with the democratic model (new paradigm approaches) and the more traditional positivistic research methods.
- Little user-controlled research has been supported or commissioned. There therefore needs to be much more discussion between service users and other researchers as to how the latter can support the former in such research without leading or taking control.

References

Baistow, K. (1995) 'Liberation and regulation: some paradoxes of empowerment', *Critical Social Policy*, vol 14, no 3, Winter, pp 34-46.

Barnes, C. and Mercer, G. (eds) (1997) *Doing disability research*, Leeds: The Disability Press.

Beresford, P. and Croft, S. (1996) 'The politics of participation', in D. Taylor (ed) *Critical social policy: A reader: Tyranny and participation*, London, Sage Publications, pp 175-98.

Campbell, P. (1996) 'The history of the user movement in the United Kingdom', in T. Heller, J. Reynolds, R. Gomm, R. Muston and S. Pattison (eds) *Mental health matters*, Basingstoke: Macmillan, pp 218-25.

Campbell, J. and Oliver, M. (1996) *Disability politics: Understanding our past, changing our future*, Basingstoke: Macmillan.

Cooke, B. and Kothari, U. (2001) *Participation: The new tyranny?*, London: Zed Books.

Faulkner, A. (2003) 'The emperor's new clothes', *Mental Health Today*, October, pp 23-6.

Lindow, V. (2001) 'Survivor research', in C. Newnes, G. Holmes and C. Dunn (eds) (2001) *This is madness too*, Ross-on-Wye: PCCS Books, pp 135-46.

Mercer, G. (2002) 'Emancipatory disability research', in C. Barnes, M. Oliver and L. Barton (eds) *Disability studies today*, Cambridge: Polity Press, pp 228-49.

Newnes, C., Holmes, G. and Dunn, C. (eds) (2001) *This is madness too*, Ross on Wye: PCCS Books.

Oliver, M. (1990) *The politics of disablement*, Basingstoke: Macmillan.

Oliver, M. (1992) 'Changing the social relations of research production', *Disability, Handicap & Society*, no 7, pp 101-15.

Oliver, M. (1996) *Understanding disability: From theory to practice*, Basingstoke: Macmillan.

Oliver, M. (1997) 'Emancipatory research: realistic goal or impossible dream?', in C. Barnes and G. Mercer (eds) *Doing disability research*, Leeds: The Disability Press, pp 15-31.

Swain, J. (2001) 'Review of: Kemshall, H., Littlechild, R. (editors) "User-involvement and participation in social care: Research informing practice"', *Disability & Society*, vol 16, no 4, pp 624-6.

FIVE

Best Value but not best interests: can service users instruct mental health advocates?

Hazel Platzer

Introduction

This chapter seeks to explore a dilemma. This is the dilemma faced by independent evaluators when they elicit views from service users which lead the evaluator to question the ethos of voluntary sector provision in mental health advocacy. A model of instructed advocacy that seeks to support mental health service users who wish to be heard dominates the mental health advocacy field. This model assumes that service users are sufficiently empowered to be able to recognise and articulate their needs and therefore to give instructions. However, the literature shows that instructed advocacy does not work well for many vulnerable and disempowered groups. Such groups need personal advocacy that comprises more support and befriending before they are able to instruct advocates. However, these forms of advocacy are inherently more expensive and less likely to be funded than instructed advocacy, which is seen as 'Best Value' in the current economic climate and consumer culture (Henderson and Pochin, 2001).

It is notoriously difficult to elicit the views of disempowered service users and to do so in a psychiatric hospital environment, with its climate of fear, is particularly problematic. I have personal experience of conducting observations and interviews with service users in the hospital environment with follow-up interviews after discharge. In some instances service users' views were at odds with the providers of mental health advocacy about the quality of psychiatric services. This has led to conflict between the evaluator and advocacy providers about how oppressive practices in psychiatric settings should be challenged. This chapter intends to stimulate discussion about the role of the evaluator in representing service users' views and how to proceed if the independence of the voluntary sector organisation has been compromised.

Henderson and Pochin (2001) have argued that the tendency for voluntary organisations to be caught up in 'contract culture' has allowed 'the Best Value approach' to influence both advocacy provision and its evaluation. They argue that this approach is fundamentally flawed and that it can corrupt the principles of advocacy because it fails to acknowledge the difficulty of finding unambiguous and measurable outcomes of success in advocacy. They argue that the outcomes aimed for and the processes by which they may be achieved are much more complex than the Best Value approach allows for. Best Value derives from a market system in which outcomes are clear and measurable. The argument is about whether Best Value approaches to service delivery and evaluation can be mapped onto advocacy. It parallels methodological debates about evaluation and the relative merits of focusing on processes or outcomes and formative versus summative evaluation. It may be useful to explore this debate further to see how evaluators can usefully work with advocacy organisations and to be mindful of political factors which may make this process more or less constructive.

Evaluating advocacy

If, as Henderson and Pochin (2001) assert, the voluntary sector is immersed in a Best Value culture, then an evaluator may find themselves being asked to conduct a goal-oriented, outcome-focused evaluation. Scott (1992) found this to be the case when evaluating a health promotion programme: health education workers can be as keen as funding bodies to narrow their scope to measurable outcomes. Robson (2000) has also stated that it is rare for funding bodies to be interested in why or how a programme works. We have to ask what is lost if this outcome-oriented approach is taken in terms of development of good practice. Scott (1992) has argued that an evaluation should critically examine the political basis of a project, take account of context and question the rationale for working in particular ways, as well as questioning the stated goals of a project. This is a potentially liberating way of working if the people involved in a project can use this as an opportunity to develop good practice and to justify and explain unintended but beneficial outcomes. However, if they are committed to a particular model of working for political reasons, perhaps tied to funding opportunities and established expertise, then the organisation may not be open to the kind of reflection required in such a process. Scott argues that such an approach needs to be negotiated and can be problematic especially if workers do not have adequate support. However, a good evaluation conducted in this way can lead to new and useful knowledge as well as helping to address and reformulate policy.

Scott's ideas about evaluation fit with approaches to evaluation where there is a commitment to understanding how outcomes are achieved. Such approaches require that the underlying theory which drives a programme is made explicit and that attention is paid to the conditions which allow certain outcomes to be realised (Pawson and Tilley, 1997; Clarke and Dawson, 1999; Robson, 2000). The theory underlying a programme is rarely explicit but can be deduced from talking to people involved in a project, looking at documents relating to a programme, drawing on previous literature and logical reasoning (Clarke and Dawson, 1999). Pawson and Tilley (1997) argue that theories are proposals about how mechanisms operate in particular contexts to produce outcomes. Perhaps, most importantly, it is not the programme activities themselves that are at stake but, rather, the response that those activities generate is the key to whether outcomes are realised. Thus an evaluation needs to question assumptions that programme activities generate the responses desired. At this point, then, it will be useful to consider the underlying theory about mental health advocacy, and in particular Patient Councils, in order to make explicit the assumptions about how certain ways of working are thought to produce desired outcomes.

Review of the literature

The review of the literature was conducted in order to look at how effective Patient Councils could be in terms of advocating for the collective issues that affect all service users in a psychiatric in-patient setting. In order to gain insight into this we need to look at the underlying principles and values which drive this approach to advocacy, the different ways in which Patient Councils can be organised and run, barriers to participation and the barriers to effecting change in the host organisations. The collective issues likely to be of concern to in-patients can easily be inferred from the evidence showing the problems in acute services. The environment is considered to be custodial and untherapeutic, with a lack of cultural sensitivity, a lack of user involvement in planning care and high levels of violence, restraint and injury (Sainsbury Centre for Mental Health, 1998; SNMAC, 1999).

Advocacy is driven by the core principle of independence from service providers and by placing value on empowerment (NHS Executive Mental Health Task Force User Group, 2000). Empowerment is an intended outcome of advocacy, but there are different approaches towards how this can best be achieved. There is a spectrum from citizen advocacy involving long-term personal and supportive relationships to technical or casework advocacy (Henderson and Pochin, 2001). There is a tendency for technical advocacy to be instructed; that is, it relies on people being able to tell an advocate what their advocacy needs are, with 'best interests' or personal advocacy and befriending at the other end of the continuum. The 'best interests' approach developed with client groups, such as people with severe learning disabilities, because they were unable to articulate needs. The model of advocacy that developed around this client group involved the development of long-term relationships with clients so that advocates could try to understand what a client would want for themselves if they were able to articulate their needs. The key feature of this, as with all other forms of advocacy, is that the advocate must not have any conflicting interests such as loyalties or concerns to the service provider. In mental health advocacy, however, instructed advocacy is the dominant model, which tends to involve casework around specific issues without a commitment to long-term involvement. It helps to provide very clear boundaries for advocates with host organisations, but it can be problematic if service users are not sufficiently empowered to be able to instruct (GLMHAN, 2001). Recent research evidence suggests that personal advocacy rather than instructed advocacy is more effective in increasing user involvement in treatment (Rosenman et al, 2000). It has also been found that instructed advocacy alone is not the most effective approach for a number of groups: women, ethnic minorities, lesbians and gay men, young people and older people, people who are very ill and people who are institutionalised (Robson, 1987; Grimshaw, 1996; Baker et al, 1997; Platzer, 2000; Ashworth Hospital Authority, 2001; Kelley, 2001; Mind in Barnet, 2001; Oliver and Warwick, 2001; Rai-Atkins et al, 2002).

It may be useful to consider why the instructed model of advocacy is dominant in mental health advocacy. Mental health advocacy schemes believe that the instructed model maintains clear boundaries and prevents advocates getting assimilated into or colluding with host organisations (that is, mental health care providers) (GLMHAN, 2001). There is also a belief that instructed advocacy in and of itself will result in empowerment, although it is also recognised that at times this is problematic if people cannot instruct (Advocacy 2000, 2001). It is also partly a result of advocacy increasingly being driven by the preference of funding bodies to commission schemes with clearly measurable outcomes (Henderson and Pochin, 2001).

The literature suggests that Patient Councils in the UK have had limited success in effecting real institutional change as far as the therapeutic environment in hospitals are concerned[1]. For instance, the claims about Hackney Patient Council (2000) were that it was not dramatic but that it fulfilled a social and support role for patients; others have found it impossible to bring about very basic improvements regarding menus and drinks (Newnes, 2001). Some Patient Councils have tended to focus on trying to effect change in the physical environment (such as security and catering) and increasing social activities within the hospital, rather than issues relating to clinical judgement and treatment (Gell, 1990). Hudson (1999) talks about the difficulties of effecting real shifts in attitude or power through Patient Councils, with hospital staff being unwilling to consider changes in policies or to reflect on clinical decision making. Where Patient Councils have extended their activities around policy issues they tend to have developed in the community, with more user involvement, rather than in in-patient settings (Gell, 1990).

Patient Councils in Holland have been established for longer and have legal recognition. They have elected representatives from each ward and take forward structural issues which have been highlighted by individual complaints. In this way, then, the Patient Council make it their remit to discuss policy issues such as the use of seclusion and Electro-Convulsive-Treatment (ECT) (Barker and Peck, 1987). It is possible, then, for Patient Councils to take forward collective issues which concern the therapeutic environment through questioning existing policies and procedures in hospitals. However, it is hard to find examples of this happening in the UK on matters relating to the therapeutic environment.

It is difficult to say exactly what the barriers are to such development. It is possible that outcomes-oriented programmes using instructed advocacy are not as empowering as the implicit theory underlying them would suggest. To refer back to Pawson and Tilley (1997), there may be a need to reconsider the mechanisms thought to bring about empowerment. The idea that providing instructions is in and of itself empowering may not be sufficient in a context where service users are so disadvantaged. From the literature already discussed it seems that a variety of approaches need to be used to facilitate and develop user involvement and participation.

Can instructed advocacy always empower?

I have conducted an evaluation over a two-year period of the effectiveness of Patient Councils in two acute psychiatric hospitals. The Patient Councils were facilitated by group advocates from an independent mental health advocacy organisation and the aim was to bring issues that were of collective concern to patients to the attention of hospital managers. During this evaluation, I discovered, through observation and interviewing, that in-patients had collective concerns about the physical and therapeutic environment in psychiatric hospitals. Although the Patient Council led to notable improvements in the physical environment, an increase in willingness of hospital and trust managers to consult users on such matters and an increase in levels of privacy for in-patients, there was less progress when matters were raised which concerned the therapeutic environment. In particular, the attitudes of hospital staff were raised on a number of occasions with emphasis on the use of excessive force during restraint and the use of medication as a threat.

It may be worth examining how concerns about restraint are dealt with by advocacy workers and by hospital staff when they are raised by service users. This is an area of vital importance in terms of whether or not a more therapeutic environment can be created. It was also a central objective of the Patient Council advocacy project to help improve relations between staff and patients about issues such as levels of restraint. When the issue of excessive force during restraint has been raised at Patient Council and then taken by advocacy workers to hospital managers there is often an investigation into what took place. This is then followed by an assurance that established hospital procedures had been adhered to in accord with current policy.

The literature and the evaluation suggest that paid advocates working with Patient Councils have not yet found a way of working which gets beyond this impasse. There was a lack of agreement between myself as independent evaluator, and the project managers, about the extent to which issues about restraint and over-medication, and their effect on the therapeutic environment were collective concerns of service users. There was also a difference between what service users said when they were in-patients, either at Patient Council or to the evaluator, and what they said once they had been discharged. It is possible that the Best Value approach, which insists on service-user consultation, in combination with the instructed model of advocacy, does a great disservice to service users who are not sufficiently empowered to clearly state their needs at the time of their incarceration. There are a number of reasons why service users are not necessarily able to clearly instruct not least of which is fear. The evaluation conducted by the author revealed the concerns of service users about the risks they took if they made their feelings known about poor treatment. The following quotations are taken from focus groups and interviews conducted with service users during the evaluation. In the first quotation, we can see that fear of retribution by hospital staff towards patients seen to be complaining about the system could prevent patients from 'instructing' advocates:

> "I got the feeling that I was in a hospital a bit like *One Flew Over the Cuckoo's Nest*. You have to be careful or you get put on heavier medication. I saw an old lady thrown to the ground by one of the staff. She was being extremely aggressive and she'd been told she couldn't go in the kitchen and then a very large fellow came out of a room and he threw her to the ground and I was disgusted. I was so upset by it I couldn't eat. I was hungry before that happened." (service user)

Another factor which may prevent service users from instructing in this context would be that they have no idea how change could be effected and this results in low expectations and low demands. The service user quoted above went on to make such a point:

> "I didn't raise it at Patient Council because I didn't really want to – I could see both sides of it. I could see the side where if you're looking after a lot of mentally ill patients, dealing with them day after day, you can't really cope, that's the time when you need to take a holiday, to take a break, but you can lose it. It is extraordinarily difficult." (service user)

What is particularly interesting about this service user is that he had not brought up the issue of violent restraint at Patient Council as he could not see where it could lead. It is this position which makes service-user consultation and instructed advocacy problematic when they are immersed in the Best Value culture as it can put the onus on service users themselves to come up with ideas about how to reform a system. If they cannot do this, and they are unlikely to have the resources to do so, then their lack of imagination or fear can be used ironically as an excuse for no action at all. So even though there is plenty of evidence and expert opinion about how much reform is needed, the lack of service-user involvement can be used by hospital managers as a reason for not improving care.

Advocacy organisations, in their efforts to be seen to be following instructions rather than assuming the best interests of their clients, may fail to close this loophole. They may even begin to acculturate their own user-volunteers who begin to adhere to the instructed model of advocacy in a way which prevents even their own views being put forward for fear of being seen as somehow unrepresentative of the user group which they are themselves part of. This is illustrated in the following extract from a focus group where two service users were discussing the need for Patient Councils to wait for issues to be raised rather than having topics presented for discussion:

> "It keeps a lot of unnecessary criticism at bay so the hospital managers can't say 'Oh, you just led them down that path, you elicited those responses from them, you've been trying to go that way already' ... I just think it has to be handled very, very cautiously." (service user acting as volunteer)

> "You mustn't be accused of putting words into people's mouths." (member of the service-user forum)

This slippage from a position where service users are supposed to be able to state their views to one in which they temper what they say to hospital managers is particularly worrying. It suggests that both a lack of service-user involvement and concerns about the representativeness of those who are involved can prevent advocacy organisations from developing a clear strategy that both empowers a broader base of users and takes forward the concerns raised by some. It is difficult to know to what extent the advocacy organisation is hampered by the position of mental health service providers on this who can use the card of 'unrepresentativeness' to dismiss concerns raised by users. Campbell (1990) has argued that this issue has never really been addressed and mental health service managers can easily undermine user participation by claiming users are not representative of the hospital population while failing to enable mechanisms that would increase representation. As Campbell maintains, the position that users are not representative is a strategy of inaction. It can therefore be used to block attempts at reform.

A particularly worrying example of how this can be used against service users is provided in the demise of the Patient Council at Ashworth Hospital. It was suggested during the Fallon enquiry (NHS Executive, 1999) that the Patient Council at Ashworth Hospital might have been taken over by patients diagnosed as having personality disorders and that this should be investigated. The subsequent investigation found this to be untrue (Ashworth Hospital Authority, 2001). However, the Patient Council was disbanded before the investigation had even taken place and was not reinstated afterwards. In the *Listening to patients* report (Ashworth Hospital Authority, 2001), the main criticism of the Patient Council by patients at Ashworth was that it was ineffective at instituting change and not that it was unrepresentative. However, the recommendations in the report were that the Patient Council should be disbanded because it did not represent patients. The fact that it did represent some patients did not seem to be taken into consideration and nor was there any attempt to make adjustments to the way the Patient Council operated. It seems sinister that a Patient Council could so easily be obliterated overnight in this way on such spurious grounds of 'unrepresentativeness' and is indicative of the problem identified by Campbell.

So, what we seem to have is a situation where the culture in the statutory mental health sector is not conducive to developing user involvement. Furthermore, there is an ironic possibility that mental health advocacy organisations mirror this through paying insufficient attention to ways of working which will empower the most disempowered service users. Their current ways of working, focusing mainly on an instructed advocacy approach, allow the involvement of relatively empowered service users. However, they can potentially be dismissed by hospital managers, or even dismiss themselves, on the grounds that they do not represent the wider patient body. If mental health advocacy organisations continue to focus their efforts on instructed advocacy and ignore other forms of advocacy that can enable and empower people to instruct, there is a danger that Patient Council projects will flounder. As Weigant (1988) has noted, Patient Councils can become mechanisms which 'oil the gears of management' rather than bringing about institutional change.

So long as an advocacy project is caught up in a Best Value culture with an outcome-oriented approach to practice and evaluation, there will be little opportunity to examine the processes which empower service users and allow them to clearly express their needs. As Henderson and Pochin (2001, p 121) have said, professionalised advocacy, which ignores the personal and befriending end of the continuum of advocacy (where empowerment can take place), is "scarcely less remote and impersonal than the health and care services to which (it was) supposed to promote access". Evaluation of these programmes needs to concentrate as much on process as outcomes, and question the underlying mechanisms if it is to make a useful contribution to developing good practice.

Overview

- A two-year evaluation of Patient Councils in two acute psychiatric hospitals raised issues about the underlying ethos driving mental health advocacy programmes.
- Evaluations commissioned within the restraints of a Best Value culture focused on goals and outcomes, can cause dilemmas for the evaluator who may be hindered from asking why a programme works and thus from discovering new and useful knowledge and helping to address and formulate policy.
- The Best Value approach in combination with the instructed model of advocacy is not conducive to developing user involvement as it enables only the involvement of relatively empowered service users.
- Mental health service providers often dismiss the views of the more empowered service users as 'unrepresentative' while at the same time doing nothing to increase representation.
- Advocacy projects need to be distanced from the 'Best Value' outcome-oriented culture in order to give opportunity to explore the processes which empower service users

Note

[1] This claim is made cautiously, since many Patient Councils will have not been formally evaluated or published reports of their activities.

References

Advocacy 2000 (2001) 'Introduction to advocacy' (website.lineone.net/~advocacy2000/welcomepage2.html).

Ashworth Hospital Authority (2001) *Listening to patients: Report on the Views and perception of Ashworth patients and staff on patient involvement and engagement.*

Baker, E.A., Bouldin, N., Durham, M., Lowell, M.E., Gonzalez, M., Jodiatis, N., Cruz, L.N., Torres, I., Torres, M. and Adams, S.T. (1997) 'The Latino Health Advocacy Program: a collaborative lay health advisor approach', *Health Education Behavior*, vol 24, pp 495-509.

Barker, I. and Peck, E. (1987) 'Dutch courage: advocacy and patients councils in Holland', in I. Barker and E. Peck (eds) *Power in strange places: User empowerment in mental health services*, London: Good Practices in Mental Health, pp 4-6.

Campbell, P. (1990) 'Mental health self-advocacy', in L. Winn (ed) *Power to the people: The key to responsive services in health and social care*, London: King's Fund Centre, pp 69-78.

Clarke, A. with Dawson, R. (1999) *Evaluation research: An introduction to principles, methods and practice*, London: Sage Publications.

GLMHAN (Greater London Mental Health Advocacy Network) (2001) *The Greater London Mental Health Advocacy Network: Who we are and where we're going – Plans for 2001-2005*, London.

Gell, C. (1990) 'User group involvement', in L. Winn (ed) *Power to the people: The key to responsive services in health and social care*, London: King's Fund Centre, pp 79-91.

Grimshaw, C. (1996) 'Awaaz: an Asian self-advocacy project', *OpenMind*, vol 79, p 13.

Hackney Patients Council (2000) *Hackney Patients Council – Report No. 13 for the period 1/2/00-30/4/00.*

Henderson, R. and Pochin, M. (2001) *A right result? Advocacy, justice and empowerment*, Bristol: The Policy Press.

Hudson, M. (1999) 'Psychiatric hospitals and patients' councils', in C. Newnes, G. Holmes and C. Dunn (eds) *This is madness: A critical look at psychiatry and the future of mental health services*, Ross-on-Wye: PCCS Books.

Kelley, N. (2001) 'Taking instructions', *OpenMind*, vol 107, p 11.

Mind in Barnet (2001) *Advocacy and older people: Unmet need*, London: Mind in Barnet.

Newnes, C. (2001) 'The commitments?', *OpenMind*, vol 107, pp 14-15.

NHS Executive (1999) *The report of the Committee of Inquiry into the personality disorder unit, Ashworth Special Hospital*, London: The Stationery Office.

NHS Executive Mental Health Task Force User Group (2000) *Advocacy – A code of practice developed by UKAN (United Kingdom Advocacy Network)*, London: NHS Executive Mental Health Task Force User Group.

Oliver, C. and Warwick, I. (2001) *The PACE Mental Health Advocacy Service: An evaluation by the Thomas Coram Research Unit, Institute of Education, University of London. Final Report*, London: PACE.

Pawson, R. and Tilley, N. (1997) *Realistic evaluation*, London: Sage Publications.

Platzer, H. (2000) *Lesbian and Gay Advocacy and Training Project: An independent evaluation of the first year of operation*, Brighton and Hove: MIND.

Rai-Atkins, A. (in association with Jama, A.A., Wright, N., Scott, V., Perring, C., Craig, G. and Katbamna, S.) (2002) *Best practice in mental health: Advocacy for African, Caribbean and South Asian communities*, Bristol: The Policy Press.

Robson, C. (2000) *Small-scale evaluation: Principles and practice*, London: Sage Publications.

Robson, G. (1987) 'Nagging: models of advocacy', in I. Barker and E. Peck (eds) *Power in strange places: User empowerment in mental health services*, London: Good Practices in Mental Health.

Rosenman, S., Korten, A. and Newman, L. (2000) 'Efficacy of continuing advocacy in involuntary treatment', *Psychiatric Services*, vol 51, pp 1029-33.

Scott, S. (1992) 'Evaluation may change your life, but it won't solve all your problems', in P. Aggleton, A. Young, D.M.K. Moody and M. Pye (eds) *Does it work? Perspectives on the evaluation of HIV/AIDS health promotion*, London: Health Education Authority.

SNMAC (Standing Nursing and Midwifery Advisory Committee) (1999) *Mental health nursing: "Addressing acute concerns"*, London: DH.

Sainsbury Centre for Mental Health (1998) *Acute problems: A survey of the quality of care in acute psychiatric wards*, London: Sainsbury Centre for Mental Health.

Weigant, H. (1988) 'Users' councils in Holland', *Asylum*, vol 2, pp 5-7.

SIX

New Deal for Communities as a participatory public policy: the challenges for evaluation

Kay Graham and Amanda Harris

Introduction

The current Labour administration has introduced a raft of policies that hinge upon public participation. While this is often limited to consultation exercises (for example, the Best Value and Crime and Disorder legislation), some policies have gone much further. One of the best examples of a highly participatory policy is the New Deal for Communities (NDC) initiative, which forms a substantial part of the government's neighbourhood renewal agenda. It stipulates that local people must be integrally and meaningfully engaged in all aspects of programme development and delivery. A further feature of the current government's approach is its sharp focus on evidence-based policy making, thus we have seen a large investment in evaluative activities. For the first time, participatory evaluation can be explored on a large scale. This chapter argues that evaluation itself can be used as a means of public engagement, but to do so it may be necessary to look outside traditional methodologies and consider more creative approaches. This chapter introduces a range of creative methods that can be used to encourage the participation of all sectors of the community.

Policy background

The NDC was launched in 1998 as part of the government's 'National Strategy for Neighbourhood Renewal' (DETR, 1998). This is now widely touted as the government's 'flagship' regeneration programme, which is costing almost £2 billion and is implemented nationally by the Office of the Deputy Prime Minister (ODPM). Its aim is to reduce the gap between the least and most prosperous areas in the country so that in ten years' time, no one should be seriously disadvantaged by where they live (DETR, 1998). In total, 39 geographically small urban areas, exhibiting extreme levels of multiple deprivation, were selected to become NDC partnerships. There were 17

'Pathfinder' NDCs announced in 1998 and a further 22 partnerships were launched the following year.

The NDC programme is a 'comprehensive' regeneration programme, which encompasses employment, crime, education, health and housing. While each partnership must include these five themes in its programme, local circumstances may influence the inclusion of others.

Aside from the thematic focus, there are a number of key features of the NDC programme which distinguish it from previous regeneration initiatives. First, partnerships should be led by local people. This is usually through representation on partnership boards and involvement in funding decisions. Another key characteristic of NDC is that interventions should be based on evidence of 'what works'. Third, and in stark contrast to former programmes such as the Single Regeneration Budget (SRB), NDC programmes should focus on *outcomes*, rather than activities or outputs. Finally, NDC partnerships are required to reshape the way in which mainstream services (such as the police, local authority services and so on) are delivered. The government hopes that, due to these factors, significant change will occur that will be sustainable long after the life of the programme. The NDC is clearly intended to be the catalyst required to reverse the generations of decline these areas have experienced.

Evaluation and NDC

An emphasis on evidence-based policy making, as well as a focus on outcomes, has led NDC to be a programme highly dependent upon evaluation. While there is an acceptance that the programme can be informed by evidence from existing sources (for example, evaluations of SRB, City Challenge), it is fairly widely accepted that NDCs are intended to be a source of evaluative evidence as well as a response to it. This means that evaluation has possibly never before been so important in public policy.

The ODPM commissioned a national evaluation of the NDC programme in 2001. The body responsible for this work comprises a number of organisations, and represents the largest evaluation ever commissioned by the government. It aims to provide critical information on what works, for whom and in which circumstances, and has a substantial formative as well as summative aspect. Each NDC partnership has a local contact from the evaluation team who researches the partnership and provides ongoing feedback. There are also teams that concentrate on generating knowledge in the five statutory theme areas partnerships are pursuing. The principal aim of the evaluation is to ensure effective delivery of the NDC programme during its life, rather than learning lessons after the event. Further support is available to partnerships (and, indeed, other practitioners and policy makers) in the form of the online resource, www.renewal.net. Established by ODPM, the system offers users access to evaluation evidence in neighbourhood renewal.

Despite the huge resource of the national evaluation, it clearly cannot provide the level of detail required to inform all partnership decisions. Individual partnerships have invested in evaluation to differing degrees; each partnership does have a statutory requirement to evaluate their position (against original baselines) at the end of years three, six and ten. Most partnerships have either relied upon the national evaluation to fulfil this obligation or they have commissioned evaluative work to local research organisations. Nottingham NDC stands out as having made an extraordinary investment in evaluation. It has a dedicated evaluation team and has adopted a rolling programme of evaluation in order to ensure that service delivery is continually informed by evaluation findings.

A participatory approach

Since local people should lead NDCs, it is a logical step to also adopt a participatory approach to the evaluation. This means that evaluation itself becomes another mechanism for public engagement. Participatory evaluation attempts to meaningfully involve all stakeholders in the examination and assessment of an intervention process (Charities Evaluation Service, 1998d). In particular, it will seek to involve those who are traditionally viewed as the least powerful in the development and implementation of interventions, namely service users and deliverers and project staff (Guijit and Gaventa, 1998).

When adopting a participatory approach, structures and processes are developed to enable everyone to play a key role within the evaluation process. Stakeholders may become involved in deciding the scope of the evaluation, designing and conducting research, analysing findings and making recommendations for change. Using a truly participatory approach, stakeholders will become involved not just as research subjects responding to research questions but also as evaluators.

Thus, the purpose of evaluation and the role of the (professional) researcher must change in a participatory evaluation. The researcher must shift their role to act as a facilitator, guiding the evaluation, but allowing others to lead; and the process of evaluation becomes a mechanism to increase the skills, knowledge and influence of others. A participatory evaluation will seek to increase the capacity of those who often have the least power, to take action and create change (OESP, 1997).

Participatory evaluation challenges the notion of objective, independent enquiry to assess an intervention. Instead, the knowledge and values of stakeholders are recognised and positively embraced. Their perceptions do not invalidate the research, rather they are openly acknowledged, and give a depth and richness to the evaluation. In a participatory evaluation, because stakeholders are directly affected by the impact of an intervention, it is they who judge its success through a process that is meaningful to them.

Box 6.1: Characteristics of participatory evaluation

- It draws on local resources and capacities.
- It recognises (or even *prioritises*) the wisdom and knowledge of local people.
- It ensures that stakeholders are a key part of the decision-making process.
- Participants *own* the evaluation process, rather than being 'subjected' to it.
- Participants work together, usually as a group, on the evaluation. A facilitator could support their work (yet only acting as a catalyst for others' ideas).
- All parts of the evaluation process are relevant to the participants rather than being imposed upon them.

Participatory evaluation offers a number of advantages for the NDC programme: local people are integrally involved in it; it builds up capacity within that community; and is based on the principles of empowerment, equity and democracy – all of which are guiding principles in the whole programme. Additionally, it affords local people the opportunity to learn new skills and encourages them to engage with local issues.

However, it is not without its problems. It is incredibly time consuming and innovative ways have to be considered when trying to persuade local people to get involved. Involving people from different backgrounds, with different perspectives can also potentially lead to conflict that may be difficult for the evaluator or facilitator to manage. Finally, participatory evaluation can lead to the feeling of loss of control – it may initially feel chaotic to the evaluator accustomed to a more traditional approach. It is for the evaluator to learn how to *be* participatory and to relax some of the controls they usually have over the research.

There are a number of ways in which to involve local people in evaluation. These can be conceptualised in the same way as Arnstein's (1969) 'ladder of participation' – from local people acting as research respondents (or perhaps even only being informed of findings) at one end to leading the evaluation at the other. Clearly, there are many different ways of participating in an evaluation, and a stakeholder's relationship to an evaluation can be viewed on a continuum. While a truly participatory approach would be further up the ladder and involve a high degree of control by service users, one has to carefully consider which forms of participation are most appropriate for an evaluation and, indeed, for the participants.

If we recognise that participation can occur at any step on the ladder, then *any* evaluation can be tailored to a participatory approach – whether it adopts a qualitative or quantitative methodology. While the former perhaps has a more obvious application to participatory evaluation, many participatory techniques can be quantified, for example service users can design, administer and analyse questionnaire surveys with support and training. This has many of the benefits of a participatory approach, yet uses a quantitative research method. Service users could also be supported to analyse secondary data sources, as their interpretations are likely to be invaluable. Involvement of service users can also be incorporated into research design in other supported or non-threatening ways such as, for example, the co-facilitation of focus groups, participation in a group to discuss emerging findings, recruiting respondents and so on. So, participation can be an underlying principle or ethos regardless of the methodological approach.

Is there a need to reconsider traditional methods?

Since participatory evaluation reflects a willingness to accept the knowledge and skills of others and to share information and control, perhaps the most popular and widely accepted research methods (surveys, interviews, focus groups, and so on) need to be set to one side so that we can consider more creative approaches. These are likely to be far less exclusionary for some of the more readily quashed voices (for example, people with English as an additional language, people with learning difficulties or disabilities, children and young people) who can communicate in ways in which they are perhaps more comfortable.

While this chapter has argued that any piece of research or research method could be participatory, if there is an openness and commitment to participation, some approaches will lend themselves more readily to a truly participatory approach than others. The selection of methods will depend, of course, upon the nature of the research questions, the local context and the interests and concerns of the stakeholders involved. It will be the role of the evaluator (as facilitator) to advise on appropriate methods for the task at hand.

An array of creative approaches can be employed in a participatory evaluation. The advantages they offer are that they are often viewed as less 'technical' and, therefore, less threatening by participants, and may spark interest and encourage participation. They do not rely on literacy or highly developed interpersonal skills, nor is there an assumption that there can be a 'right' or 'wrong' answer. Participants may also feel much more involved in the process. There are potentially a limitless number of creative approaches that may be tailored to evaluative purposes. Here follows a discussion of some that have been attempted at Nottingham NDC.

Photography

Photography can be used in a variety of ways. These include:

- diary or storyboard shots, which could represent 'a day in the life of ...';
- 'before and after' photographs, for example to show changes in the physical environment;
- action shots can be used to record project activity or an event;

- imagery (images can be used to invoke feelings or evaluate people's perceptions. An image is selected to represent a person's response to a posed question); and
- mapping: participants could be asked a question, such as 'What does the area you live in mean to you?' They are then required to explore and report back using photography.

Sculpture

The shape, form and texture of sculpture can be used to record events and communicate emotions. Participants can be provided with a range of materials (soft clay, building bricks, Plasticine, and so on) and asked to record their feelings or experiences in response to a particular question. As with many creative methods, if participants are working in a group, their discussions while they are creating their sculpture can often be as revealing as the product itself. Evaluators can take the opportunity to prompt and probe (for example, 'Why are you doing that?' or 'What does that mean?', and so on). Participants should be allowed time to create and recreate their sculpture, while the evaluator or observer records process and change.

Textiles

We make associations with colour and texture, which can be used as a form of expression. The selection of materials and their positioning can reveal perceptions and emotions in relation to a posed question (such as 'How do you feel about …?'). Again, questioning participants while they are creating their pieces can reveal what certain aspects mean to them. Participants should be provided with a range of materials (feathers, felt, sandpaper, fabric, corrugated cardboard, metal, beads, and so on) and fastenings in many colours, both bright and pale.

Storytelling

Storytelling may record a person's thoughts, feelings and experiences. It is a way of learning about a project or its impact through the voices of participants and stakeholders. It can also corroborate other sources of data and information and provide a more personal insight into a project's achievements. Stories capture progress by focusing on one person's or organisation's account of change. It can be particularly useful for depersonalising traumatic events through the use of metaphor and characterisation.

Social mapping

This involves participants constructing a 'map', using a variety of images. Images are selected, positioned and grouped to represent key themes, community structures, local organisations and networks, or the life of the project (for example, using key stages such as 'securing funding', 'recruitment', and so on). Mapping tells a 'story' and provides invaluable insights into interactions (or lack of) within the community, the resources that are available and access to them. Participants can work in facilitated groups to interpret the maps created. Evaluators should be careful to ensure that interpretations take into account the characteristics of participants. For example, when constructing mental maps, elderly residents may include local features that are no longer present.

Drama

A variety of movement and 'sculpting' exercises can be used to assess values, perceptions and emotions (see University of Manchester, 2002, for examples of exercises). Participants will need to be 'warmed up' (for example, "Position yourself across this line depending upon how much you agree with X", "Stand up and swap seats if you like chocolate") as drama can be daunting for some participants. Eventually, participants can be asked to work in groups to create a scene in 'statues', while other participants interpret their positions, facial expressions, and so on. Care should be taken to respect gender, age and cultural difference.

Creative approaches can offer a number of advantages for (participatory) evaluation. First, by their very nature, they allow the creator to express emotions, experiences or aspirations. Creative 'products' are highly symbolic, often telling us more about the creator themselves than the product. People often feel less inhibited expressing themselves through a medium other than speech or writing. Second, they offer a way of not only collecting information, but *presenting* it. It makes a visual impact, so participants can more readily take part in the interpretation of the pieces – both theirs and those created by others. Third, creative approaches have the potential to engage different groups of people, particularly those who have communication difficulties (including inhibitions) or those who communicate differently to one another. As mentioned earlier, they can be particularly helpful in multicultural groups, with people with learning difficulties or disabilities and with children and young people. Fourth, they offer safer spaces for expression by depersonalising emotional stories (for instance, when working with metaphor). Fifth, while participants engage in creative activities, there is an opportunity for evaluators to ask questions, prompt and probe to add to the richness of the data collected. The process, therefore, is as important as the participants and the products.

Finally, and actually very importantly, creative methods are fun! Some participants are often much more likely to want to take part in, say, creating pieces of sculpture than a structured interview. Although creative approaches appear to offer great promise, their application in evaluation remains in its infancy. It should also be remembered that unless they are introduced and managed well, they could potentially be exclusionary to some groups. One further challenge is the interpretation of findings. The evaluation community is comfortable with narratives and numbers, but when presented with, say, images, some of the skills of art criticism may need to be drawn upon and incorporated into our evaluative methodologies. Evaluators also have to be mindful of the need to impute the *process* of creation into the interpretation of findings, in the same way an ethnographer would.

In Nottingham NDC, people have, in the main, been receptive to these 'fun ideas'. They have definitely considered them less threatening and found ways to build them into project activities more readily than the 'burdensome' traditional approaches to evaluation. People are also beginning to recognise evaluation as another way of engaging local residents in the programme. It is true that people are often initially sceptical, but most actually begin to enjoy and value the evaluative process.

Box 6.2: A project evaluation using multiple creative methods

Project background

The Creating Learning Links project (supported by Nottingham NDC) sought to put extra support staff in local primary schools. It was originally envisaged solely as an intervention to raise educational achievement. The project has been successful in recruiting African Caribbean and Asian communities, and men into the teaching profession, and is now as much a positive action recruitment initiative, as it is an educational one. There are 12 teaching assistants in accredited training, placed within ten local primary schools. Of these, 11 are from minority ethnic communities, five are male and four are local residents.

Evaluation challenges

The principal challenge was to include a range of stakeholders in the evaluation, including local children. This meant that a variety of methods were required to appropriately work with children of different ages.

Research methods

Nursery

Two persona dolls were used and introduced to the children. Information about 'Jack' and 'Anisah' and their school was told to build up character and introduce discussion. Using puppets to introduce discussion is commonly used in education and youth work, and was an approach with which this group of children were familiar. The puppets were used to introduce discussion, about the classroom, the playground, favourite activities and their teacher (for example, "Jack likes to do X, what do you like to do at school?"). The children were shy (and, in retrospect, more time was needed to build relationships), but spoke of their favourite activities, named their teachers and the things they and

---

their teachers did together. The children talked of how they had seen their teaching assistant play football with bigger boys, had put a plaster on their knee when they fell and played dinosaurs, sand and building with them.

Year 3

The children had a number of postcards, each with a half statement, and a selection of words and pictures to use to complete the statement (they had about 15 options). They also had pens to write or draw their own options if they wished.

When I am with Mr/Miss .... we ....

Mr/Miss .... has helped me to ....

When I am with Mr/Miss .... I feel ....

I would like Mr/Miss .... to ....

I don't like it when Mr/Miss ....

Having two teachers means that ....

The children stuck the statements onto the postcards and then posted them into a postbox. The children were supported in this task by some gentle probing while they were busy creating. Afterwards, postcards were selected randomly by the children and discussed. The children had also drawn some pictures of their school and teachers that we discussed.

Year 6

A graffiti-wall exercise was used. The following statements were displayed on sheets of paper:

Describe Mr/Miss .... What is he/she like?

What work do you do with Mr/Miss... ?

Mr/Miss .... has helped me to ....

What makes a good teacher?

What is the worst thing that adults/teachers do?

Having two teachers means that ....

Afterwards each sheet was discussed.

Discussions with Years 3 and 6 were recorded. The children were very at ease with the recording equipment, and enjoyed listening to their own voices.

A number of issues arose from employing this creative approach. More time was needed to build up relationships with the younger children, and great care was needed to explain the purpose of the research, and issues of confidentiality and anonymity, with all the different age groups. In the older age group, the boys tended to dominate the discussion, and so we would probably advocate single sex groups in the future. Gender differences did not seem to be such an issue with the other groups, but smaller group work with the Year 3s may have been better (there were eight in a group, with two facilitators), and more one-to-one work with the younger children. The 'informal' discussion that took place while creating was as important as the 'official' discussion time afterwards. The use of recording equipment proved very popular (the older children all sang a song into the microphone afterwards!) as did making postcards, and writing about the worst things that adults do!

These methods were developed by referring to examples of good practice, and in negotiation with project and school staff, and with Play Development Workers. This work, although adopting a creative approach that enabled children to exhibit considerable control over the research process, was not as participatory as it could have been, since the children themselves were not involved in the development of research methods. An evaluation of the children's experience in this research needs to take place, as does the further involvement of children in developing appropriate research methods.

Conclusion

Many public policies now place beneficiaries and service users at their heart. Arguably, the NDC programme is currently one of the most participatory public policies, where local people are intended to control and drive its delivery. Evaluation is critical to such programmes and, due to their participatory nature, we argue that there is a need to embrace less conventional approaches so that the evaluation process itself can become a vehicle for engagement. Engaging people in evaluation means allowing service users the opportunity to control the evaluation, offering different and perhaps more appropriate methods to explore their experiences, needs and aspirations.

The use of participatory methods, although often highly interactive, should not exclude the use of more traditional (or even quantitative) methods. Depending on the initiative, it might be beneficial to combine various methods and approaches. The thoughtful evaluator will find ways to build in public participation. It is not enough, however, simply to advocate participation – one must *be* participatory. Being participatory involves more than using a particular technique or approach. It reflects an attitude towards human interaction. It means exhibiting a willingness to share decision making and power.

We have argued that creative approaches to evaluation can offer significant benefits for increased public participation. If adopting such approaches, there is the issue of balancing what is considered to be credible and valid data with what is 'good enough'. The approach may challenge what people consider rigorous data collection. Adopting creative approaches requires accepting new, less rigid standards of what is relevant and valid data. While what is conventionally accepted as 'rigour' may be viewed as being compromised, the service, project or policy gains so much through truly engaging those whose views matter in a way which is less threatening than traditional research methods. Generally, the findings will not be neat and quantifiable, but the richness of the data can be unparalleled. If resistance to creative methods is too high, evaluators can consider mixing their methods to boost the validity and reliability of findings. However, to completely fail to engage with these methods could lead to compromising the depth of understanding and excluding some beneficiary groups.

Participatory evaluation can be used to build skills and knowledge and can contribute to empowering local communities. It can also be used to ensure evaluations address locally relevant questions, contribute to strengthening local projects and support the development of sustainable partnerships. We believe that the evaluation community and policy makers need to properly embrace more creative, participatory methods which can offer very significant spin-offs for public policy development and the evaluation discipline.

Overview

- Policies requiring a high degree of public participation should seriously consider participatory approaches to their evaluation, thereby allowing another opportunity for engagement.
- In order to fully engage all parts of the community, particularly those groups which may be marginalised, creative approaches offer great potential.
- Creative methods may encourage local people to participate as they are often seen as less threatening than traditional approaches and more enjoyable.
- Examples of creative methods include photography, sculpture, textiles, storytelling, social mapping and drama.
- The participatory/creative approach does raise a number of challenges, but these should be faced, as to fail to engage with them could lead to compromising a depth of understanding and excluding some beneficiary groups.

References

Arnstein, S.R. (1969) 'A ladder of citizen participation', *American Institute of Planners Journal*, vol 35, pp 216-24.

Charities Evaluation Service (1998a) *The purpose of evaluation*, Discussion Paper 1, London: Charities Evaluation Service.

Charities Evaluation Service (1998b) *Different ways of seeing evaluation*, Discussion Paper 2, London: Charities Evaluation Service.

Charities Evaluation Service (1998c) *Self-evaluation*, Discussion Paper 3, London: Charities Evaluation Service.

Charities Evaluation Service (1998d) *Involving users in evaluation*, Discussion Paper 4, London: Charities Evaluation Service.

Charities Evaluation Service (1998e) *Performance indicators: Use and misuse*, Discussion Paper 5, London: Charities Evaluation Service.

Charities Evaluation Service (1998f) *Using evaluation to explore policy*, Discussion Paper 6, London: Charities Evaluation Service.

Children in Need (1999) *Guide to self evaluation*, London: Children in Need.

Connell, J., Kubisch, A., Schorr, L. and Weiss, C. (eds) (1995) *New approaches to evaluating community initiatives*, Washington, DC: The Aspen Institute (www.aspenroundtable.org).

DETR (Department of the Environment, Transport and the Regions) (1998) *Bringing Britain together: A national strategy for neighbourhood renewal*, London: Neighbourhood Renewal Unit.

Fetterman, D.M. (2000) *Foundations of empowerment evaluation*, Thousand Oaks, CA: Sage Publications.

Fetterman, D.M., Kaftarian, A.J. and Wandersman, A. (eds) (1995) *Empowerment evaluation: Knowledge and tools for self-assessment and accountability*, London: Sage Publications.

Guijit, I. and Gaventa, J. (1998) *Participatory monitoring and evaluation: Learning from change*, Institute of Development Studies (www.ids.ac.uk/ids/bookshop/briefs/Brief12.html).

New Economics Foundation (2000) *Prove it!*, London: New Economics Foundation.

OESP (Office of Evaluation and Strategic Planning) (1997) *Who are the question-makers? A participatory evaluation handbook*, OESP, UN Development Programme (www.undp.org/eo/documents/who.htm).

University of Manchester (2002) *Artpad*, Manchester: Centre for Applied Theatre Research, University of Manchester.

Van der Eyken, W. (1993) *Managing evaluation*, London: Charities Evaluation Service.

SEVEN

Discovery through dialogue and appreciative inquiry: a participative evaluation framework for project development

Glynis Cousin, Judith Cousin and Frances Deepwell

Introduction

The requirement of funding bodies for projects to report on the delivery of their outputs is clearly acceptable because it is reasonable to require a project to demonstrate contract compliance. At the same time, an evaluation that is limited to such a report is trapped in 'audit logic' (O'Neill, 2002) which is incapable of fully supporting project development. Indeed, we argue that a listing of outputs constitutes little more than an audit and barely deserves the name evaluation if it cannot capture process or so-called soft outcomes (Dewson, 2000) or a statistical report of deliverables.

We accept, however, that many evaluations that do focus on such outcomes are burdensome on the project members' time and energy. This chapter explores ways in which these can be evaluated manageably and creatively to support project development. In making this exploration, we first discuss the posture of the evaluator and, second, we present some ideas and illustrations from the perspectives of realistic evaluation (Pawson and Tilley, 1997) and appreciative inquiry (Ludema et al, 2001) respectively.

The evaluator's posture

Project teams are often under pressure to secure the services of an external evaluator who will take up an objective stance. We fully accept that an external evaluator needs to keep some 'reflective distancing' from the project (Wadsworth, 2002a, 2002b) in that s/he needs to be capable of standing outside of the project even while working alongside its members. But we do not accept that an external evaluator should see the evaluation site as a research field that she visits dispassionately for the gathering of data, as if researcher distance guaranteed objectivity and reliability.

The call for objective external evaluation is often tied to the positivist belief that there is a 'truth' to be got at through the deployment of an impartial evaluation capable of identifying the 'facts' that are thought to correspond to truths. We think that it is more realistic to approach evaluation research as a means by which increased understanding about a project and the issues it addresses is developed (Baume, 2003). We are aware that some project members feel that they have neither the time nor the inclination for this kind of evaluation, either because the obligation to evaluate has been imposed upon them or because funders have already prescribed how an evaluation must be conducted. Clearly, external evaluators must work within these constraints but in our experience, project teams can be persuaded to expand on the formal requirements of a funder's prescriptions if they are offered manageable methods for such an expansion. We now turn to our discussion of how we think this can be done, using examples from our own practice.

Less is more

Pawson and Tilley's (1997) framework avoids a data-driven evaluation strategy on the grounds that this tends to overwhelm the evaluator with the job of collecting anything and everything that can pass as data. There is a popular conflation in the data-driven perspective of data with evidence. This is particularly so if the evaluator is following an inductive method in which she is expecting the analysis to emerge from the data (Strauss and Corbin, 1997). Within this researcher-centred method, the burden on project members is to hand over the data (focus groups, interviews, and so on), while the burden on the evaluator is to cut and paste this data on her/his dining room floor or in her/his software package in order to second-guess what the data segments might mean. This is a laborious and time consuming process. The evaluator may eventually offer a draft report of her/his findings but s/he has already processed her/his data in a particular direction. In contrast, Pawson and Tilley's 'theory-driven' perspective is dialogic in that it variously positions the evaluator and project members as teachers and learners within a shared research project that invites a more thoroughly iterative process with stakeholders. In this model, early impressions, drafts and ideas can be circulated in documentary form or orally presented for project team comment. This method also enables critical observations from the evaluator to be discussed in solution-oriented ways rather than in judgemental ones.

In the theory-driven model, the evaluator brings into the project insights and provisional hypotheses taken from her/his knowledge of the relevant field. S/he initially positions her/himself as 'teacher' and raises questions with stakeholders which are aimed at testing her/his theories about what may be happening. Unlike many researchers, however, s/he shares her theoretical thinking with stakeholders. For instance, in evaluating a higher education project on linking teaching and research, Glynis Cousin summarised some key theoretical ideas about the nature of contemporary research and circulated these to the project team. She felt that these ideas were of particular relevance to the project and that engagement with them would be enriching. At a project team meeting, members discussed the extent to which these ideas may be applied to their context and they in turn taught the evaluator about their specific experiences and perspectives. This approach gets the evaluator and the stakeholders talking and reflecting on what works or what is happening within an exchange of expertise. This expertise may be bookish, experiential, formally or informally acquired; the issue here is to find an evaluation context for its exchange.

There would be many projects where the production of discussion documents, as in the example given earlier, would be entirely inappropriate. One method Judith Cousin has used for stimulating dialogue concerned young people with poor social and basic skills. These youths were provided with lots of household paint colour strips and asked to use the colours to express their experience of the project. The evaluator discussed the results by exchanging ideas with the young people as to what they might mean and by eventually producing explanatory captions with them.

For many researchers, letting 'interviewees' into the secrets of their theories or assumptions incurs a high risk of suggestion. To pose a question such as, 'I think the children may be truanting because they have never felt that they belonged to the school' is felt to channel the response and to block out a more spontaneous and apparently more truthful one. But to worry about suggestive questions like this is to displace the problem. As Pawson and Tilley (1997) argue, researcher anxiety about constructing the carefully crafted question that can elicit uncontaminated responses from people is based on a view of humans as answering machines. Much more dangerous to the risk of suggestion is the power relation which inheres in interviewer–interviewee interactions (Oakley, 1981) and which affects the quality of the response. In contrast, the drift of Pawson and Tilley's model of research is one of establishing adult-to-adult relations, of privileging dialogue and of yielding data from a reflective process in which theories about what works and what is happening can be built collaboratively and with productive exchanges between different kinds of expertise. This perspective also chimes well with Robert Stake's (1981) notion of 'responsive evaluation' (see Greene and Abma, 2001), Deepwell and Cousin's (2002) conversational approach and MacLure and Stronach's (1997) 'report and respond' methods. In each of these methods, provisional evaluations are drawn up by evaluators and presented to the stakeholders for their responses.

To summarise, the three benefits of dialogic methods of the kind we have outlined are that:

a) the data tends to be very rich;
b) it tends to be more manageable because the analysis is shared; and
c) the establishment of a teacher–learner dialogue offers strong support for the development of a project.

In borrowing from appreciative inquiry (Ludema et al, 2001) for the collection of positive stories, we hope to show further ways in which to keep the data collection and analysis both manageable and rich.

What gives life here?

Researchers, including evaluation researchers, tend to be attracted to problem-oriented questions. For instance, in her work in establishing a 'dialogue conference', Palshaugen (2001, p 213) begins the first session of such a conference with the question, 'What do you consider are, respectively, the biggest problems and the greatest potential for improvements at your enterprise?'. The negative is thought to be balanced with a positive here, reflecting the kind of 'strengths and weaknesses' or SWOT (strengths, weaknesses, opportunities and threats) vtype analysis that drives much Western-based project development discussion. Citing the weaknesses of a project, however, often leads to a protracted and less coherent account of problems and leaves little space in a discussion for the negative balance to shift towards the positive. In contrast, Ludema et al (2001) argue in their article, 'Appreciative inquiry: the power of the unconditional positive question', for a different kind of guiding research question, namely 'What gives life here?'. How we pose questions, they write, has a great bearing on the quality of data we get:

> If we devote our attention to what is wrong with organisations and communities, we lose the ability to see and understand what gives life to organisations and to discover ways to sustain and enhance that life-giving potential. (Ludema et al, 2001, p 189)

In these writers' view, the dynamic of appreciative inquiry enables participants to value what they have done and to think expansively about opportunities and possibilities beyond the formal outcomes set for a project. While we accept that all projects have what Perkins and Wilson (2002) call 'blow up factors' (that is, tensions, conflicts, setbacks and resistances, for example), we agree with Ludema et al's (2001, p 197) premise that a focus on the half-full cup rather than the half-empty one, produces different kinds of project energy and outlook:

> Appreciative inquiry is a collaborative effort to discover that which is healthy, successful and positive in organisational life. By definition, such a project is a radically participatory approach, designed to include an ever-increasing number of voices in conversations that highlight strengths, assets, hopes and dreams.

In the spirit of this position, we have found that capturing data by using the 'discovery' phase of appreciative inquiry of particular usefulness. Had we asked the kind of question Palshaugen asked earlier, we think that we would have been overwhelmed with 'barrier' data. Indeed, when one of us (Judith Cousin) recently evaluated a Single Regeneration Budget-funded Capacity Building

Project following the question, 'Can you describe what has particularly worked well and what have been the barriers to participation and development?', a great deal of time and energy was spent in both one-to-one interviews, focus groups and workshop situations on the barriers. Participants clearly felt more comfortable giving voice to those issues that have genuinely caused them difficulties. When pushed to concentrate on what worked, the data gathered was far shorter, less detailed and participants had to be encouraged and facilitated much more to contribute suggestions, and often their responses would switch back again to barriers. The richness and success of what they were achieving was somehow devalued and given far less importance than the space they took to express their frustrations and difficulties.

We should stress here that the point of appreciative inquiry is not to repress news about setbacks and difficulties. Rather, it is to allow the system to *discover*, amplify and multiply the alignment of strengths in such a way that weaknesses and deficiencies become increasingly irrelevant (Ludema et al, 2001, p 198). In our view, working with project members towards such a discovery is the most productive role an evaluator can take (as we hope to show next). First, however, we will briefly outline three more 'Ds' of appreciative inquiry from Ludema et al (2001) before returning to our own emphasis on discovery.

Following the 'discovery' stage, the second stage for appreciative inquiry is called the *dream*. This is where project members are asked to think about useful ways to describe how they see their project going. For instance, they can be invited to offer graphic and metaphoric representations. These alternatives to written descriptions can be more socially inclusive and appropriate for some project members. The third phase is *design*, where project members discuss 'what social architecture would translate the dream into reality'. One way of doing this would be to pose provocative propositions to stimulate ideas (for example, 'What if we asked the drug users to run a "drugs fair?"'). The 'design' challenge is to think as big as possible and then to stay open to further possibilities. Some project members may object that they do not have the flexibility to design their project because its parameters were set before their appointment or through constraints on the funding. However, the design phase is intended to help a project flesh out what it will do to achieve its aims and to identify any revisions from its original design it may be able to make. Finally, the last stage of appreciative inquiry is that of *destiny*. In this phase, a project is celebrating and evaluating its achievements. In the spirit of appreciative inquiry, members are asked to discuss the extent to which they have shifted the issues they have addressed 'from vocabularies of deficit to vocabularies of possibility'. The aim is to shift towards a 'can do' culture? It is the evaluator's task to turn the discussions and observations from this phase into project recommendations for sustaining the work of the project beyond its formal life cycle.

Returning then to the 'discovery' phase of research, Ludema et al (2001, p 193) offer the following questions to begin a cycle of appreciative inquiry:

1. What in this particular setting or context makes organising possible? What gives life to our organisation and allows it to function at its best?
2. What are the possibilities, latent or expressed, that provide opportunities for even better (more effective and value-congruent) forms of organising?

Ludema et al's work is with community projects and they offer case studies of community development projects to show how the procedures of appreciative inquiry are of immense use in opening up a language of possibilities and positive relationships. They also show how data can be gathered very creatively with participants with low literacy skills. Our example is very different and this exemplifies, we hope, how methods chosen for specific settings can often be adapted for other contexts. We also hope to show how appreciative inquiry can be conducted through the collection of stories.

As part of a European Project (EQUEL) into the implementation of online learning in higher education, Glynis Cousin and Frances Deepwell (two contributors to this chapter) have adapted the questions raised by Ludema et al by asking academic colleagues, within a workshop setting, to write a story about their experiences of online learning, using the following initial prompts:

> Identify moments when things clicked? When you were enthused by something? Excited? What has engaged your interest and attention recently?

Two notable things emerged from this workshop. First, although we received quite short stories and thus 'limited' data in terms of bulk, we think it was a case of 'less is more', because we got some very rich stories about 'what works' which we were able to analyse in terms of success variables. Here are some extracts:

> "This story is about a middle-aged lecturer with a certain degree of optimism. She used to hate computers till the tender age of 24, but then she saw the light of the BBC micro and made it her mission in life to make sure that students could be part of her 'illumination'. There were major jumps over the years, from BBC Micro to Toolbook to Internet, but WebCT truly brought some 'disco' lights to her teaching. She found discussion mind-blowing and students' unsolicited electronic praise of the online environment to support their studies exciting." (a language teacher)

> "Although I really enjoyed developing the Information Skills tutorials with Kathy, the real excitement began when I used the tracking facilities in [the online environment] and realised how heavily the students were using the resource. The survey results, too, were astonishing, with nearly half of the students responding. And those responses were very positive. It was then that I felt that I was doing something worthwhile and had produced something that could be expanded. The responses from my peers within other institutions have also been very positive." (a librarian)

"With developing technology, one could provide pictures. I bought some relatively cheap software from Serif to use at home and discovered how easy, though time-consuming, it was to produce animations. I was enthused again. Animations are particularly helpful in building up the steps to solving a maths or stats problem. The then new website for the Maths Support Centre gave others and myself the vehicle for using these ideas. More enthusiasm. Flash animations with voice-overs (for dyslexic students) on solving algebraic problems seemed another tremendous and cheering advance. Exciting." (a lecturer in maths and statistics)

The stories here relate to encounters with technology within the same institutional context. By gathering a constellation of such stories, we are able to build a sufficiently coherent understanding of the processes and systems operating at this level within the organisation. What is particularly noteworthy about the stories we gathered in the spirit of appreciative inquiry concerns the emotional content to them. The stories capture the mood within the organisation. Inviting people to recount their experiences in the story genre appears to create licence for colleagues to express themselves freely, (something that professionals such as these are not always good at). The descriptive vocabulary used in the stories in part echoes back to us the words used in the question ('exciting', 'astonishing', 'enthused again'), but it goes beyond this and reveals the intensity of positive feelings towards their experiences. For one, the experience was 'tremendous and cheering', for another even 'mind-blowing'. The personal commitment to making a change for the better is evident in the stories, which also point to the environment and the good relationships (with peers, with students, with technology) necessary for this improvement to happen.

By recounting their past enthusiasm, it was also the case that it was rekindled. The storytelling was an opportunity taken by the participants to reaffirm their own beliefs in what they are doing and to realign their work efforts. The storyteller's enthusiasm for the medium in each case is awakened by their discovery not of the technology in its own right, but of what it might do for them and their students. The prime purpose of using technology in this organisational context reveals itself here to be to improve the learning potential of their students. In the workshop, the stories were shared in small groups and the discussions moved on to the 'dream' and 'design' stages of appreciative inquiry, with new insights and shared understandings of the organisation and how the individual ties in with the institutional project mission.

The idea of 'stories' rather than interviews comes from the field of narrative inquiry (see, for instance, Savin-Baden, 2000), which has as its premise the view that we are all storied individuals and the veracity of our stories is irrelevant because they are true for us. What people think and feel is happening is of particular importance for project development. As the next example shows, the story genre also gives people an easy rhetorical structure in which to explain their own history of change:

"Once upon a time I was an ordinary lecturer delivering fairly ordinary lectures with photocopied handouts, standard coursework and dreaded exams. The student experience would have been OK, but perhaps a bit boring, and there was something lacking....Then came the web. Anyplace, anytime accessibility, and the vision of providing alternative materials as supplementary help for students. Students learn in different ways and at different paces; here was a way of providing a variety of approaches, accessible at a variety of levels, for students within my presence." (a lecturer in languages)

We have found that using questions in the spirit of appreciative inquiry means that we can concentrate on an understanding of success variables. We are aware that there is a utopian risk of promotionalism in the framework of appreciative inquiry. However, in our experience we have found that responding to a positive question has been empowering and motivating for members of the project and this method is particularly suitable for formative evaluation.

Conclusion

Our aim in this chapter has been to share with readers how they might tackle the questions of creating partnerships with project teams in order to develop evaluation activities that support them. Through the approaches of theory-driven and appreciative inquiry, we have tried to show how this support can be offered in ways that are economic, manageable and developmental. In our view, these approaches can complement a quantitative account of a project's outcomes. The examples cited come from public sector projects involving many stakeholders. The evaluation activities described work for us in a number of ways. First, by engaging with the project members in determining what is working well we are able to start to identify the success variables. Second, the project members are encouraged to share their achievements within the project and thereby assess for themselves where they are in relation to the declared project outcomes. And third, the discussion invites the project to think beyond these declared outcomes to a greater gain for their organisation.

Overview

- Evaluations are often limited to a statistical report of deliverables as methods focusing on 'soft outcomes' or attempting to capture processes are often considered burdensome. However, project teams can be persuaded to expand upon quantitative requirements if offered manageable methods to do so.
- The 'theory-driven' rather than the laborious and time consuming 'data-driven' model is recommended for this kind of evaluation.
- The 'theory-driven' model may need to incorporate creative methods when working with groups (such as young people) that are potentially difficult to engage.

- An 'appreciative inquiry' approach is advised in order to avoid becoming overwhelmed with barriers. This can be conducted through the collection of stories, which reflect 'what works' and can be analysed in terms of success variables.
- One benefit of 'appreciative inquiry' is its empowering and motivating potential where members of a project are responding to positively rather than negatively framed questions.

Acknowledgements

During the preparation of the conference paper on which this chapter is based, one of its co-authors, Stephen McGrath, tragically died. This chapter is written in his memory. The authors would like to thank those colleagues who gave us their stories to support our research in the EQUEL Project (tecfaseed.unige.ch/equel/equel.php).

References

Baume, D. (2003) *Enhancing staff and educational development*, London: Routledge Falmer.

Deepwell, F. and Cousin, G. (2002) 'A developmental framework for evaluating institutional change', *Educational Developments*, March, vol 3, no 1, pp 24-6.

Dewson, S., Eccles, J., Tackey, N.D. and Jackson, A. (2000) *Guide to measuring soft outcomes and distance travelled*, London: The Institute for Employment Studies for the DfEE.

EQUEL (Virtual European Centre for research into innovation and research into e-learning) tecfaseed.unige.ch/equel/equel.php.

Greene, J. and Abma, T.A. (eds) (2001) *Responsive evaluation* (New Directions for Evaluation 92), San Francisco, CA: Jossey Bass.

Ludema, J.D., Cooperrider, D.L. and Barrett, F. (2001) 'Appreciative inquiry: the power of the unconditional positive question', in P. Reason and H. Bradbury (eds) *Handbook of action-research: Participative inquiry and practice*, London: Sage Publications, pp 189-99.

MacLure, M. and Stronach, I. (1997) *Educational research undone: The post-modern embrace*, Buckingham: Open University Press.

O'Neill, O. (2002) *BBC Reith Lectures: A question of trust*, BBC Radio 4 (www.bbc.co.uk/radio4).

Oakley, A. (1981) 'Interviewing women: a contradiction in terms', in H. Roberts (ed) *Doing feminist research*, London: Routledge and Kegan Paul, pp 30-61.

Palshaugen, O. (2002) 'The use of words: improving enterprises by improving their conversations', in P. Reason and H. Bradbury (eds) *Handbook of action-research: Participative inquiry and practice*, London: Sage Publications, pp 209-18

Pawson, R. and Tilley, N. (1997) *Realistic evaluation*, London: Sage Publications.

Perkins, D.N. and Wilson, D. (1999) 'Bridging the idea action gap', *Knowledge directions: The Journal of the Institute of Knowledge Management*, vol 1, no 1, pp 65-77.

Savin-Baden, M. (2000) *Problem based learning in higher education: Untold stories*, Buckingham: SRHE/Open University Press.

Stake, R. and Pearsol, J.A. (1981) 'Evaluating responsively', in R.S. Brandt (ed) *Applied strategies for curriculum evaluation*, Alexandria, VA: ASCD.

Strauss, A. and Corbin, J. (1997) *Grounded theory in practice*, London: Sage Publications.

Wadsworth, Y. (2002a) 'Becoming responsive – and some consequences for evaluation as dialogue across distance', in J. Greene and T.A. Abma (eds) (2001) *Responsive evaluation, New Directions for Evaluation 92*, San Francisco, CA: Jossey Bass, pp 45-58.

Wadsworth, Y. (2002b) 'The mirror, the magnifying glass, the compass and the map: facilitating participatory action-research', in P. Reason and H. Bradbury (eds) *Handbook of action-research: Participative inquiry and practice*, London: Sage Publications, pp 420-32.

EIGHT

Evaluating projects aimed at supporting the parents of young people: "I didn't learn anything new, but ..."

Debi Roker

Introduction

This chapter reviews the issues that arise in parenting projects and interventions, which are designed to offer information and support to the parents of teenagers. In the last few years, a large number of new initiatives have been set up by the government, as well as the statutory and voluntary sectors. These initiatives aim to provide information, advice and support to the parents of young people. These services are in a variety of formats, and include written materials, telephone helplines, parenting courses and specific projects to help particular groups, such as fathers or lone parents.

I have been involved in both designing interventions to support parents, and evaluating projects set up by other organisations. During this time, a number of difficult and contested issues have arisen in these projects, which are central to the politics of evaluation. This chapter highlights a number of points in relation to the evaluation of parenting interventions, using Trust for the Study of Adolescence (TSA) projects to illustrate the points made. For readers unfamiliar with the author's organisation, TSA is an independent charitable organisation, which works to improve the lives of young people. It does this through applied research, training and development, and publications (for further information, see its website: www.tsa.uk.com).

The chapter is divided into four main sections:

1. a background to the recent policy and practice developments in relation to supporting parents;
2. TSA's evaluations in these areas;
3. a range of issues that have arisen in these projects, in relation to the 'politics' of evaluation; and
4. some general conclusions and suggestions for addressing some of these issues.

Background: supporting parents of teenagers

During the past five to six years, there has been an increasing focus on the needs of the parents of young people. Prior to this, the focus within parenting support had been on parents of young children. There is now a growing body of literature that demonstrates the needs of the parents of young people, and different practical strategies for offering these parents information, advice and support (see, for example, Coleman, 1997; Coleman and Roker, 2001; Gillies et al, 2001; Roker and Coleman, 2001).

The last few years, therefore, have seen an increase in policy initiatives aimed at supporting practitioners who are working with parents, and directly to support parents themselves. Such initiatives have included the establishment of the National Family and Parenting Institute (NFPI), an extension of the ParentLine Plus telephone helpline to a 24-hour service and policy initiatives such as funding for innovative projects from the Family Policy Unit (recently moved from the Home Office to the Department for Education and Skills). The recent establishment of a new Parenting Fund is a further recognition of the importance the current government attaches to parenting support. The establishment of Parenting Orders has also been a key development in relation to parenting within the youth justice context (Henricson et al, 2000; Lindfield and Cusick, 2001). (A detailed commentary on these developments is outside the scope of this chapter, and interested readers are referred to the references cited earlier for further information.) What is central to the topic of this volume, however, is that an evaluation of many of these new projects has been commissioned. The TSA has been involved in many of them, and a summary is given below which is followed by a discussion of the issues involved in relation to evaluation that have arisen from these projects.

TSA's evaluations of parenting support projects

The evaluation of the YMCA's 'Parenting Teenagers' Initiative

This three-year project, undertaken 1998-2001, was evaluated by TSA. The project was run by YMCA England, and funded by the Family Policy Unit (then part of the Home Office). It involved setting up 30 different projects in YMCA centres and elsewhere, to provide information and support to the parents of young people. The projects set up were diverse, and included mediation schemes, group-based courses, information evenings and 'Dads and Lads' events to bring men and their sons together. A report on this project has been completed (Roker et al, 2000), and a journal article has also recently been published (Roker and Richardson, 2002).

Two school-based projects looking at the effectiveness of offering parents different types of information and support

The TSA recently completed two school-based interventions and evaluations, both of which were designed to look at the effectiveness of offering parents different types of information and support. Both projects were run in schools, and involved parents being offered three different types of support over the course of a year, the first of which was information in the form of videos, books and audiotapes; the second was joining a group-based parenting course; lastly, there was access to one-to-one support from a parent adviser. A detailed evaluation of both these projects was undertaken, involving interviews with parents before and after the intervention, and interviews with those providing the services. A variety of organisations funded these projects including Kent Social Services, the Carnegie UK Trust and the Lloyds-TSB Foundation. (Further details are available from TSA about both these projects. In particular, see Roker and Richardson, 2001.)

An evaluation of newsletters as a form of parent support

The TSA also recently completed a two-year project funded by the Family Policy Unit, which looked at an innovative form of support for the parents of young people. This project used newsletters to provide information, advice and sources of support to parents. Four newsletters were produced in total, and included research findings, hints and tips, a 'young people's page', agony aunt pages and lists of organisations and resources. The evaluation of this project involved 5,000 parents drawn from four diverse secondary schools in England and Wales. A final report on this project is now available from TSA, and a paper is also available (Shepherd and Roker, 2001). The following project involved developing this form of support further.

The community newsletters project

Following the successful completion of the newsletter project, the TSA received further funding from the Family Policy Unit to develop this work. This current project is addressing the fact that the newsletters produced in this previous project were universal, and not targeted at the needs of particular groups. Our new project is addressing this by working with ten specific community groups to produce newsletters specifically for parents of young people in those groups. Organisations involved to date include lone parents, parents of disabled teenagers, parents of children with special educational needs, parents of gay and lesbian young people, fathers of teenagers and disabled parents of teenagers. A detailed evaluation is being undertaken to assess the effectiveness of providing parents with information and support in this way.

The evaluation of the YMCA's 'Dads and Lads' project

Following the completion of the Parenting Teenagers Initiative (described earlier), the YMCA secured funding to continue one element of this work. They have now set up and run 30 'Dads and Lads' projects throughout the country, where sport is used as a 'hook' to engage fathers and male carers in parenting support work. The TSA undertook the evaluation of this initiative, and a copy of the final report is available.

An evaluation of a 'parent mentoring' scheme

This new project is an evaluation of an initiative being run by the National Council for Voluntary Child Care Organisations (NCVCCO). This organisation is working with three sites in different parts of the country to run a parent mentoring scheme. This involves parents of older young people acting as mentors to parents of younger young people, in particular those who are experiencing difficulties. This evaluation is ongoing.

An evaluation of materials for parents of young people with an eating disorder

A recently commissioned project being undertaken by the Eating Disorders Association (EDA) involves the TSA working on the evaluation of a new project. The EDA has funding to produce some materials, aimed at providing information and support to parents of young people who are diagnosed with an eating disorder. The TSA is undertaking the evaluation of the development of the materials, and the impact of them on parents and young people. This is a three-year project due to be completed in 2005.

The politics of evaluation

As stated earlier, rarely is any new funding round mentioned without the specific link to evaluation. Evaluation is now a key component of activity in government, and in the statutory and voluntary sectors. In undertaking each of the projects listed above, TSA's staff has had to address some very fundamental issues around research, evaluation and ethics. Many of these issues are now being raised by other organisations within this field.

Alongside the increase in the amount of evaluation has been an increase in the difficult, contentious and 'political' issues involved in doing evaluation. A number of researchers and practitioners are raising issues to do with aims, measurement and participation in evaluation research, as well as issues such as power and ownership (see, for example, Broad, 1999; Chahal, 1999; Crawshaw et al, 2000). These are the important and contested aspects of evaluation, and the TSA has also been faced with these issues. In particular, our work to evaluate parenting initiatives has raised some important issues for us, central to the topic of this book. Some of the main issues we have identified, drawn from the TSA projects listed earlier, are now detailed.

Issues involved in evaluating projects to support the parents of young people

A number of points have arisen from TSA's projects in relation to the politics of evaluation.

The views of funders and senior staff about the aims of interventions and evaluations

A key issue that has arisen in TSA's evaluations of parenting initiatives has been the often differing views of senior staff, and/or funders involved, about the aims and purpose of the evaluation. We have often found that some practitioners and organisations believe that there is a single approach to evaluation, and that being asked to 'do the evaluation' of a new project is sufficient to ensure this. An example of a project that we evaluated recently demonstrates this well. Three senior staff on the project had supposedly agreed the aims of the evaluation. However, in speaking to each of them, it was clear that they had very different aims and objectives in mind:

> I'm looking mainly for facts and figures – numbers who came along, whether they liked it, things that will help justify our funding for this project.

> [The evaluation should] be about helping people to see how it went, what went well, what was difficult, that sort of thing. What we can learn from it really.

> Did it have an impact? Did it meets its objectives? That's the main thing we need to know.

In highlighting these very diverse aims in relation to the evaluation of one project, it is by no means intended to criticise any of those involved. Rather, these quotes clearly demonstrate that those within the same organisation may well want very different things from the evaluation. This reflects different professional backgrounds, experiences, ideologies and interests. Crucially, the views of senior staff may, in turn, be different to those who are providing the funding for a project or evaluation. We have often found that funders and senior staff on projects have very different ideas about what the evaluation is for, and how it should be undertaken. It is clearly important to clarify the aims and objectives of the evaluation early on. This links in with the views of others involved in projects, and this is dealt with next.

The views of stakeholders and participants

As stated earlier, all those involved in evaluations may each have very different views of the purpose and nature of an evaluation. Thus, in the case of TSA's work in the field of parenting support, we have sometimes found that funders, practitioners and parents have very different views of project aims, and what is needed from an evaluation. The diverse views of senior staff on one project, quoted earlier, are often mirrored for other stakeholders in the evaluation. This is often complicated by the fact that we, as researchers, may only have contact with funders and/or senior staff when designing and preparing the evaluation. Therefore, there is often tension between the views of different stakeholders, and this needs to be reflected both in the evaluation, and in the final report.

A key issue in relation to stakeholders, particularly practitioners who are running projects, is their perception of what the evaluation might conclude. In parenting support projects, as with all new initiatives, practitioners have often invested a great deal of time, effort, expertise and organisational commitment. Many evaluators will be familiar with the anxiety expressed by workers in new initiatives that the evaluation may be critical (or at least not overwhelmingly positive), and thus affect their future employment or funding. This is a pressure on evaluators that is all too rarely articulated, and that should not be ignored. One worker in a TSA evaluation stated to the author that he "had to focus on the positives, because I need a really positive result on this". This anxiety is all too understandable in an environment of short-term funding, and the rapid development of new projects and initiatives. It is important to address with funders and with practitioners the impact that an evaluation might have on the future of a new initiative.

Understanding 'impact' and outcomes

There are many ways of conceptualising and theorising evaluation (see, for example, Broad, 1999; Simons and Usher, 2000). However, in terms of types of evaluation, most researchers would distinguish between *process* evaluation, and *outcome/impact* evaluation. The TSA's experience in the field of parenting support suggests that both elements are essential. Process evaluation is important because of the innovative nature of much of the work, where the recording of the process of setting up a new project is valuable, and contributes to the development of good practice. Most organisations want to learn how to do things better in the future and help other organisations learn from errors and difficulties. However, outcome and impact evaluation is also clearly essential in order to identify what happened as a result of an innovative project. Did it meet its aims and objectives? Were there other unintended outcomes of the project? Was the project cost-effective? These are essential questions in any evaluation. We therefore encourage organisations, where possible, to address both process and impact/outcome aspects, even where they might state that they had planned to look at only one or other of these types of evaluation.

Related to this, there is also a keen debate underway about the methods used to evaluate parenting support interventions. There is sometimes pressure to focus on quantitative outcome indicators, in order to demonstrate whether an intervention has had impact on (a fairly narrow range of) particular attitudes or behaviours. However, much of the work within parenting support is new and innovative, and so it is also important to understand the broader processes and outcomes involved. In the evaluation of the YMCA's Parenting Initiative (described earlier) for example, many of the projects were struggling to recruit participants into their activities. During the course of the evaluation of their projects, a great deal was learnt about marketing and advertising of activities, and factors that encouraged and discouraged parents to get involved. In terms of quantitative indicators (measured in terms of numbers of participants) success was described as limited for many projects. The more qualitative information about process, however, identified important learning points for future work. Only now, several years on, are many of those projects achieving success in terms of numbers. Without the inclusion of the process element of the evaluation, the essential learning from these projects would have been lost. Thus, the length of evaluations are also important: short-term evaluation can often miss crucial long-term benefits and outcomes.

One mother raised a related issue about the aims and objectives of evaluation. Her quote is used in the title of this chapter. This woman was attending one of the first parenting courses for those subject to a Parenting Order. She was therefore required by law to attend the course. During the interview conducted with her at the end of the eight-week course, she stated that she "didn't learn anything new …" on it. Indeed, she had rated the course very low on a self-completion questionnaire administered by course organisers in the last session. However, a significant "… but" was added to her statement. This mother did, in fact, give a long list of positive outcomes from attending the course, in particular getting social support from other participants, and feeling less isolated. This parent had increased in confidence, and felt able to start to address some of the issues related to her son's offending. However, the emphasis of much evaluation of Parenting Orders at the time was on parents 'learning' new skills from courses. Without the broad focus given in the interview with this (and other) parents, the quantitative results might have indicated that the programme was 'unsuccessful'.

The role of young people in evaluations

In the parenting support projects that TSA was involved in during its early days, it was common for *parents only* to be involved in the evaluation. However, this is now changing, both at TSA and elsewhere. Children and young people's views are increasingly being taken into consideration, and indeed seen as a key part of the evaluation (Alderson, 1995; Clarke et al, 1996; Crawshaw et al, 2000; David et al, 2001). In the two school-based projects that were described earlier in this chapter, our approach was clearly evolving. In the first project, only parents were involved in the evaluation. In the second project, we were much more aware of the right of young people to express their views about the project, both when it was being set up and when it was completed. Indeed, in the field of parenting support, it might be argued that the views of young people are particularly important, in that the aim is to provide support to the parent–teenager relationship. More and more projects in the parenting support field are involving young people, and the evaluations of such projects need to reflect this.

Assessing young people's views in evaluation raises a wide range of methodological and ethical issues. It is notable that in the school-based intervention and evaluation described earlier, some interesting findings were made with regard to the young people's views. One in particular is worthy of mention here. The large majority of young people (90%) were extremely positive about the project, believing that parents of adolescents should have more information and advice in relation to the teenage years. The remaining young people (approximately 10%), however, were extremely negative and opposed to such projects, believing that it was offensive and intrusive to provide interventions that were in many ways 'about them'. This raises many issues, in particular how the voices of the minority are included in evaluations, and reflected in final reports and dissemination.

Issues of confidentiality and anonymity

As in all research projects, the issues of informed consent, and of confidentiality and anonymity, are central to parenting support evaluations. It is often the case that parents reveal very personal and sensitive information during fieldwork to evaluate parenting support interventions. In many of the evaluations TSA has undertaken (listed in this chapter), parents became involved in the projects because they were experiencing difficulties in the relationship with their children. The information collected has therefore often been very personal, collected at a time when parents were in crisis. One parent told the author that she had completely "bared her soul" in an interview about the problems she was experiencing with her daughter. She added that she had provided much more personal information "to a stranger" than she would normally. As a result, evaluations undertaken in this area have to be particularly careful about securing informed consent, and making sure that participants fully understand what is happening and how the information they provide will be used. This relates to issues of confidentiality and anonymity, and highlights the importance of spending time with parents and other stakeholders at the start of the project in order to properly address these issues. This issue is returned to later.

The use made of results from evaluations

Finally, as was highlighted earlier, for many practitioners and project workers, evaluation of their work or project can be extremely threatening. There is often a concern that evaluation results will directly and negatively impact on jobs and funding. This point is closely tied to the issue of how evaluation results are reported and used. Evaluators are in a difficult position in this respect, in that a final report, once handed over, is often taken out of the hands of those who wrote it. Evaluation reports are sometimes, therefore, used as a basis for justifying funding cuts or changing posts within organisations. While it is often difficult for evaluators to control the way in which their material is used, it is important to discuss and agree these points at the beginning of the project. This issue is also raised later in this chapter.

Addressing 'political' issues

This chapter has briefly addressed some of the main contentious and difficult issues that the TSA has faced in undertaking evaluations of parenting support projects. It is evident from this analysis that evaluation is a 'political' issue, in the sense that it is contested and subject to the influence of power and personal interest. This needs to be acknowledged and addressed by all those involved in undertaking evaluation.

The main recommendation that I make is the importance of addressing issues and areas of difference early on in evaluations. Evaluators need to recognise and acknowledge the different (and often competing) views of all those involved. In the case of parenting projects, that includes parents, young people, practitioners, evaluators, organisations and funders. Each of these are likely to have a different expectation of the aims, objectives, methods, outcomes and uses of an evaluation. Thus at the start of all evaluations, time must be given to exploring these different views in an attempt to reach an understanding of the role and purpose of the evaluation. Only in this way will all those involved feel some sort of ownership over the evaluation. It must also be acknowledged, however, that this can be very difficult given the short-term nature of many projects, and the short lead-in time allowed before projects start.

In summary, a number of things have been found to be important in TSA's evaluations of parenting support projects, which for us are the 'lessons learnt', and we hope that they are useful for others working in this field. These are as follows:

The importance of planning

In each of the earlier sections, the importance of time for planning evaluations was repeatedly stressed. Many of the difficult and political issues that were encountered at TSA in evaluating parenting interventions have arisen when there has been a very short lead-in time. Indeed, projects are often up and running (or very close to being so) before TSA is approached to undertake the evaluation. The TSA has often found that, by this stage, key decisions have been made about the aims and design of the project. These frequently have a considerable impact on the evaluation, and are often irreversible. Many of the political and difficult issues that have been raised in this chapter have been a result of evaluation being something of an 'add-on'. There will be times, of course, when this is inevitable, and evaluators have to work quickly to catch up. However, TSA is working hard to encourage practitioners, funders and organisations to plan as early ahead as possible, and engage evaluators in key decisions. This is something that we would encourage all evaluators to do.

Engaging all those involved in planning and designing the evaluation

Related to the need to plan evaluations as early as possible is the importance of consulting as many people as possible in planning the evaluation. Engaging all those involved is obviously beneficial in terms of making people feel part of the evaluation. However, this wide consultation is also a valuable way of raising any tensions and differences in terms of the *aims* of the evaluation. While this wide consultation can be very time consuming, it is essential if problems are to be avoided later on in an evaluation. An example was given of three senior staff on the same project who were each expecting something very different from the evaluation. These different perspectives had not been evident before, even during the early stages of negotiating the evaluation. Spending time with each individual meant that the evaluators from TSA could refine and agree the evaluation aims.

In concluding this learning point, it is acknowledged that it is not always possible for evaluators to speak to all those involved in a new project or initiative. Clearly for large-scale or national projects, other systems must be used to engage all those involved in a project. Strategies that could be used include line management systems within organisations, email correspondence from evaluators and group workshops or briefing events. The TSA's experience suggests that early effort at this stage pays off later in the evaluation.

Agreeing methodologies and the implications of these decisions

It has also been stressed throughout this chapter that evaluation design, methods and tools need to be negotiated with the organisations concerned. In this respect, it is very important to assist projects and stakeholders to see the implications of decisions made at this stage. In one of our parenting intervention evaluations, for example, the stakeholders concerned wanted long qualitative interviews undertaken with those participating in a parenting programme. In exploring this further at a follow-up meeting, it became clear that the project workers had also agreed to provide quantitative data to their funders, in the form of attitudinal measures in number form. It was evident that, reflecting on the previous discussions, they felt that these quantitative measures would 'emerge' from the qualitative data. Similarly, we have worked with organisations that have asked for the evaluation to include only simple quantitative measures, which do not take long to collect. However, we always encourage projects to think through the implications of this decision for the final report on the evaluation. When stakeholders do so, they often indicate that they also want to include more qualitative material such as quotes.

It should be stressed that, in this field, some funders are taking responsibility for helping parenting practitioners to think through the implications of decisions made early on in an evaluation. For example, the Children and Families Directorate in the DfES funds many innovative parenting projects every year, undertaken by a range of voluntary organisations. It now provides evaluation workshops and advice as part of its funding, to enable workers in these projects to plan and undertake their own evaluation, or to work knowledgeably with external evaluators in this respect.

Discussing and agreeing how the evaluation results will be used

It has also been stressed throughout this chapter that evaluations and projects must communicate effectively about the end point; that is, how the results will be written up and how they will be used. These discussions need to be held, and include agreement about such aspects as:

- To what extent does the project or organisation expect to be able to comment on or change the evaluation report?
- Will the report be confidential to the funders and/or organisation concerned, or can it be widely distributed? To what extent can the evaluators disseminate the results in articles and other publications?
- How will issues of confidentiality be dealt with? Do stakeholders or parents involved have the same views about this?
- How may the results be used by the funders or the organisation concerned? What ramifications could there be of a poor evaluation of a project or service?

These sorts of issues, while complex, must be addressed early on in the evaluation with all of those involved.

Conclusion

This chapter has aimed to address the 'political' issues involved in the evaluation of projects and initiatives, which are designed to support the parents of young people. Many of these projects are new and developing, and there is a considerable amount of evaluation now being undertaken. However, as already described, TSA's experience is that evaluations of parenting support projects can raise difficult and contentious issues which must be addressed by evaluators. Evaluation is not, and cannot be, an objective activity which is undertaken by people who are divorced from the real world. Evaluation is a political activity. In concluding this chapter, it is necessary to stress that evaluation has a key role within the field of parenting support, and a great deal has been learnt from it. Projects and initiatives have been improved and developed as a result of the evaluations undertaken. It is hoped that TSA's experience in this field will help to improve and develop both research and practice in this area.

Overview

- Evaluations of new initiatives providing support and advice to parents of teenagers have raised a number of issues. These include how to address differing views among stakeholders regarding the aims and methods of the research and how to include the voices of the minority.
- These evaluations have been evolving to increasingly include, for example, the views of children and young people.
- Both process (largely from qualitative data) and outcome (mostly quantitative) information is important. Without the former the meanings from data and essential learning from projects may be lost.
- Key elements of the evaluation must be negotiated with stakeholders at an early stage. These include the evaluation design, methods, aims and objectives, issues such as confidentiality and anonymity and ways in which research findings will be written up and used.
- Evaluators should also be engaged early on in key project decisions as these may impact on the evaluation aims and design.

References

Alderson, P. (1995) *Listening to children: Children, ethics and social research*, London: Barnardo's.

Broad, B. (ed) (1999) *The politics of social work: Research and evaluation*, Birmingham: British Association of Social Workers.

Chahal, K. (1999) 'Researching ethnicity: experiences and concerns', in B. Broad (ed) *The politics of social work: Research and evaluation*, Birmingham: British Association of Social Workers, pp 59-73.

Clarke, K., Glendinning, C. and Craig, G. (1996) *Children's views on child support*, London: The Children's Society.

Coleman, J. (1997) 'The parenting of teenagers in Britain today', *Children and Society*, vol 11, pp 45-52.

Coleman, J. and Roker, D. (2001) *Supporting parents of teenagers: A handbook for professionals*, London: Jessica Kingsley.

Crawshaw, P., Mitchell, W., Bunton, R. and Green, E. (2000) 'Youth empowerment and youth research: expertise, subjection and control', *Youth and Policy*, vol 69, pp 1-16.

David, M., Edwards, R. and Alldred, P. (2001) 'Children and school-based research: informed consent or educated consent?', *British Educational Research Journal*, vol 27, no 3, pp 347-66.

Gillies, V., Ribbens-McCarthy, J. and Holland, J. (2001) *'Pulling together, pulling apart': The family lives of young people*, York: Joseph Rowntree Foundation.

Henricson, C., Coleman, J. and Roker, D. (2000) 'Parenting in the youth justice context', *Howard Journal of Criminal Justice*, vol 39, pp 325-38.

Lindfield, S. and Cusick, J. (2001) 'Parenting in the youth justice context', in J. Coleman and D. Roker (eds) *Supporting parents of teenagers: A handbook for professionals*, London: Jessica Kingsley, pp 77-106.

Roker, D. and Coleman, J. (2001) 'Setting the scene: parenting and public policy', in J. Coleman and D. Roker (eds) *Supporting parents of teenagers: A handbook for professionals*, London: Jessica Kingsley, pp 7-21.

Roker, D. and Richardson, H. (2001) 'The evaluation of the "Living with teenagers ... supporting parents" project', in J. Coleman and D. Roker (eds) *Supporting parents of teenagers: A handbook for professionals*, London: Jessica Kingsley, pp 163-79.

Roker, D. and Richardson, H. (2002) 'Innovations in parenting support', *Children and Society*, vol 16, pp 143-53.

Roker, D., Richardson, H. and Coleman, J. (2000) *Innovations in parenting support: An evaluation of the YMCA's Parenting Teenagers initiative*, London: YMCA.

Shepherd, J. and Roker, D. (2001) 'Newsletters as a form of parent support', *The Psychology of Education Review*, vol 25, pp 27-31.

Shepherd, J. and Roker, D. (2004) 'The parenting of young people: using newsletters to provide information and support', *Children and Society*.

Simons, H. and Usher, R. (2000) *Situated ethics in educational research*, London: Routledge.

Part Three
Partnerships and evaluation

Evaluating interagency working in health and social care: politics, policies and outcomes for service users

Audrey Leathard

Introduction

Since 1997, interagency working has taken centre stage in the new initiatives for health and social care. An increasing number of collaborative endeavours have been set up but, with some exceptions, little has been evaluated, even less where the views of service users have been involved. This review presents the issues surrounding evaluation where interagency working is concerned. In this light, some relevant projects that have been assessed will be considered. The political issues relevant to interagency evaluation will be set out, followed by the place of the policy arena with the focus on the assessment of collaborative health and social care provision. The views and outcomes for service users will be discussed in order to perceive ways forward towards a more integrated form of interagency evaluation. It has to be appreciated at the outset that in the field of interprofessional, multidisciplinary and partnership working between health and social care, initially little was addressed with regard to the place of evaluation, so we set off into somewhat innovative territory.

The pathway for analysis

The evaluation of interagency working: purpose and responsibility

In seeking the purpose of evaluating interagency work, one problem is that rarely have projects been set up with evaluation in mind which comes (if and when) some while after the initiatives have been installed. For example, the need for agencies to work together could come about as a result of an organisational merger whose main purpose is usually to cut costs. The place of evaluation is therefore not an immediate issue. Other recent developments have come through one of the numerous initiatives and changes brought in by recent government policy: care trusts would be one example whereby a new level of primary care trust has been encouraged to integrate health and social services into one organisation by common agreement from April 2002 (DH, 2001). Just how far a meaningful evaluation of care trusts can be undertaken remains to be seen, as does the purpose of such an exercise together with the responsibility involved. Other key questions for interagency evaluation need to be established at the outset, alongside the purpose of such an exercise, as well as the responsibility involved:

- By who and for whom is the exercise intended?
- Who should be responsible for undertaking and/or funding interagency evaluation: jointly or by an outside agency and with what intended outcome?
- For whose benefit is evaluation at the end of the exercise?

Some outcomes and further questions in the process of evaluation

The outcome of evaluation can raise further implications. For example, is joint action appropriate in addressing the problems identified by the evaluation process for interagency working? However, in looking at the outcomes of some relevant research, the more problematical matters become.

One recent example draws from a substantial study undertaken by the Health Services Research Unit at the London School of Hygiene and Tropical Medicine. The findings, based on mergers throughout 1998-99, covering acute hospitals, mental health services and community provision, showed that hospital mergers and other NHS services delayed improvements for patients by at least 18 months, failed to deliver promised savings and did nothing to improve staff recruitment or retention. From the setting of nine trusts (from a cross-sectional study) and four case studies on trusts in London, no clear evidence could be shown that any savings had been reinvested into services nor even achieved, while any savings in management costs took at least two years. The only advantages to be found were the presence of a bigger pool of professional staff, which allowed larger teams of clinical specialists; improvements in training; and less fragmentation in mental health care. However, the research team (Fulop et al, 2002) made some final telling points:

- that results of mergers are disappointing;
- that it takes a long time for positive results to show;
- that research on mergers should begin before mergers take place formally; and
- that the longer the time frame used, the more difficult the assessment becomes to attribute to the merger process within a turbulent environment of change across the health and social services.

Precisely who is to address the listed shortcomings remains to be clarified.

The next question to be raised is, what body is appropriate to evaluate interagency working? The illustration given earlier draws on work from an established Health Services Research Unit, which reflects one type of evaluative body used for assessments. Another approach is to turn to the Charity Commission. With growing competition for funds, partnerships between a charity and a commercial company are becoming increasingly common. However, many such partnerships are failing to comply with charity law; these cases are now coming before the Charity Commission wherein commercial partnerships formed 22% of all the commission's evaluations and investigations in 2001 (McCurry, 2002).

By January 2003, new powers of observation and scrutiny were to come into effect, when local authority scrutiny committees would have powers to refer decisions about health service changes to the new Independent Reconfiguration Panel and to the secretary of state. The new scrutiny arrangements were intended to promote partnership and service improvement but, as Bradshaw and Walshe (2002) warn, the changes could degenerate into a blaming and point-scoring exercise.

Overall, an ever-increasing number of bodies, agencies, research units, commissions, user-controlled research programmes and groups of individuals are involved in the place of evaluation across interagency and partnership working. Will a scrutineer then be needed for all these developments? This review now turns to some interagency projects which have been assessed and evaluated in order to bring forward some of the key issues and outcomes.

Some assessed interagency projects reviewed

The sequence starts by looking at two of the very few early evaluations. First, a taxonomy of collaboration was valuably constructed by Gregson et al (1992), adapted from work by Armitage (1983), on joint working in primary care (Table 9.1).

Table 9.1: A taxonomy of collaboration

1. No direct communication	Members who never meet, talk or write to each other
2. Formal, brief communication	Members who encounter or correspond but do not interact meaningfully
3. Regular communication and consultation	Members whose encounters or correspondence include the transference of information
4. High level of joint working	Members who act on that information sympathetically; participate in general patterns of joint working; subscribe to the same general objectives as others on a one-to-one basis in the same organisation
5. Multidisciplinary working	Involvement of all workers in a primary health care setting

The results showed a relatively low level of joint working between doctors and nurses (24%) and an even lower score for doctors and health visitors working together (8%). At the highest level of collaboration – multidisciplinary working – for both groups, the scores were the same and minimal in both cases (3%). Among the key issues for today, this type of evaluation could usefully be applied to the ever-widening base of primary health care, now in conjunction with social care, across a wider arena of professionals and agencies. A sixth level could also be added to relate to an evaluation of care trusts within this context; but a dilemma could arise over different interpretations of what actually counts as collaboration across the rating elements for interagency working (Leathard, 2003).

A second initial approach to evaluation came from the Centre for Social Policy Research and Development at the University of Wales, when McGrath (1991) set out to examine the different models of community mental handicap teams in Wales, as well as to assess the implementation and outcome of multidisciplinary teamwork mainly from the viewpoint of team members. Despite certain inherent difficulties in teamwork across agencies, the evaluation showed the clear advantages of teamworking through:

- a more efficient use of staff resources (for example, professional collaboration);
- a more effective service provision (for example, through improved assessment procedures); and
- a more satisfying work environment (that is, maximising use of skills).

From the evaluation, one key issue to emerge for the future was that successful multidisciplinary teamwork required collaboration at both agency and frontline worker level.

Throughout the mid-1990s, the issues for evaluation tended to concentrate on the Conservative government's health and welfare policy, which placed an emphasis on competition and quasi-markets rather than on joint working. With the arrival of Blair's New Labour government in May 1997, partnerships that placed a high value on collaboration took centre stage. With the width and depth of the programmes introduced, so the complexities for evaluation have increased. Two examples underline these developments.

Health Improvement Programmes (HImPs)

The first illustration comes from Health Improvement Programmes (HImPs) introduced with the publication of *The new NHS* (Secretary of State for Health, 1997). The intention was for HImPs to be led by each (then) health authority, with a main responsibility to draw up a HImP to tackle root causes of ill health and to plan care for patients, but significantly, in consultation with NHS trusts, primary care groups, other primary care professionals (dentists, opticians, pharmacists), the local social services, the public and other partner organisations. At this stage, therefore, interagency working had now become an ever-widening proposition which set out to assess the health needs and health care requirements of the local population as well as the range, location and investment needed to meet the needs of local people.

Box 9.1: The six challenges identified by the King's Fund

- work and time overload;
- changing roles and responsibilities;
- the lack of resources;
- public involvement and accountability;
- measuring progress; and
- interagency partnerships.

A fairly extensive evaluation programme was undertaken by the King's Fund (Arora et al, 2000) which located six challenges (Box 9.1). From this background, one major issue for evaluation, where various agencies are involved, has been how to ensure that partner organisations remained signed-up when the reduction of health inequalities is sought which requires long-term goals. Second, interagency partnerships can introduce unevenness of commitment where health authorities have regarded HImPs as part of the public health department – thus marginal to the organisation as a whole – while local authorities and primary care groups felt the need to be better equipped with public health skills. Then again, different cultures and ways of working have also provided barriers between the different organisations involved. However, a third aspect has become even more significant whereby new initiatives, such as HImPs, have hardly secured initial evaluation when significant changes are made to the overall context. From 2002, HImPs have been repositioned to become part of the Health Improvement and Modernisation Plans (which have now altered the initials to HIMPs) to underline the importance of interagency involvement for health improvement, reducing health inequalities, but within the modernisation agenda. So, one issue for evaluation here is the continuously evolving nature of the exercise where earlier evaluations may only have some relevance for later developments as can be further illustrated by the next example.

Health Action Zones (HAZs)

In 1998-99, 26 Health Action Zones (HAZs) were designated to develop and implement joint strategies between the NHS, local authorities, the voluntary and private sectors and community groups as well as to tackle health inequalities in some of the most needy areas of the country (Secretary of State for Health, 1997). Higgins (1998) quickly pointed out that HAZs were part of a long tradition of area-based social programmes and economic regeneration projects in Britain, where lessons should be heeded if HAZs were to avoid past pitfalls. However, subsequently, Powell and Moon (2001) contended that HAZs did address the main criticisms of the earlier area-based policies since they were based on place and location rather than on the poverty of people. Nevertheless, although intended as a seven-year HAZ programme, already by 2001 the government's announcement of new local strategic partnerships appeared to suggest that health action zones could disappear. The new partnerships would form part of a neighbourhood renewal strategy targeted at England's most deprived areas as well as a possible rationalisation of partnerships, plans and initiatives, so that HAZs could be integrated with local strategic partnerships to strengthen the links between health education, employment and social exclusion (SEU, 2001).

Initially, among the HAZ outcomes, Peck (1998) showed that nurturing partnerships took time. Rather differently, Owens (1998) pointed out that collaboration might be tested by legal constraints but, significantly, while the Department of Health placed stress on local accountability, NHS bodies were at best only indirectly accountable to the local public.

Meanwhile, HAZ programmes were to be extensively evaluated by the Personal Social Services Research Unit at Kent University, where one of the top priorities was to look at the interagency partnership and governance arrangements as well as the nature of community involvement (Judge, 1999). In the light of the HAZ experience, Judge (2000) subsequently raised some fundamental points for evaluation in the future. Illustrated by the HAZ evaluation programme, Judge (2000) has aptly described the arena as "testing evaluation to the limits". The tests were set by the need to manage and deliver the objectives, which was far from easy as HAZs were set broad goals that depended on achieving significant change. Furthermore, the goals tended to alter over time to respond to circumstances. Then again, the programmes were focused on communities with complex open systems, which are difficult to disentangle when many forces can influence the pathway and outcomes of the initiatives. As a result, new approaches to evaluation are needed, for which Judge (2000) suggests the concept of 'realistic evaluation', which seeks to understand "why a programme works, for whom and in what circumstances" in order to increase knowledge about the context and outcomes so that "better policies can be developed in the future". One positive outcome, claimed by Kent University's evaluation, has been the knowledge assembled by the HAZ evaluation programme to show how the contexts, strategies and interventions can contribute to addressing health inequalities (Judge, 2000). However, Barnes and Sullivan (2002, p 94) subsequently pointed out from the HAZ experience that partnership cannot of itself equalise power imbalances between stakeholders.

Some evaluated projects which have featured the views of service users with regard to collaboration between health and social care:

1. A project at King's College (London) undertook a two-year evaluation of integrated working between the health and social services for joint

commissioning and provision of mental health services in Somerset. Peck et al (2002) showed that the process was less than seamless, while the benefits to users were not significant. Further, users considered that access to services had actually deteriorated with no alternative to hospital admission in crises. Users felt less involved in care planning than previously, even though both users and carers had been included as non-voting members of the commissioning board. Significant structural innovation with good political support and some high quality management had been evident but, although some helpful initiatives had taken place to help user involvement and to support networking among unpaid carers, there had been no shift of power towards users.

2. From the National Primary Care Research and Development Centre at the University of Manchester, Glendinning and Rummery (2003) have been engaged in an ongoing study as to how primary care groups/trusts (PCG/Ts) have been tackling the new collaborative agenda with social services, with particular reference to developing services for older people. At this stage, the evaluation has shown that there is evidence that interprofessional and interagency barriers between primary health and social services are beginning to break down within the community, although organisational 'turbulence' remains a continuing threat to improved collaboration. The PCG/T boards still appeared to consult their professional colleagues rather than the older people themselves, in contrast to the values and perspectives of the social services professionals, with regard to their willingness to listen to older people as well as to involve this client group with planning, developing, monitoring and reviewing new service developments.

3. A third illustration draws on one of the few studies of evaluated work specifically concerned with service users. Turner and Balloch (2001) have highlighted the Wiltshire and Swindon Users' Network to show how an effective model of user-controlled organisations can develop and be supported. The network effectively began in 1993 following the county's first Community Care Development Plan. The main purpose of the network has been to build up a membership organisation of service users to become involved in the planning, delivery and evaluation of services; to provide a support network for service users in Wiltshire; to facilitate direct links between the service users and the Social Services Department; and to employ development workers to involve service users in the programme in which the project has been firmly based on a community development approach. Throughout the 1990s, funding for the network has been secured variously from Wiltshire county council, the Wiltshire Health Authority for projects on advocacy and information, the Wiltshire Independent Living Fund for special funds for user-controlled research, alongside other specifically focused funds from the Joseph Rowntree Foundation to undertake a user-controlled

'Best Value review' of Wiltshire's direct payment scheme with which local disabled people have been involved in the review.

The Wiltshire Users' Network has been held up as a model for user involvement in evaluating services, which has stretched more widely than the immediate services in health and social care provision to take in community safety and the quality of pavements among other local services. However, as Turner and Balloch (2001) point out, most user groups are concerned in particular with the represented needs of disabled and older people, people with learning difficulties, mental health service users and, in some areas, young people in care. Despite a tendency towards service evaluation concentrating on other better represented groups, nevertheless the value of joint working between the different user groups and voluntary organisations has been increasingly recognised.

Various questions are raised for evaluation with user involvement. The list would include:

- lack of funding (especially with local authority funding cuts to voluntary groups);
- how to ensure that the process of user involvement is appropriate for evaluation;
- how to counteract discrimination among user involvement with evaluation (where the better represented groups can more readily ensure effective outcomes); and
- to what extent are health and social services prepared to go to empower service users to ensure their evaluated needs are met?

A further point of interest to emerge has been the recognition that, in contrast to user involvement with social services, as with the second example given earlier, the health services still remained further behind on user involvement and relevant evaluation (Turner and Balloch, 2001).

Having looked at three evaluated aspects of projects based on user involvement, this chapter returns to some wider aspects on the perspective of service users in the conclusion. Next, some political factors in evaluating interagency working are considered, followed by an overview of certain issues which have arisen in the policy arena.

Some political factors in evaluating interagency working

One fundamental matter at stake is the continuation of a deep structural divide between the health and social services. Health services continue to be funded and run by a centralised system under the Department of Health (DH), while social services remain funded and run by locally elected authorities, but responsible to the DH overall, as is the Social Services Inspectorate. Despite various policy moves to bring the two sectors together (as the following section of this chapter shows), the financial divisions remain, which can create both questions and problems for the evaluation of joint working. Should interagency initiatives be jointly funded? Who should take responsibility for evaluated outcomes: both services working together?

A second political issue concerns the place of private–public concordats. In this instance, a different sector altogether comes into play to provide interagency health and welfare services. On the positive side of evaluation, in East Surrey, Bryson et al (2001) claimed that health needs could not be met through the NHS facilities available locally, which meant that cooperation with private hospitals had therefore been beneficial. Then again, the first survey of the £100 million evaluation, from the National Audit Office (2001), showed that the government considered that 80 of the first 100 private finance initiatives (PFI) projects delivered a good service or better value for money than conventional funding. However, public–private concordats have also presented various problems for evaluation, which include practical dilemmas with regard to regulation, accountability, safeguards and even partnership working itself, with the temptation to under-regulate to encourage market entry (Pollock et al, 2001).

A third political arena for evaluation concerns the place of boundaries across interagency working: where does evaluation begin and end? How far can partnership responsibility enable effective programme implementation to be evaluated and at what stage? Further, the findings from evaluated studies then need action. However the merger research study (Fulop et al, 2002), discussed earlier, may present a classic case which ends with the published research only.

Above all, a fourth political issue for evaluation concerns money and funding. What is the most appropriate funding base: a joint exercise between agencies? Outside sources? Government money? Many options exist. The next question is: at what point should financed evaluation be brought in? The early outcome, by August 2002, to launch a £100 million NHS Bank rescue package for three (of the 28) Statutory Health Authorities which were only introduced in April 2002, in order to produce balanced budgets and to solve underlying deficits (Stephenson, 2002), indicates an absolute failure to evaluate what was needed, within a manageable financial outlay, from the start.

The policy arena

Closely linked to political factors is the outcome in the policy arena for evaluation. The major challenge is the constant pattern of change in service delivery for both health and social care provision. Hardly has one development taken place (with or without time for evaluation) than the next round for change takes place.

Recent innovations

With respect to interagency working, an array of developments have been introduced to enable services to work together under joint programmes, more particularly in England, which include from 2000 onwards (Leathard, 2003):

- *Intermediate care* to enable older people to lead more independent lives at home, through a range of integrated services to promote faster recovery from illness, to prevent unnecessary acute hospital admission, long-term residential or continuing NHS in-patient care. Care is therefore supported by interagency approaches and multidisciplinary teams across primary care trusts, hospitals and local authorities, all working together with a collaborative response from general practitioners, nurses, care workers and social workers (Laurent, 2001).
- *Care trusts* to commission health and social care in a single organisation (DH, 2001) under the 2001 Health and Social Care Act, although by mid-2002 only some 15 care trust pilots were to start work by April 2003. As primary care trusts concentrated on the delivery of improved services, so care trusts began to be regarded as only one of a number of ways to move towards health and social care integration (Hudson, 2002).
- *Integrated care pathways* to make explicit the most appropriate care for a patient group based on the available evidence and consensus of best practice with a multidisciplinary approach to the care pathway.
- *One-stop health and social care services* to provide a single care network to assess needs with staff working alongside each other with a primary care and community health care team as part of a single network.
- *NHS direct and Care direct* to work jointly as a one-stop approach to information by phone round the clock.

All of the above developments open up questions for evaluation:

- Who should fund an assessment of the changes?
- What happens if the intended programmes do not fulfil expectations?
- How far can service users take part in any evaluation?

Potential hazards ahead: cross-charging

By July 2003, policy developments began to look more problematical for interagency working. First, under the 2003 Community Care (Delayed Discharges) Act, social services departments would be required to reimburse NHS hospital trusts (some £100-£200) for every day a patient was delayed in hospital after a two-day discharge deadline. From the start of 2004, the 2003 Community Care (Delayed Discharges) Act has come into force, with reference in the press being made to a two-day discharge deadline as distinct from three days earlier on. The act says:

Regulations may prescribe a period as the minimum interval after a notice under section 2 is given, but that period must:

a) begin with the day after that on which the notice under section 2 is given and

b) be a period of at least 2 days (8)
   Until 31 March 2005, the period of two days referred to in subsection (7) is exclusive of Sundays and public holidays in England and Wales.

Following opposition to the bed-blocking bill in the House of Lords, the government conceded that guidance would be needed to check on patients' home care packages within two weeks of their return home to ensure adequate support. The act required the NHS to notify social services when a patient, needing home care, was due to be discharged while social services had to carry out an assessment as well as arrange a care package.

The programme was to operate without payment from 1 October 2003, then to be fully implemented in January 2004. Despite the provision for local jointly devised protocols between health and social care 'partners' which would cover: notification and cross-boundary arrangements; local hospital beds defined as providing acute care; informing and consulting with patients and relatives during the care planning process; and agreement on whole systems investment arising from local authority reimbursement of £100 million for each full year (www.doh.gov.uk/reimbursement), the proposed pathway between health and social services could be hazardous. Much would depend on the commitment to joint working. Financial tensions and disagreements over such complex but critical factors could quickly undermine effective interagency arrangements, which require agreed purposes, goals and outcomes, underpinned by adequate resources. Cross-charging impecunious social services departments by the NHS could well render apart the notion of working together for the benefit of service users. No trial evaluation has been suggested to test out the proposals, nor for the following new hospital developments.

Foundation hospitals/trusts

Under the 2003 Health and Social Care Bill, a further threat to interagency working comes with the proposals to create foundation hospitals. The key distinction between the present 318 NHS hospital trusts and the proposed foundation trusts is local autonomy. In theory, foundation trusts would be more accountable and responsive to their local communities, run by locally elected boards with representatives from hospital staff and primary care trusts, with more financial freedom and incentives to be entrepreneurial, innovative and free of regulation from central government. An independent regulator would vet financial plans and adjudicate on complaints. By July 2003, 25 hospitals were being considered for foundation status – half the number eligible under the government's criteria (Wintour, 2003).

So what could be the threat to interagency working? Far from working together on locally elected boards, some have dismissed the elections as a 'sham democracy' that would rival the legitimacy of local councillors (Hurst, 2003). Next, tension at the heart of foundation trust developments could emerge as policy points in two directions (not one overall interagency outlook). On the one hand, the government has presented foundation trusts as independent entrepreneurial organisations but, on the other has sold the venture to sceptical MPs and the public as a new form of local representative organisation. Then again, although foundation trusts would have, in theory, greater freedom over pay, recruitment, financial control and tailoring services to meet local needs, interagency working could also be jeopardised by the potential for foundation trusts to promote inequality and NHS fragmentation (Prentis, 2003). Furthermore, as Hunter (2003) has pointed out, relations between primary care trusts and acute trusts are often marked by suspicion; links with local government are little better. Cooperative networks do not therefore seem within immediate range to further interagency working with foundation trusts, although primary care trusts will be commissioning services from these newly independent health care providers. However, Walshe (2003) has recently argued that, as foundation trusts develop, new joint ventures, partnerships and other enterprises could emerge or even link up with other non-health care organisations given that foundation trusts will be able to retain the income from such new ventures.

Regulation

Meanwhile, the government has sought to tighten up on inspection and audit across health and social care provision. The proposed changes include a Commission for Healthcare Audit and Inspection to investigate the performance of NHS organisations as well as the registration and inspection of private and voluntary hospitals; to include the Independent Healthcare functions of the National Care Standards Commission; the functions of the Commission for Health Improvement; and the health value-for-money work of the Audit Commission. Furthermore, a Commission for Social Care Inspection will combine the powers of the DH's Social Services Inspectorate and the social care functions of the National Care Standards Commission, as well as to review the performance and quality of local authority social care provision. One flaw can be spotted immediately for interagency working: all the measures for inspection, audit and regulation continue with separate bodies for health and social care evaluation.

Conclusion: the key points to emerge from the evaluation of interagency working

First, with regard to input, the extent of evaluation has been limited. Only by the 21st century has a quietly increasing number of studies addressed the outcomes of partnership working and collaborative endeavours across health and social care provision. The present chapter has focused on the health and welfare services but it has to be recognised that relevant interagency working also extends across ever-wider areas as well, such as social deprivation, New Deal for Communities and the government's neighbourhood renewal policy (Neighbourhood Renewal Unit, 2002).

Second, even across the present evaluation arena under consideration, some key points emerge:

1. Once evaluated, little appears to have taken place in response to the findings of projects that have addressed agencies working together across the public, private and voluntary sectors.

2. One significant factor has been the constant process of change. Hardly has one initiative been installed than new moves are made towards modification or reorganisation. Health Improvement Programmes come into this category as does the National Care Standards Commission, concerned with the inspection and audit of the social services which, introduced in April 2002, barely lasted a few weeks before new changes were set out for the future of this commission.

3. With a range of bodies, organisations, individuals and research teams, all variously and separately involved with evaluation in this field, no overall targets nor commonly agreed interagency objectives have been established. Separate elements are individually and selectively assessed. What, however, could be an overarching basis for evaluation? Some suggestions could include: achieving financial targets; reflecting user expectations; or measuring how far the original objectives have been met overall.

4. Meanwhile, El Ansari et al (2001), in looking at the evaluation of collaboration and partnerships, have questioned the quality of the evidence which argues that partnerships are beneficial to the communities they serve. However, the authors contend that if targets are being achieved through joint working, more precise evidence and evaluation of the effectiveness of collaborative working could then lead to an improvement in interagency working and the practice of partnerships.

5. A remaining challenge for interagency evaluation is the continuing structural divide between the health and social services. Significant differences continue across financial patterns; professional outlook, values and competition for

domains; procedural matters (budgetary and planning cycles); as well as status and legitimacy between elected and appointed agencies. One way forward would be to work firmly towards an integrated service to reconcile the differences. As Humphris and Macleod *(Health Service Journal, 2002)* have argued, workforce planning, funding and regulation should be combined across health and social care. Finally, there remains the question, initially set in this chapter, for whom is evaluation intended? One approach may be to suggest that the outcome has to be financial viability – the intention therefore being to respond to the political agenda.

On this basis, the pathway forward could be set at a tough level. Cooper (2002) has recently suggested that, in the financial market, "funds should match fees to results"; in other words, that fund managers should cut their fees as millions of investors languish in expensive schemes that have plunged in value. *Should health and social care funds match budgeted public and private expenditure to evaluated results?* Then, should successful interagency working be rewarded and others penalised?

However, former health secretary Alan Milburn's (2002) agenda was somewhat different:

> We could choose transformation, recognising that extra spending alone is insufficient to deliver improvements in public services. Reform needs to go further, using resources to deliver not just improved services but a different sort of service – one where users are in the driving seat. (p 18)

As one service user pointed out in response *(The Times, 2002)*, Mr Milburn recognised that the NHS has become a monopoly provider, hamstrung by political dogma, with little choice for patients. The only way forward was to put the money squarely behind the user, so that resources were harnessed under contract between the provider and patient. However, where would such a striking development leave interagency working? To make such a suggestion meaningful, service users would need information. As Maynard (2002) has argued, consumer information should be tested with care, as experience has shown that to develop information for consumers takes time and also needs to be conducted with a cautious, evidence-based approach. Moreover, to what extent would financially supported service users be able to perceive an interagency pathway was for their benefit?

Overview

- The extent and response to evaluations of interagency working have been limited.
- Barriers have included the shifting policy context, the often late involvement of an evaluator in a project, the structural divide between health and social services and the lack of commonly agreed objectives.

> • Questions raised include: who is an appropriate body to undertake interagency research? For whom is it intended? Who should take responsibility in addressing the outcomes?

References

Armitage, P. (1983) 'Joint working in primary health care' (Occasional Paper), *Nursing Times*, vol 79, pp 75-8.

Arora, S., Davies, A. and Thompson, S. (2000) 'Developing health improvement programmes: challenges for a new millennium', *Journal of Interprofessional Care*, vol 14, no 1, pp 9-18.

Barnes, M. and Sullivan, H. (2002) 'Building capacity for collaboration in English Health Action Zones', in C. Glendinning, M. Powell and K. Rummery (eds) *Partnerships, New Labour and the governance of welfare*, Bristol: The Policy Press, pp 81-96.

Bradshaw, D. and Walshe, K. (2002) 'Powers of observation', *Health Service Journal*, vol 112 (5801), pp 28-9.

Bryson, K., Williams, E. and Bell, C. (2001) 'Public pain, private gain', *Health Service Journal*, vol 111 (5771), pp 24-5.

Cooper, K. (2002) 'Funds should match fees to results', *The Sunday Times* (Money Supplement), 11 August, p 1.

DH (Department of Health) (2001) 'Care trusts: emerging framework' (www.doh.gov.uk).

El Ansari, W., Phillips, C. and Hammick, M. (2001) 'Collaboration and partnerships: developing the evidence base', *Health and Social Care in the Community*, vol 9, no 4, pp 215-27.

Fulop, N., Protopsaltis, G., Hutchings, A., King, A., Allen, P., Normand, C. and Walters, R. (2002) 'Process and impact of mergers of NHS trusts: multi-centre case study and management cost analysis', *British Medical Journal*, vol 325 (7358), p 246.

Glendinning, C. and Rummery, K. (2003) 'Collaboration between primary health and social care – from policy to practice in developing services for older people', in A. Leathard (ed) *Interprofessional collaboration: From policy to practice in health and social care*, London: Routledge, pp 186-99.

Gregson, B., Cartledge, A. and Bond, J. (1992) 'Development of a measure of professional collaboration in primary health care', *Journal of Epidemiology and Community Health*, vol 46, pp 48-53.

Health Service Journal (2002) 'Combine workforce planning across health and social care', vol 112 (5808), p 8.

Higgins, J. (1998) 'HAZs warning', *Health Service Journal*, vol 108 (5600), pp 24-5.

Hudson, D. (2002) 'Silence is golden', *Health Service Journal*, vol 112 (5792), p 18.

Hunter, D. (2003) 'Enter at your peril', *Health Service Journal*, vol 113 (5842), p 18.

Hurst, G. (2003) 'Labour rebels defy plea to back hospital reforms', *The Times*, 9 July, p 12.

Judge, K. (1999) 'National Evaluation of Health Action Zones', in A. Bebbington and K. Judge (eds) *PSSRU Bulletin, Canterbury: Personal Social Services Research Unit*, Canterbury: University of Kent, pp 18-20.

Judge, K. (2000) 'Testing evaluation to the limits: the case of English Health Action Zones', *Journal of Health Services Research and Policy*, vol 5, no 1, January, pp 3-5.

Laurent, C. (2001) 'Independence way', *Health Service Journal*, vol 111 (5751), pp 22-3.

Leathard, A. (ed) (2003) *Interprofessional collaboration: From policy to practice in health and social care*, London: Brunner Routledge.

Maynard, A. (2002) 'A double-edged sword', *Health Service Journal*, vol 112 (5798), p 20.

McCurry, P. (2002) 'Selling points', *The Guardian* (Society Supplement), 17 July, p 12.

McGrath, M. (1991) *Multi-disciplinary teamwork: Community mental health handicap teams*, Aldershot: Avebury.

Milburn, A. (2002) 'We have to give the voters more than this', *The Times*, 7 August, p 18.

National Audit Office (2001) *Managing the relationships to secure a successful partnership*, London: The Stationery Office.

Neighbourhood Renewal Unit (2002) *Bending the sp£nd*, London: Haymarket Professional Publications Ltd.

Owens, D. (1998) 'Trouble Zones', *Health Service Journal*, vol 108 (5593), p 9.

Peck, E. (1998) 'Share of the action', *The Guardian*, 25 February, p 17.

Peck, E., Towell, D. and Gulliver, P. (2002) 'Going Halves', *Health Service Journal*, vol 112 (5801), pp 26-7.

Peck, E., Gulliver, P. and Towell, D. (2002) *Modernising partnerships: An evaluation of Somerset's innovations in the commissioning and organisation of mental health services: Final report*, London: King's College.

Pollock, A., Shaoul, J. and Rowland, D. (2001) *A response to the IPPR Commission on public private partnerships, health policy and Health Services Research Unit*, London: University College.

Powell, M. and Moon, G. (2001) 'Health Action Zones: the 'third way' of a new area-based policy?', *Health and Social Care in the Community*, vol 9, no 1, pp 43-50.

Prentis, D. (2003) 'Rocking the foundations', *Health Matters*, Summer, vol 52, pp 8-10.

Secretary of State for Health (1997) *The new NHS: Modern, dependable*, Cm 3807, London: The Stationery Office.

SEU (Social Exclusion Unit) (2001) *A new commitment to Neighbourhood Renewal: National strategy action plan*, London: Cabinet Office.

Stephenson, P. (2002) 'NHS Bank to launch £100m rescue package', *Health Service Journal*, vol 112 (5816), p 4.

The Times (2002) 'The Register', 12 August, p 9 (debate@the times.co.uk).

Turner, M. and Balloch, S. (2001) 'Partnership between service users and statutory social services', in S. Balloch and M. Taylor (eds) *Partnership working: Policy and practice*, Bristol: The Policy Press, pp 165-79.

Walshe, K. (2003) 'No holding back', *Health Service Journal*, vol 113 (5863), pp 18-19.

Wintour, P. (2003) 'Blair to double foundation hospitals scheme', *The Guardian*, 30 July, p 4.

TEN

Reflections on an evaluation of partnerships to cope with winter pressures

Susan Balloch, Alison Penn and Helen Charnley

Introduction

This chapter reflects on an evaluation of partnership working between health and social care services in West Sussex. In evaluating projects to combat 'winter pressures', it outlines the mapping of the main relationships between stakeholders, findings from a questionnaire sent to senior, middle management and frontline staff and an analysis of evaluation forms. It shows how national policy drove the projects and how local politics contributed to as well as impeded their success.

Winter pressures are governmentally recognised special problems experienced in winter by both health and social services as a result of a higher incidence of illness, especially among older people, and a consequent increase in emergency admissions. Special funding to meet these pressures was introduced in 1997 for local health and social care communities through Local Winter Planning Groups (LWPGs).

The LWPG provided a prime example of partnership working. Its broad representation included the relevant Health Authority, Social Services Departments, Trusts (acute, mental health, community, learning disability and ambulance services), Primary Care Trusts and Groups, Local Representative Committees, Out of Hours' Cooperatives, Deputising Services, NHS Direct, Community Health Councils (CHCs)/Patient/Public representatives and members of the voluntary and private sectors involved in health and social care.

National criteria for local winter planning required each health and social care community to submit a single local winter plan to its health and social care region at the end of the July of that year for agreement by the end of September (DH, 2000). In 2000 national criteria focused on flu immunisation, hospital services (critical care and acute services), community and mental health services, ambulance services, intermediate care, social care and primary care.

Further issues covered included contingency plans for escalation/control procedures, human resources and communications.

Box 10.1: Six broad areas of action being taken to prepare for winter, as set out in the 'Winter Plan'

- Promoting self-care and preventing ill health;
- investment in capacity and change;
- service improvement and design;
- staffing;
- better preparations and strengthened partnerships; and
- managing the winter.

The Winter Report 2000-01 found many examples of good progress, as well as areas still requiring considerable attention. Its recommendations, however, signalled a greater focus on year round capacity planning as the key to improved services:

> Local planning for winter should explicitly include preparations to manage elective as well as emergency demand. LWPGs should operate all year round. (DH, 2001a, para 58)

> [T]o ensure capacity planning across the whole system is more effective LWPGs should map available capacity across the system eg in the local NHS, Social Care and private health care sector throughout the year. (DH, 2001a, para 59)

On this basis, the NHS Executive South East then set out a plan for emergency care for 2001-02 and beyond (NHS Executive South East, 2001). This political change of direction altered the parameters of an evaluation being carried out by the Health and Social Policy Research Centre (HSPRC) at the University of Brighton for two of West Sussex's LWPGs.

West Sussex Health Authority commissioned HSPRC in March 2001 to assess the effectiveness of selected winter pressures projects in West Sussex in relieving the pressures on health and social services and to assess the outcomes for patients and service users. The independent evaluation was to take place retrospectively for winter 2000-01. However, some projects continued after the winter funding stopped and were resourced from other budgets. A further task, not discussed here, was to develop a toolkit for self-evaluating projects in the future (Balloch and Penn, 2003).

The agreed objectives of the work were to describe the processes involved in the planning, decision making and implementation of winter pressures schemes; identify the outputs associated with winter pressures schemes; identify outcomes associated with selected schemes; and identify the cost consequences associated with the use of winter pressures funding. The evaluation adopted a 'realistic' approach aiming to maximize the number of stakeholders involved.

Study design

Two of the four West Sussex LWPG areas (Coastal and Northern) were selected by the health authority to participate in the evaluation exercise. The Coastal Group encompassed health and social services agencies in Worthing, Adur and Arun. The Northern Group similarly included health and social services agencies in Crawley and Horsham. Chanctonbury, located between the two groups, was represented on both LWPGs.

The two selected areas had different community profiles that affected the nature of services demanded. The Coastal area, particularly in Arun and Worthing, had a large population of elderly people, with pockets of deprivation, particularly around Littlehampton in Arun. As a seaside area, it attracts many older people on holiday in the summer months. The Northern Group covered a more urbanised area, with a small but growing population of older people and a large population of young people. It contains, mostly in Langley Green in Crawley, the largest ethnic minority population in the county, mainly from India, Pakistan and Bangladesh. High rates of teenage pregnancy characterise both Littlehampton and Crawley (see Health in West Sussex, 2000).

Each of these areas used winter pressures monies to fund a wide range of residential and community-based initiatives through health and social services with a very small proportion of resources supporting voluntary sector initiatives. The private sector was indirectly involved through commissions for 'step down' facilities for older people leaving hospital.

Projects were selected by the LWPGs from the wide range of those implemented. Projects selected were generally those thought to be useful and successful. One or two projects initially selected for evaluation were taken off the list because they had failed to get off the ground. In one case this was because of a failure to recruit the necessary staff – unsurprising as most services in the South East were experiencing, and continue to experience, recruitment problems. Projects finally included are listed in Box 10.2.

Box 10.2: Projects included in the evaluation

Coastal group:
- Nursing home beds with rehabilitation support.
- Additional bed management/discharge nurse support.
- Community support services following hospital discharge (Worthing).

Northern group:
- Purchase of additional nursing home placements.
- Funding for additional beds in medical assessment unit.
- Community support services following hospital discharge.

This sample of schemes enabled us to achieve a comparative analysis of broadly equivalent projects in the two areas:

- the purchase/provision of additional beds in nursing homes and community hospitals to provide step down and/or rehabilitation facilities following discharge from hospital;
- the funding of additional assessment beds, enhanced bed management arrangements and discharge support designed to increase throughout; and
- enhanced community support services provided through social services.

A difficulty that emerged with evaluating the two projects was comparability. This was made difficult by two factors in particular:

1. the idiosyncratic use of terminology, such as 'step down beds', 'rehab beds' and, more recently, 'intermediate care beds', which was inconsistent between the areas; and
2. the different methods and categories used for collecting data for monitoring and evaluation.

This inconsistency also extended to definitions of units of outcome.

Mapping the stakeholders

Preliminary discussions were held with key actors in the selected projects to identify and map the schemes and the relationships between them. Diagrammatic maps of both areas were prepared. This began with the focus on the provision of extra beds, in both nursing/residential homes and in hospitals. The community support services following hospital discharge were then added in. These maps (Figures 10.1-10.2) also do not include the Chanctonbury part of the provision, which is a key link between the coastal and northern areas.

The maps represent a summary only of the relationships involved in the three types of schemes funded by the respective LWPGs and included in HSPRC's research. Each area ran a large number of schemes. Furthermore, it needs to be remembered that the winter pressures schemes were themselves part of a much wider picture of health and social care provision.

The maps indicate the political and organisational complexities within which staff had to work in order to make the schemes function and meet their objectives. Staff themselves were not always aware of the full picture and it took researchers some time to identify the main interrelationships. The lack of coherence made rational policy implementation difficult. Also, the maps suggest there is a strong focus on hospital-based or hospital-oriented schemes, which is unsurprising given the origins of winter pressures funding to relieve the admissions of elderly people to hospital.

Figure 10.1: Coastal

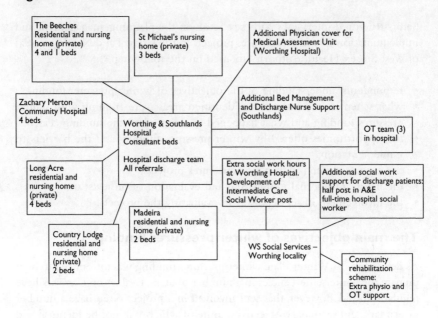

Figure 10.2: Northern

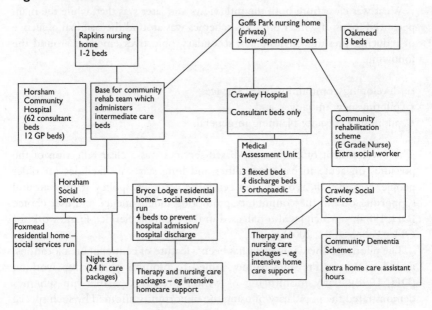

Interview findings

Semi-structured interviews with key actors in the planning, management and implementation of winter pressures projects in the Coastal and Northern areas of West Sussex Health Authority focused on the following:

- respondents' understanding of the objectives of winter pressures funding;
- what schemes under the three identified areas were running with winter pressures funding and what happened to them when the funding ceased;
- the opportunities offered by winter pressures funding and the barriers to implementation;
- the costs associated with winter pressures projects;
- the nature of internal monitoring and evaluation of projects; and
- the involvement of service users in evaluating the projects.

The main objectives of winter pressures funding

As defined in the Winter Plan, winter pressures funding was introduced to help prepare for winter emergencies in a number of areas. Evaluation exercises have regularly found, however, that staff involved in a project often have a number of primary and secondary objectives, some of which will not be identical and may even be in conflict. In our interviews, therefore, we asked respondents what they saw as the main objectives of winter pressures funding.

What was clear from both the interviews and later was that, while the main perceived focus of winter pressures schemes was around the original objective of reducing pressure on hospitals, secondary objectives emerged around the following:

- developing community-based services;
- piloting new initiatives; and
- addressing capacity planning in general.

The development of community-based services was a clear reflection of the pressures on acute in-patient facilities and long stay care facilities for older people. However, it also reflected central government policy framed around supporting care in the community, promoting independence and user choice (DH, 1989) – principles also reflected in the National Service Framework for Older People (DH, 2001b).

The piloting of new initiatives has been a feature of central grant allocations, including Winter Pressures Money, aimed to promote partnership working (DH, 1998). Early monitoring of winter pressures partnership schemes demonstrated the popularity of using the opportunity afforded by such special funds to develop innovative approaches to respond to greater or more complex demands on services (Healy, 1999).

Reference to increasing capacity and capacity planning illustrated the realisation, at both central and local levels, that year-round capacity planning was needed "to ensure winter is planned for within the wider year round agenda" (DH, 2001a).

Opportunities and barriers presented by winter pressures funding

Opportunities and benefits

Respondents from Coastal and Northern areas shared some experiences of key opportunities and benefits brought by the schemes. These common experiences were related to processes of joint working, increased financial resources and opportunities for innovation.

Joint working between health and social services was a real bonus. The pooling of resources for the greater good represented a sea change and had enabled the growth of trust. One respondent stated:

> "there have been major successes on the ground with people working together and there are examples of real partnership working."

Such findings are not uncommon where personnel from different agencies join forces on specific projects, where close contact becomes part of the structure of working and where resources are applied to the same group of beneficiaries (Charnley, 2001; Williamson, 2001). As Huxham (1993) has argued, effective partnership working is driven by trust.

A joint approach to planning and funding winter pressures schemes offered further potential for expanding dialogue and influence between health and social services. One social services representative expressed the view that:

> "we have addressed the primary care issues, discussions have focused on acute hospitals. We need to look at GP services too. Social Services do not hold the lion's share of resources, but we oil the wheels to keep the system working."

While a partnership approach is an integral part of the allocation of winter pressures monies, the availability of extra funding in itself was considered a key opportunity and helped to alleviate the pressures experienced as a result of underfunding. This was expressed particularly acutely in relation to social care services:

> "there has been an increase in funding to social care projects which have been chronically underfunded."

A third common observation was that the injection of new money in the system *gives opportunity to do new things*. In a context of under-resourcing, the will to spend money from core budgets on innovative approaches, in other words to take risks, is low. New money for specific projects offers a relatively low risk possibility of developing innovative approaches (Healy, 1999; Martin and Sanderson, 1999) that may be replicated where they are successful.

Further reports of opportunities in each of the two areas were related to specific projects. Each, in its own way, refers to issues of joint working, additional resources or innovative approaches.

In the Coastal area

Step down beds were popular and evaluated positively by older patients and their families, although there were reports of initial scepticism that this represented the introduction of a second-class service. This finding is related to 'acceptability' of services, one of the key factors with direct implications for questions of user and carer involvement in both the planning and evaluation of services.

The combination of physiotherapy support and intensive home care was also perceived as being really effective in promoting independence among frail older people. This observation was related directly to the outcome of the service, the impact of the intervention on individual users.

These two service-related comments from the Coastal area are linked closely to questions of quality and remind us of the important link between process and outcome. Quality of service provision is viewed differently by planners, professionals, users and carers who place different values on the processes and outcomes of care (Nocon and Qureshi, 1996). In examining the notion of quality assurance, Maxwell (1983) has argued that differences in value attached to particular outcomes are reflected in the value placed on different elements of quality assurance: appropriateness, equity, accessibility, effectiveness, acceptability and efficiency. Appropriateness and acceptability are seen as key elements in achieving quality, without which the outcome-related elements will not be achieved (Ranade, 1994). The argument is that positive outcomes are more likely to be achieved where service users feel that the services they receive are closely matched to their needs and expectations (Øvretveit, 1992).

In the Northern area

Health access to social services equipment via buffer stores was a bonus and demonstrated the collaborative capability between organisations (Huxham, 1993). The use of flexible beds in the acute admissions unit enabled people to move through the system faster. While this indicated an increase in output it did not necessarily indicate greater efficiency in the use of resources. To establish improved efficiency would require knowledge about the medium- and longer-term outcome for individuals who had used this service and the impact this had made on other parts of the health and social services system.

Horsham Social Services Intensive Home Care scheme dedicated to rehabilitation was perceived as having been very successful. With staff able to visit up to four times a day, it was felt that *there is a focus where help is really needed.* This matching of resources to needs has been a central concern of community care policy for over a decade and is echoed in the National Service Framework for Older People that states:

> services sometimes fail to meet older people's needs ... by allowing organisational structures to become a barrier to proper assessment of need and access to care. (DH, 2001b, p 2)

Commenting on the community rehabilitation scheme, one respondent spoke of how "liaison and rapport with GPs and District Nurses was excellent – they really appreciated having just one point of access". This is a common finding of schemes designed to improve links between primary health care and social services for the benefit of elderly service users requiring both health and social services in their own homes (Charnley et al, 1998).

Barriers

Respondents from both areas offered a range of insights into the barriers to implementing winter pressures schemes effectively. Their comments fell into four categories:

1. **The processes surrounding the selection of schemes to be funded, continuity and evaluation.**
   - A lack of clear criteria for selection of bids for schemes to extend capacity.
   - Unrealistic timescales for the bidding process and for getting schemes up and running (a feature often associated with time limited sources of funding for specific areas of work). The time limits placed on funding led to:
     - the stop-start nature of schemes with negative effects on staff morale when projects ceased; and
     - the crudeness of monitoring and evaluation tools that led to difficulties in demonstrating effectiveness and arguing the case for particular interventions to be replicated as part of mainstream provision.

2. **Shortfalls in resources of different kinds that could not be improved simply by making money available.**
   Examples included:
   - Staff shortages in nursing, occupational therapy and social work, a problem linked to wider workforce problems of recruitment and retention of appropriately trained staff (see Balloch et al, 1999).
   - An acute shortage of nursing home beds in the Northern area reflecting the national supply crisis in residential care for older people as private home owners find it increasingly difficult to make a viable business or indeed go out of business (Henwood, 2001).

3. Inappropriate use of resources that tackled symptoms but not causes.
This was argued in the case of:
• Step down and intermediate care beds being used primarily to clear hospital beds, simply shifting the problem from hospital based services to community based services.

4. Cultural differences between health and social service organisations.
This was less related to professional differences and more to political and funding differences that had led to:
• The introduction of eligibility criteria in social services in an attempt to ensure that resources were concentrated on those in greatest need. Establishing eligibility involves a professional assessment of need, and this often implies a long wait, particularly where an older person is deemed to be in a safe place such as a hospital.

In the Coastal area additional barriers were experienced in relation to:

• *A neighbouring Primary Care Group whose geographical area was covered by two different LWPGs.* This PCG was perceived to be reluctant to contribute to the pool of resources to relieve winter pressures if benefits would accrue to service users outside their own area. But there was no reluctance to benefit from winter pressures funded schemes based at the District General Hospital that benefited service users across all Primary Care Group areas.

• *Step down beds that were also thought to be located in too many places.* This perception was made by a professional respondent and reflected problems of control over operations that are physically removed from the centre. It is important to remember, however, that users and carers also have interests in spatial aspects of service provision, and that needs-based planning is increasingly concerned with the tension between the advantages and disadvantages of central and local service provision (Foley, 2001; Haynes, 2001).

In the Northern area two further specific barriers were noted:

1. *Frontline staff of the Community Rehabilitation Team experienced difficulty in sticking to agreed task criteria for professional involvement with service users.* In particular, staff felt it was sometimes difficult to 'say no' when dealing with clients. This reflects growing tension between theoretical claims to holistic models of care in both health and social services, and the tightly defined task and time criteria that govern the provision of home based support services. The experience in this scheme was in contrast to the experience of a neighbouring local authority joint continuing care project in which the contracting of private agencies to provide intensive home care led to frontline workers cutting corners both in terms of time and allocated tasks (Charnley et al, 1998).

2. *Problems of communications were endemic.* Despite approved funding of £20,000 for therapy in the additional beds funded in the Admission and Assessment Unit there was a delayed start to the provision of the beds and the availability of funding for therapy was not communicated until the funding period was almost over. This meant that there was a limited period to assess the impact of such a scheme. The importance of effective communication both within and between agencies, between special schemes and mainstream services cannot be overestimated and has the potential to make or break the effective implementation of projects (Williamson, 2001).

The costs associated with winter pressures projects

One aim of this study was to identify the cost consequences associated with the use of winter pressures funding. The costing of health and social care services has become a great deal more challenging over the last decade. In line with policy changes, responsibility for service provision has shifted from large single public service agencies to a more complex set of service providers from different sectors, agencies, informal carers and service users themselves. These changes require constant adaptation in approaches to the determination of costs (Netten and Beecham, 1993), which organisations find difficult.

Our interviews showed that there was a lack of shared meaning or understanding of costs, both between and within agencies and that little attention was paid to costing exercises in any internal evaluation of winter pressures schemes. Where costs were identified, they were narrowly defined in terms of budget allocations, or direct financial costs such as salaries and overheads. Broader perceptions of costs such as levels of worker morale were not articulated. The implication of this narrow focus was that costs are divorced from outcomes and, therefore, from measures of effectiveness and efficiency. Accordingly, a broader appreciation of costs, to include savings to other agencies, or the long-term savings linked to preventative schemes, was not evident. The implications of reduced per capita costs were not recognised. Nor were opportunity costs central to respondents' thinking. There was no consideration, for example, of the opportunity costs arising from unallocated funds. The superficial attention paid to questions of cost was due, in part, to the timescales involved in project planning, implementation and evaluation. As one respondent indicated, "projects are tabled and they are dealt with so quickly no one can scrutinise". However, another important factor in the scant attention paid to costs lay in the lack of explicit recognition that costing exercises require specific skills that are not common among health and social care practitioners. One respondent suggested that costing should properly be left to health economists. The development of capacity to enable reliable and valid costing exercises to form part of project evaluations is vital if the value of innovative schemes is to be understood comprehensively. This requires not only access to appropriate skills, but also the development of systems for recording the information that is required in order to make cost calculations.

Internal monitoring and evaluation of projects

As part of the mapping process and semi-structured interviews, information was sought on what information was being collected within existing systems. This was an area receiving increasing attention. For example, the Chief Inspector of Social Services had noted in the 10th Annual Report that:

> [p]roblems also exist in the ability of health partners to share information with social services partners in order to improve service effectiveness and in a way that will help social services to plan. Information held by health authority area cannot be disaggregated for many councils.... For example, in our performance monitoring we asked about information on delayed discharge passed by health authorities to councils to get an idea of how routinely information is shared to facilitate effective joint work.... Only 40 per cent of councils confirmed that information in relation to residents affected within council areas was made available on a routine basis. In 26 per cent of councils, the NHS was unable to supply full information about delayed discharges within council areas. (DH, 2001c, paras 5.36-5.38m, p 54-5)

The following table indicates the types of information collected in the areas concerned. While there was some apparent overlap, for example, total patients, number of allocated beds, average length of stay; both areas collected information on a slightly different basis. They also used different definitions. For example, one area used bed days 'saved', the other bed days 'used'. Such differences make it very difficult to draw comparisons as a result we were unable to compare the success of property between areas. Table 10.1 illustrates the types of information being collected.

This collection of statistics represented a considerable amount of personal investment by the staff concerned; that is, over and above their normal workloads and in some cases in the absence of funded support for basic IT equipment and software to facilitate good use of monitoring systems.

Internal evaluation of winter pressures schemes

This subsection presents respondents' views on the role of evaluation in the schemes with which they were concerned. Activities referred to as evaluation were largely concerned with the monitoring of outputs such as numbers of patients or service users, treatments and services allocated. Little attention was paid to the measurement of outcomes other than destinational outcomes.

The following quote offers a flavour of the difficulties experienced in evaluating service provision and the challenges to be faced:

> "We are not good at this ... most effort goes into implementing not evaluating. We struggle with the outcomes of intervention."

Table 10.1: Data collected in selected areas

| | Coastal
(Jun 2000-Feb 2001) | Northern
(Sept 2000-Mar 2001) | |
	Worthing	Horsham	Crawley
Total patients	239	14	53 or 55
Type of acute bed referral: Surgery Medicine Dome Orthopaedic	110 47 43 39		
Average length of stay [days]	11.6	15.5	13
Bed days saved	2,781		
Readmissions	27	1	
No of allocated beds	18 [block contract]	1 to 2 [spot contract]	5 or 3 [block contract]
Bed days used	0	217	673 [out of 741 days available]
Average age of patients		87.5	82.2
Discharge venue: eg, Home, RIP, Hospital Long-term care, Residential rehabilitation			
Outcomes at four weeks discharge from beds		Stayed at home: 5	Stayed at home: 32
Source of referral: GP DN A & E I/Care Team	10 1 2 1	44 5 1	
Reasons for admissions: eg, fractures, falls and so on			

This view was clearly reflected in the types of data that had been collected in internal evaluations of winter pressures schemes. These data focused mainly on outputs (such as services provided, numbers of patients treated, bed days saved) with some mention of processes (for example, source of referral, reason for admission). Evaluation of outcomes was limited to destinational outcomes showing the institutional or community based locations of individuals following particular interventions. There was no evidence of qualitative outcomes such as change in condition, ability or quality of life. There were attempts in some schemes to determine degrees of user satisfaction. User satisfaction may be linked to, but is not synonymous with, outcomes. Moreover, many of the methods used to measure user satisfaction, including telephone interviews that were used in one scheme, raise significant problems of reliability and validity (Nocon and Qureshi, 1996).

A second quote, "we need a template to give substance to developments so they're not just somebody's good idea", suggested a level of frustration at the inability to draw on comparable evaluative information to learn valuable lessons about the effectiveness of different interventions or approaches in varying contexts.

Another problem mentioned was the use of evaluative information, with particular concern expressed that the information collected was not always used. Finally, as described earlier, little attention was paid to the calculation of costs associated with particular outcomes. One respondent argued that costing exercises should be the responsibility of audit rather than commissioners or providers of services, a view based partly on the need for specialist skills for costing that are not always available among teams of health and social care professionals.

The role of evaluation

The immediate purposes of evaluation were understood in relation to monitoring standards and benchmarking, measuring outputs, measuring outcomes, informing future resource allocation and deciding on schemes that might usefully be adopted as part of mainstream practice. However, wider discussion of respondents' aspirations for evaluation revealed a broader set of purposes linked to different types of outcomes, processes, equity, appropriateness and acceptability of services to users. It was felt that evaluation could, for example, measure the impact of particular interventions on patients; illuminate the impact of schemes on other parts of the health and social care system; aid understanding of how services operate; identify groups who may be marginalised or excluded from schemes; and identify whether the schemes provided reflect the interests and preferences of older people.

Additionally, evaluation might identify key themes and facilitate comparison with other areas and generate effective measures for new projects. However, respondents recognised that any evaluation needed to be inbuilt from the beginning of any project or scheme; be transparent and objective; be clearly understandable; be clear about objectives; and reflect the values associated with the interventions being implemented, such as person centredness and partnership.

Most evaluations, of course, do not approximate such ambitious standards, particularly when added on to already completed projects as in this instance.

The involvement of service users in evaluating projects

Exploring the involvement of service users in evaluating winter pressures schemes reflects the priorities of the HSPRC and was not explicitly requested by the commissioners of this report. User involvement is a complex and much debated issue. While arguments for user involvement emphasise aspects of human and civil rights, it is important to remember that user involvement is directly linked to questions of service effectiveness. Service users are best placed to inform policy makers, planners and practitioners about the acceptability and appropriateness of services. Services that are considered appropriate and acceptable by service users are more likely to be associated with positive outcomes (Øvretveit, 1992; Ranade, 1994).

Despite a decade of developing older people's and carers' involvement in planning and evaluating community care services (Thornton, 2000), users and carers were conspicuous by their absence in the planning or evaluation of winter pressures schemes other than as respondents in satisfaction questionnaires or the source of an occasional complaint. The inclusion of Community Health Councils (CHCs) on the LWPGs offered an opportunity to observe the processes of decision making, but did not offer effective representation of patients. Moreover, the imminent demise of CHCs had effectively reduced motivation and possibilities for active participation.

Respondents acknowledged the marginalisation of users and carers, and demonstrated awareness of the challenges of achieving effective involvement and participation. One said:

"We never ask users and carers a great deal. The complexity of issues marginalises users and carers ... but they need support to be involved."

Another respondent expressed some frustration that, "They hardly ever complain – I wish they would". This comment was of particular interest given the claim that one way of obtaining user views could be an examination of formal complaints. But as Nocon and Qureshi (1996, p 43) have argued: complaints are generally only made when services fall well below a minimally acceptable standard and, even then, not all users will feel sufficiently emboldened to make a complaint. Their high threshold and unsystematic nature preclude their use for evaluation.

Differences in organisational and professional cultures in health and social services also gave rise to different views on the involvement of users in decisions about the services they received. Central government policy reflects a generalised rhetoric of user involvement, but this has been adopted more easily in social services than health services where the language of empowerment has not assumed the same profile, particularly in relation to older people (Thornton, 2000). User involvement presents particular problems for managers who are faced with competing pressures to deliver services in a cost-efficient way and to respect service-user choice. One example of these competing pressures was expressed by a health manager who believed that social services' adherence to the ideal of 'client choice' had become a luxury given the shortage of local nursing home beds and pressure to discharge older people from acute hospital beds.

Suggestions for ways in which older people might become more involved included Citizen's Panels, which have been used to include older people in consultations on a wide range of issues, and Patient Advisory Liaison that have now replaced CHCs. A review of developments in older people's involvement (Thornton, 2000) presents evidence of varying preferences for forms of involvement and stresses the need to consult older people locally about how they wish to be involved rather than expecting them to respond positively to external, top-down suggestions for involvement.

The National Service Framework for Older People (DH, 2001b) makes it clear the NHS should shape services around the needs and preferences of patients, and that older people and their families should have a voice through patient forums and patient councils. Person-centred care, one of eight standards outlined in the framework, is based on the commitment that older people and their carers should receive person-centred care and services which respect them as individuals and which are arranged around their needs (DH, 2001b, p 23).

Reflections

This evaluation was initiated primarily as a requirement of government funding though there was no doubting the sincerity of the participants' wish to learn from their experiences. As in many other cases, the evaluation was commissioned retrospectively when most of the projects in question had run their course and had been terminated when funding had dried up. In a few cases only had projects continued, usually because of their perceived success and because of powerful backing.

Assessing the effectiveness of projects retrospectively is always difficult. This task was made more complex by the diversity and patchiness of information collected. Areas could not be compared with each other because they were using different terminology and different measures (for example, for 'bed days') and no comprehensive information system had been thought through. This is scarcely surprising given that the Department of Health itself is still grappling with this problem. In West Sussex, the lack of coherent information was partly a reflection of the lack also of a centralised health and social care authority. As elsewhere, health services were split between acute and primary care, social services were contracting with voluntary and private providers and, as Figures 10.1 and 10.2 of the interface between agencies show, there was no pivotal, central point of coordination. Thus policy implementation flowed through a diverse range of channels and perspectives.

The impossibility of evaluating winter pressures projects in terms of their original aims and objectives was also a continuing difficulty. This was partly because the original aims and objectives were unclear and had a number of dimensions dependent on local politics and also because the goalposts were effectively shifted away from winter pressures planning to year-long capacity planning by central government. All evaluations take place in a shifting political context, but this context was one from which emanated considerable nervousness. Both health and social services were under pressure to reduce bed blocking and achieve targets within a very short timescale.

It was understandable that major anxieties were being generated at a time of rapid organisational change when many people's jobs were in question. The creation of a new Strategic Health Authority and the movement from Primary Care Groups to Primary Care Trusts was imminent and all services were being challenged to improve services without greatly increased budgets. All this was, of course, directly related to the changing national policy context. Social services based within the county were also being called on to modernise within the seven districts and boroughs of West Sussex and work out their strategies within Local Strategic Partnerships for community development as well as in partnership with health agencies. Even in affluent West Sussex, such partnerships have to take account of relatively deprived communities, particularly in pockets along the South Coast and in Crawley, as well as meeting the needs of the very high percentage of people aged 65+.

In the winter pressures projects that we evaluated, there was evidence of partnership working and increasing trust and communication between different types of practitioners but this could not eliminate the tensions between health and social care services, with impatience in the health trusts provoked by the perceived slowness with which social services reacted to bed blocking. It is hardly conceivable that the system of fines now proposed for social services will alter this situation, which stems from an acute lack of resources for an ageing population rather than dilatoriness. Problems were and still are being exacerbated by the closure of numbers of private care homes – a combined result of soaring property values encouraging owners of homes to sell and new requirements for the training and qualification of care staff and their managers. These factors have made it even more difficult to find accommodation for those not well enough to return from hospital to their own homes while a shortage of home care staff and the tightening of eligibility criteria has meant that those well enough to return home cannot always receive necessary support. This is the political context in which health and social services must operate.

Such pressures inevitably meant that the presence of the university as an evaluator was sometimes resented. Substantial opposition had to be overcome in more than one instance to continue with the evaluation process. Such was the intensity of feeling that some staff were actually forbidden to come to join the discussions in our validation seminar. We were gratified that they came anyway! However, such animosity does challenge evaluators and they need their own support system to counter it judiciously.

A further concern was the almost complete lack of information on users' views. The terms of the evaluation were reflective of a 'top-down' approach to service planning and delivery with serious questions raised about capacity to consult and involve service users meaningfully. At the end of the evaluation, this became more of a problem as planning for Patient Advice and Liaison Services and more serious consideration of clinical governance came onto the agenda. Since none of the projects to be evaluated had involved users to any great extent, a participatory approach to evaluation was ruled out. This raises an interesting issue: whatever the methodological preferences of evaluators, it is probably only possible to engage in participatory evaluation to the extent that the project under scrutiny has itself attempted to involve users. The more top-down the project, the more difficult it is to identify and communicate with any service users it may have affected.

If all this sounds very negative, it should be stressed that there were several positive developments towards the end of the evaluation. Participants realised that they needed more information on the evaluation process and to that end requested preparation of an evaluation toolkit. Interestingly, once this had been prepared and published, questions arose about the extent to which internal staff could themselves make use of it. In spite of initial resistance to outside evaluation, external evaluators were recognised for their potential independence and ability to distance, if not disengage, themselves from the political processes involved. As noted in the introduction to this volume, we return to a social science paradigm which acknowledges the ability of researchers to negotiate understandings and provide alternative views of what appears to be working and what is not.

Additionally, this evaluation became a small part of the process through which the emergent Adur, Arun and Worthing PCT, the Worthing and Southlands NHS Trust, the county social services and other agencies, began to develop their joint strategic programme, *Vision 2010*. Although still at an early stage, this has shown how evaluation, reflection and strategic partnership working can pay dividends in increasing understanding of the problems faced and the alternative routes that can be followed.

Overview

- West Sussex Health Authority commissioned the Health and Social Policy Research Centre (HSPRC) at the University of Brighton to evaluate the effectiveness of selected winter pressures projects in the county. Two of the four West Sussex Local Winter Planning Groups were selected to participate.
- Problems encountered by the evaluators related to the retrospective nature of the study; the shifting political context; the lack of clarity in its aims and objectives; the inadequacy of information collected (which disabled comparison); a 'top-down' approach to the initiative (ruling out the use of a participatory approach); and opposition to the evaluators due to political pressures.
- A positive development was that participants realised their need for more information on the evaluation process and thereby requested an evaluation toolkit.
- The evaluation exercise emphasised the need for evaluation to be inbuilt from the beginning of a project, to be clear about objectives and to reflect the values associated with the interventions being implemented.

Acknowledgements

The authors would like to thank the staff of the Adur, Arun and Worthing Primary Care Trust and West Sussex social services who funded and contributed to the evaluation.

References

Balloch, S. and Penn, A. (2003) *An evaluation tooklit*, Health and Social Policy Research Centre: University of Brighton.

Balloch, S. and Taylor, M. (eds) (2001) *Partnership working: Policy and practice*, Bristol: The Policy Press.

Balloch, S., McLean, J. and Fisher, M. (1999) *Social services: Working under pressure*, Bristol: The Policy Press.

Charnley, H., Kocher, P., Prentice, S. and Williamson, V. (1998) *The Joint Continuing Care Project: An evaluation of innovative joint working*, Brighton: Health and Policy Research Centre.

Charnley, H. (2001) 'Promoting independence: a partnership approach to supporting older people in the community', in S. Balloch and M. Taylor (eds) *Partnership working: Policy and practice*, Bristol: The Policy Press, pp 143-64.

DH (Department of Health) (1989) *Caring for people: Community care in the next decade and beyond*, London: HMSO.

DH (1998) *Partnership in action: New opportunities for joint working between health and social services*, London: The Stationery Office.

DH (2000) Health Service Circular (2000) 16; Local Authority Circular (2000) 14: Winter 2000/01 Capacity planning for health and social care: Emergency care and social care, London: The Stationery Office.

DH (2001a) 'Issues to be addressed in capacity planning for 2001/2' (www.doh.gov.uk/winter/hsc200114.htm).

DH (2001b) *National service framework for older people*, London: The Stationery Office, (www.doh.gov.uk/nsf/olderpeople.htm).

DH (2001c) 'Modern social services: a commitment to deliver', the 10th Annual Report to the Chief Inspector of Social Services Inspectorate, London: The Stationery Office.

Foley, R. (2001) 'GIS and caring: a common and compatible approach?', in D. Taylor (ed) *Breaking down barriers: Reviewing partnership practice*, Brighton: Health and Social Policy Research Centre, pp 206-19.

Haynes, P. (2001) 'Spatial considerations in multiagency and multidisciplinary work', in S. Balloch and M. Taylor (eds) *Partnership working: Policy and practice*, Bristol: The Policy Press, pp 261-81.

Healy, P. (1999) 'Fancy brickwork', *Health Service Journal*, vol 21, January, pp 12-13.

Henwood, M. (2001) *Future imperfect? Report of the King's Fund Care and Support Inquiry*, London: King's Fund Publishing.

Huxham, C. (1993) 'Collaborative capability: an inter-organisational perspective on collaborative advantage', *Public Money and Management*, July–Sept, pp 21-8.

Kelson, M. (1997) *User involvement: A guide to developing effective user involvement strategies in the NHS*, London: College of Health.

Martin, S. and Sanderson, I. (1999) 'Evaluating public policy experiments: measuring outcomes, monitoring progress and managing pilots', *Evaluation*, vol 3, pp 245-58.

Maxwell, R.J. (1984) 'Quality assessment in health', *British Medical Journal*, vol 288, pp 1470-2.

Netten, A. and Beecham, J. (eds) (1993) *Costing community care: Theory and practice*, Aldershot: Ashgate.

Nocon, A. and Qureshi, H. (1996) *Outcomes of community care for users and carers*, Buckingham: Open University Press.

Øvretveit, J. (1992) *Health service quality: An introduction to quality methods for health services*, Oxford: Blackwell.

Pratt, J., Gordon, P. and Plamping, D. (1998) *Working whole systems: Putting theory into practice in organisations*, London: King's Fund.

Ranade, W. (1994) *A future for the NHS? Health care in the 1990s*, London: Longman.

Thornton, P. (2000) *Older people speaking out: Developing opportunities for influence*, York: Joseph Rowntree Foundation.

Williamson, V. (2001) 'The potential of project status to support partnerships', in S. Balloch and M. Taylor (eds) *Partnership working: Policy and practice*, Bristol: The Policy Press, pp 117-41.

Appendix I
Interview topic guide

Evaluation of Winter Pressures Projects, 2000-2001

YOUR ANSWERS WILL REMAIN CONFIDENTIAL TO THE
INTERVIEWERS AND WILL BE ANONYMISED IF USED IN ANY
REPORT

Name and title of interviewee: _____

_____

Interviewer: _____

Date of interview: _____

Time (start and finish): _____

Question One

What do you see as the main objectives of winter pressures funding?

_____

Question Two

What LOWPAG schemes are you managing/implementing? Do these involve
you in working with other agencies and, if so, which agencies/officers?

_____

Question Three

What opportunities and problems have arisen from the winter pressures funding?

_____

a) What has gone well?

_____

b) What has been difficult?

_____

Question Four

Have you any information on the costs of services provided with the winter pressures funding and implicated costs/savings for other services?

_____

Question Five

What has happened to service provision when winter pressures funding has stopped?

_____

Question Six

What role do you see for an evaluation of the schemes with which you are involved? Do you yourself currently use any evaluation methods or forms and, if so, can you give us copies of these?

_____

Question Seven

Have you involved service users in any way in evaluating a service(s) received as a result of winter pressures funding?

_____

Question Eight

Is there anything else you would like to discuss in relation to our evaluation of winter pressures funding?

_____

ELEVEN

Evaluating a partnership approach to supporting people into employment

Hilary Arksey

Introduction

The government is keen to support disadvantaged groups into employment. Partnership is also a central plank of UK government policy. This chapter reports the findings of an evaluation study of an employment project called People into Employment (PIE). In the words of its promotional literature, "[PIE] hopes to assist people back into employment, on an individual, unpressurised, informal basis, in a manner which suits them". The client groups that the project supported were disabled people, carers and former carers. The PIE project offered a tailored package of support, comprising information, advice and practical help on jobs, training and benefits provided through the only member of staff, the Project Development Officer, who worked on a one-to-one basis with PIE clients. If appropriate, referrals were made to other agencies.

The PIE was a 'partnership' project (see later in this chapter). Partners were determined that PIE should continue beyond its initial two-year funding period, and the Social Policy Research Unit at the University of York was commissioned to evaluate the project. The independent evaluation was prompted by the wishes:

- to obtain information on performance and effectiveness;
- to review activities and goals, and to use the results to modify practice;
- to obtain public relations material;
- but in particular to inform bids for further external funding.

The full findings are presented elsewhere (Arksey, 2002; see also Arksey, 2003). The analysis presented here focuses on partnership activity at both the policy and operational level. The chapter is organised as follows. First, some background information about the PIE project and how the partnership arrangements worked is given. The research methods for the evaluation are then described. The next section documents key findings relating first to the facilitators to partnership working, and second to the barriers (internal and external) to partnership working. The chapter concludes with a short discussion about

PIE's model of partnership working; how PIE is boosting social and other forms of capital in its locality; the role of the Project Development Officer; and changes in partnership behaviour as a result of the interim evaluation report. Finally, some ideas for improving partnership arrangements are offered.

The project

The PIE project was located in Sunderland, an urban area in the north east of England falling within the 6% most deprived local authority districts in the country. Relevant agencies in the City of Sunderland were very keen to submit a bid to the New Deal for Disabled People Innovations Schemes. The bid, however, was unsuccessful. The agencies who had worked together were still keen to implement the proposed new initiative to improve employment opportunities in Sunderland, and managed to acquire funding from a variety of sources: the Local Authority Prevention Grant, the Local Authority Strategic Initiatives Budget, the Health Action Zone and the NHS Training Consortium Grants.

The PIE project started as a pilot project in April 2000, with just one member of staff (the Project Development Officer) and a budget of £40,000 per year for two years. This was a 'shoestring' budget, and people taking part in the study described PIE as "a bit of a begging bowl" and "it's a case of having to beg, steal and borrow from all sources".

Its remit was to provide support to disabled people, carers and ex-carers, with a particular emphasis on helping 'hidden' individuals who would not normally access mainstream services and employment options. The PIE project adopted an open recruitment policy, and sought to work with all-comers; this meant that very often it helped the least 'job-ready' people. Potential clients were referred to the project by a range of bodies, such as user and carer groups in regular contact with the targeted audience.

The PIE project was hosted by ETEC Sunderland Ltd, a 'not-for-profit' company and one of the largest training providers in Sunderland. ETEC was responsible for managing the PIE project and the Project Development Officer, but did not receive any funding for this management function.

The partnership

As noted earlier, PIE was a partnership project. The partnership approach that was adopted grew out of Sunderland's well-established approach to wider strategic partnership activities that had been developed between key agencies through the City of Sunderland Partnership. The PIE partnership brought together the voluntary, public and private sectors as key stakeholders. Members of the partnership were primarily those who had been involved in the unsuccessful New Deal for Disabled People Innovations Schemes bid.

The partnership was initially established in two different formats: the multiagency Employment for People with Disabilities Steering Group and the

PIE Working Group. The steering group comprised representatives from up to 17 organisations[1]. The steering group met on a quarterly basis, overseeing all aspects of the project, providing strategic direction and monitoring progress. Generally, members comprised individuals with a managerial role in their respective organisations.

In addition, an operations group was established called the PIE Working Group. In comparison to the steering group, the working group met more often, and was smaller (about ten members). It was less formal, but decisions made by the working group had to be agreed by the steering group. The working group provided an opportunity for PIE's Project Development Officer to discuss operational problems with fieldworkers in similar job support agencies in the area. There was quite a lot of overlap in the membership of the steering group and working group. Agencies common to both groups were: ETEC, City of Sunderland Social Services Department, the Employment Service's Disability Services, the Princess Royal Trust Sunderland Carers Centre, City Hospitals Sunderland NHS Trust, Physical Disabilities Alliance, Regeneration Team/Job Linkage and Littlewoods Home Shopping Group. However, in some instances managerial staff sat on the steering group, while development workers from the same agency sat on the working group.

The partnership in its two forms brought together a wide range of skills, experience and expertise. The underlying notion was that partners worked together towards a common end, namely to support PIE clients into employment, and in this way collaborated to produce a new service. Activities that partner agencies were involved in included:

- taking referrals from and referring to PIE;
- offering guaranteed job interviews and/or work experience;
- facilitating workplace visits; and
- providing funds for training, travel and childcare expenses, or clothing for work.

These additional resources were crucial, given PIE's limited funding, but the project also gained from partners' experience, networks and credibility. Benefits were two-way, however, as partners' own interests were served. For instance, cross referrals meant that staff workers from other job search agencies could utilise the Project Development Officer's (and each other's) expertise and specialist knowledge. The personal networks of development workers provided mutual support and friendship. Agencies could market and advertise each other, and share expensive equipment (one agency had just purchased a mobile unit that it intended to make available to others).

Employers in the partnership gained, for example recruiting disabled people or carers helped fulfil equal opportunities policies.

Most importantly, clients benefited from the partnership as PIE offered a single point of entry to a range of employment, training and advice agencies/ services, including financial support.

Research methods for the evaluation

One approach to the evaluation would have been to try to answer the question, 'Is PIE working?', but any answer was likely to raise further questions about why PIE worked (or not, as the case might be). Instead, a 'realistic evaluation' approach was adopted; this involves taking the views of all the key stakeholders into account to find out *what works, for whom and in what circumstances* (Pawson and Tilley, 1997). It is an approach where the *process* of implementing a programme is as important as evaluating the *outcome*. As far as the PIE evaluation was concerned, it facilitated learning the lessons of PIE from the point of view of all stakeholders: PIE clients, the Project Development Officer, the partnership and employers. The PIE Working Group was involved in the overall research design, and the construction of the two questionnaires. The evaluation used mixed methods to collect both quantitative and qualitative data at two points in time: between May and July 2001 (Time 1) and in February 2002 (Time 2).

Data collection: Time 1

1. **Postal survey of PIE clients: Questionnaire 1**
   A self-completion questionnaire (Questionnaire 1) was distributed to 59 current and former PIE clients; 26 usable copies were returned. It covered issues related to joining the project, experiences of, and satisfaction with, different PIE activities and overall appraisal of the effectiveness of PIE.

2. **Face-to-face interview with Project Development Officer**
   A face-to-face interview was conducted with the Project Development Officer. This covered the PIE partnership, the project itself, staffing and an overall assessment of the first year of PIE.

3. **Telephone interviews with partner agencies and employers**
   Telephone interviews were conducted with six partner agencies and employers. Topic areas included involvement with PIE, funding and resource issues, staffing, strengths and weaknesses, improvements and the future development of PIE.

Data collection: Time 2

1. **Postal survey of newly registered PIE clients: Questionnaire 1**
   Questionnaire 1 was distributed to 18 clients who had registered with PIE since the first round of data collection. Ten questionnaires were returned (giving a combined total of 36).

2. **Follow-up survey of PIE clients: Questionnaire 2**
   A follow-up survey was implemented, focussing on the type and quality of jobs that PIE clients were obtaining, as well as how PIE was judged by

clients. Questionnaire 2 was distributed to a total of 70 current and past PIE clients. (Note: the 18 new PIE clients received Questionnaire 1 and 2 simultaneously.)

3. Face-to-face or telephone interviews with PIE clients

Face-to-face interviews were conducted with three PIE clients, and telephone interviews with a further six. Areas covered included how PIE helped in obtaining work, comparisons between PIE and other agencies, the perceived strengths and weaknesses of PIE and an overall assessment of PIE, including what was seen as 'special'.

4. Face-to-face interview with Project Development Officer

The Project Development Officer was interviewed again. The majority of the time was spent discussing progress and/or changes since her previous interview, likely new developments and overall assessment of PIE's achievements.

5. Telephone interviews with partner agencies and employers

Follow-up telephone interviews were conducted with the six partner agencies and employers who had taken part in Time 1. This set of interviews provided the opportunity to obtain an update on key issues raised previously, to identify the benefits and drawbacks of collaborative work with the project and to consider future developments.

Data analysis

The questionnaire data from Times 1 and 2 were analysed with the widely used statistical analysis package, SPSS. All interviews were audiotaped, with permission, and comprehensive notes made. The analysis of the qualitative data used the 'Framework' technique (Ritchie and Spencer, 1994), which involves familiarisation with the material collected, followed by the identification and interpretation of key topics and issues that emerge from the accounts.

Outputs

An interim evaluation report, based on the Time 1 findings, was produced in September 2001. The final report (Arksey, 2002) was published in May 2002.

Key findings

The evidence from Time 1 showed that overall PIE was working well. It was achieving its aims or *outcomes* in relation to helping disabled people and carers obtain jobs. Likewise, the *process* of supporting clients into work was effective. At the same time, however, there was evidence that the partnership was not realising its maximum potential. First of all, however, what factors were identified as key to supporting the effective working of the partnership arrangement?

Cooperation – not competition

Partner members included similar organisations whose remit was also to help local people who were out of work to find jobs. Even so, there was evidence of cooperation rather than competition between the different agencies, helped no doubt by the fact that common clients could be a statistic for both PIE and the other agency(ies), as long as there was no duplication of existing provision. Only one partner raised the issue of possible rivalry by these different bodies supporting individuals (disabled people, especially) into work who might then think, to quote: "Do we really want PIE to succeed? Because if it does, how did they manage it? Was it at our expense?".

Commitment to the partnership

The partnership was ambitious; it required time, effort and commitment for it to work to its full potential. One or two members did indicate at Time 1 that in their view the partnership seemed to have divided into a core group of enthusiastic PIE proponents, and a more peripheral/less proactive group (but see later in this chapter). Interviewees expressing such views seemed to be judging the success of the partnership in terms of being involved in decision making and members' physical presence at meetings. For instance, when there was low levels of attendance at Steering and Working Group meetings, one person asked: "Is the partnership really working if people don't attend?".

In spite of this, the Project Development Officer believed there was a "real willingness to help" among most partnership members. This view might reflect the fact that from the development officer's point of view contributing towards practical delivery issues and effective working with other fieldworkers was more important than partners' presence at meetings. It is often the case that partners bring quite clear yet inconsistent ideas about what working in partnership means, and therefore their actions may appear uncooperative to others but perfectly obvious and sensible to themselves.

The Project Development Officer

As the only member of staff, the Project Development Officer had to deal with a wide range of areas including clients, employers, the partnership and the administration/promotion of PIE. Undoubtedly, her skills, qualities and commitment were crucial to supporting PIE clients into work and partners readily acknowledged how effectively the Project Development Officer performed her role. She could be conceived of as a *boundary spanner* (Katz and Kahn, 1966; Aldrich, 1979), an individual engaged in networking tasks, coordinating and integrating activities across organisational boundaries and generally progressing working relationships aimed towards (joint) service development.

Shared learning/new knowledge

Partner members were motivated by the wish to share lessons learned through PIE, to exchange information and to apply new knowledge to their own particular organisation (although this was not happening in as structured a way as some would have wished). One example related to the design of sick-pay schemes, where it was discovered that one large employer did not pay ancillary staff who were absent through sickness during the first four months of their employment. Other agencies in the partnership were then able to check their own organisation's procedures in this regard. Another organisation had been able to use statistics and other information produced through the project in a bid to obtain further funding for their particular organisation.

In contrast, the following factors created barriers to the effective working of the partnership arrangement. These have been divided into 'internal' problems (such as those created by the process of working together) and 'external' problems (that is, those created by the action – or inaction – of external bodies and that were generally beyond the control of the partners to solve).

Internal problems

Confusion over PIE's aims

Like other employment projects that focused on 'hard', quantitative outcomes, PIE had numerical targets to meet: employment opportunities for 20 disabled people and ten carers for each of its two years of funding. However, at Time 1 it was clear there was some controversy and disagreement among partnership members over whether what counted was to get the specified number of people actually into work, or instead to progress them closer to work. This caused some ill feeling within the Steering and Working Groups, not to mention creating uncertainty for the Project Development Officer. The ongoing debate about target figures at Time 1 had resolved itself by the time of the follow-up interviews. The partnership had reached the view that the targets had been met, and in hindsight appreciated that the initial targets were unrealistic in view of the type of clients PIE was dealing with, individuals who were generally far from 'job ready'.

Clarity over partners' roles and responsibilities

At Time 1, a common view was that more clarity at the outset about partners' roles, responsibilities, commitments and accountability to the project would have been helpful. This gap possibly reflected the fact that the Steering Group evolved from the working group responsible for the original New Deal for

Disabled People Innovations Schemes bid. At the time, no significant consideration was given to the role/aims of the partnership with regard to the new PIE project. Matters came to a head when both Steering Group and Working Group members arrived for the same meeting, only to discover some time into the ensuing discussions that some of them were at the wrong Group/meeting and that none of them really knew which group they sat on, or why or what the difference was between the two groups!

The interim evaluation report appeared to trigger off self-reflection by partner agencies, and the Time 2 study revealed changes in the wake of issues highlighted by the first phase of the research. Interviewees believed that the Steering and Working Groups were now more focussed. Membership of the two groups had been looked at; some changes had taken place, and it was felt that current members had more of a sense of ownership, understanding and commitment to the project. The Steering Group was heavily involved in Sunderland's Welfare to Work for Disabled People Joint Investment Plan. This had prompted a decision to rename it the Welfare to Work Partnership, in order to reflect the full nature of the work it was now involved in. Simultaneously, the Working Group's name was changed to the ACE/PIE Management Group, again to reflect new developments. There was a belief that these name changes helped clarify the respective purposes of the two bodies, and individual members' roles and responsibilities.

External problems

Funding

As indicated earlier, PIE worked on a shoestring budget, and resource limitations clearly restricted the activities that the Project Development Officer could undertake with clients. This had the potential to put greater pressure on the partners to help fill the gaps in supporting clients.

The PIE project received funding from diverse sources. These bodies all employed different methods of auditing and required different monitoring information and progress reports from PIE. Given the lack of administrative support, it was sometimes the case that PIE was not easily able to meet these requirements to claim its funding. Late submissions to try to reclaim outstanding funding then meant even more work, which PIE just did not have time for. Even worse, on a couple of occasions the promised funding did not materialise. For instance, a verbal agreement made with a representative from one particular organisation was not honoured when that person later left to take up employment elsewhere. A dedicated source of funding would have overcome these sorts of problems.

Not honouring guarantees

One particular member of the partnership ('Organisation A' for the purposes of anonymity) was causing a good deal of disquiet at Time 1. When PIE was first established, Organisation A had promised to recruit approximately 15 PIE clients for each year of PIE's two-year life. The target numbers for getting PIE clients into work had been significantly influenced by this guarantee, and Organisation A had received quite considerable funding from the local TEC to deploy two members of staff to work part-time on recruitment issues relating to PIE clients. However, the company had not fulfilled its promise (at the end of year one, it had recruited just two people from PIE) and over time its levels of commitment and interest had decreased. The probable explanation for this apparent shift in policy was that personnel changes in Organisation A meant that its original member on the Steering and Working Groups had now taken up a post with a different company and since then the PIE project appeared to have slipped down the company's agenda. By the Time 2 interviews, all contact with Organisation A had ceased. The Project Development Officer summed up the lessons of the experience:

> "We learned from that never to rely on one employer, and never to believe it if anyone said they could get us jobs because it just didn't work. That was a large learning exercise because it twisted the project targets."

Conclusion

What model did the partnership adopt? Drawing on Maureen Mackintosh's (1992) work and her three models of partnership, the 'Budget Enlargement' model probably comes closest. On the one side is PIE suffering from financial constraints and needing additional resources. On the other side is a range of public, private and voluntary sector organisations who can see opportunities from taking part in the partnership. But at the same time, given that partner members also used the partnership to achieve their own ends (for instance, drawing knowledge and information to help their own organisation; employing PIE clients to help achieve diversity in the workplace) the partnership also resonates with Mackintosh's (1992) 'synergy' model, where the essence of a joint venture is to create 'added value' from complementary assets, skills and powers.

Piachaud (2002) distinguishes five forms or types of capital: financial capital, physical capital, human capital, public infrastructure and social capital. According to Piachaud, these phenomenon are all capital in the sense that they require investment to build them up. Each may accumulate, and each affects prosperity and poverty; for example, low levels of some or all of them result in poverty and social exclusion. If individuals, communities and nations are to survive and grow, then a combination of different forms of capital is needed. The example of the PIE project can be used to put some flesh on Piachaud's conceptual framework. For instance, PIE brought in a small amount of financial capital, which was then used to boost human capital in the form of increased levels of confidence, skills and abilities of PIE clients. Furthermore, there is a case for viewing the goodwill, strong networks and mutuality between PIE and the other agencies in the partnership as social capital. By trading on the well-established social capital in Sunderland, exemplified in existing networks facilitated through the City of Sunderland Partnership, PIE boosted bonding and bridging and in this way enhanced social capital still further (for example, shared learning). Seen in this light, the different forms of capital accumulated and built on each other, and it is clear that PIE achieved a good deal more than just placing people into jobs.

The Project Development Officer clearly played a key role in PIE's success, and while this was readily acknowledged by partners (see earlier in this chapter), one or two did raise the question of whether PIE worked because its sole member of staff was personable and had established a solid network of contacts or alternatively whether there was a willingness in Sunderland to help carers and disabled people on a localised, multiagency basis. The former could be a cause for concern and the view was expressed that "we have to make PIE work, irrespective of personalities". The potential pitfall of relying on one extremely energetic and dedicated individual was that it was questionable how easily someone else could pick up the contacts the Project Development Officer had cultivated, or the local labour market knowledge she had developed, should she be knocked down by the proverbial bus.

On the basis of the Time 1 evaluation, a list of key messages or recommendations was compiled and included in the interim evaluation report. Those that could be taken forward were addressed immediately, while others had to wait for funding issues to be resolved. What was interesting was how the report had focussed minds, and as indicated earlier in the chapter many issues were no longer problematic by the Time 2 fieldwork. Most importantly, the changes to the Steering and Working Groups outlined earlier had helped give focus and impetus to the partnership; enthusiasm and attendance at meetings had increased and funding for a further two years (that is, until May 2004) was secured – helped to a degree by the Final Report of the PIE evaluation (Arksey, 2002), which was submitted with funding bids.

While partners did try to change their behaviour, prompted in part by the interim evaluation report, it was also easier to influence the 'internal' factors or problems rather than the 'external' ones. This raises an interesting question: is it the case that, unless partnerships are created and working within a wider economic and social context of support and acceptance (from, say, other funders, agencies, the local authority), then it does not matter how well they work as stand-alone bodies because they will inevitably find it difficult to accomplish the task they set themselves? This is important in terms of the 'realistic evaluation' approach (Pawson and Tilley, 1997), where understanding all the stakeholders' perceptions is perhaps futile if the wider or macro-context within which they work is not supportive or helpful.

Setting aside that slightly cynical note, and to finish on a more practical theme, the following key messages (Box 11.1) about how to improve partnership working arrangements emerged from the PIE evaluation. If implemented, there is more likelihood that partnership arrangements will not only work effectively, but also realise their maximum potential. There is no reason to think that these are not applicable to other similar partnership situations.

Box 11.1: Ways to improve partnership working

- Define the aims and principles underlying the project.
- Clarify the roles and responsibilities of partnership members.
- Persuade seemingly less committed members of a partnership to increase their levels of involvement, including regular attendance at meetings.
- When one person leaves the partnership, their place should immediately be taken by someone else from the same organisation showing the same level of commitment. Alternatively, for key organisations, there should be more than one representative.
- Members should develop a more active role in respect of monitoring and policy making. This would encourage 'ownership' and increase commitment to the project.
- Avoid reliance on one sole member of staff, irrespective of how committed they may be.
- Ensure that funding arrangements are confirmed in writing.
- Shared learning should take place on a structured, ongoing basis rather than at some unspecified time in the future.

Overview

- The evaluation of the partnership project, People into Employment (PIE), was prompted by the wish to obtain information on performance and effectiveness, to review activities and goals, to use the results to modify practice, to obtain public relations material and in particular to inform bids for further external funding.
- A 'realistic evaluation' approach was adopted, which involved taking the views of all key stakeholders into account to find out what works, for whom and in what circumstances.
- The evaluation found that overall PIE was working well but that there were barriers that were preventing it from reaching its full potential. These included confusion over PIE's aims, a lack of clarity regarding the roles and responsibilities of partners and resource limitations.
- Key messages emerged through the evaluation as to how to improve partnership-working agreements. (These are presented in Box 11.1 of this chapter.)
- A number of positive internal developments took place as a result of the evaluation interim report; for example, in terms of reviewing the structure of the partnership. An issue that arose however was the difficulty with influencing external factors that were outside of the partners' control.

Note

[1] These organisations included ETEC, City of Sunderland Social Services Department, the Employment Service's Disability Services, the Princess Royal Trust Sunderland Carers Centre, City Hospitals Sunderland NHS Trust, Priority Healthcare Wearside NHS Trust, Sunderland Health Authority, Sunderland Council for Voluntary Services, Physical Disabilities Alliance, Rehab UK, City of Sunderland Training and Enterprise Council, City of Sunderland College, Regeneration Team/Job Linkage and Littlewoods Home Shopping Group.

Acknowledgements

I would like to thank all those people who took part in the study: PIE clients, partner agencies, employers and in particular Gill Charman, PIE's Project Development Officer. ETEC very kindly helped with the data inputting for the two postal surveys. Colleagues, and in particular Michael Hirst and Lisa O'Malley, made helpful suggestions on an early draft of the chapter.

References

Aldrich, H.E. (1979) *Organizations and environments*, Englewood Cliffs, NJ: Prentice-Hall.

Arksey, H. (2002) *People into Employment project: Final report*, York: Social Policy Research Unit, University of York.

Arksey, H. (2003) 'People into employment: supporting people with disabilities and carers into work', *Health and Social Care in the Community*, vol 11, no 3, pp 283-92.

Katz, D. and Kahn, R. (1966) *Social psychology of organizations*, New York, NY: John Wiley & Sons.

Mackintosh, M. (1992) 'Partnership: issues of policy and negotiation', *Local Economy*, vol 7, no 3, pp 210-24.

Pawson, R. and Tilley, N. (1997) *Realistic evaluation*, London: Sage Publications.

Piachaud, D. (2002) *Capital and the determinants of poverty and social exclusion*, CASEPaper 60, London: CASE, London School of Economics and Political Science.

Ritchie, J. and Spencer, L. (1994) 'Qualitative data analysis for applied policy research', in A. Bryman and R.G. Burgess (eds) *Analysing qualitative data*, London: Routledge, pp 173-94.

Part Four
Learning from evaluation

TWELVE

Evaluation and the New Deal for Communities: learning what for whom?

Ian Smith and Lucy Grimshaw

Introduction

New Deal for Communities (NDC) is the flagship urban regeneration initiative of the Neighbourhood Renewal Unit (NRU), launched in 1999 and due to run until 2010[1]. It is distinctive because of the espoused strong emphasis on 'community involvement' in the formulation and delivery of the initiative within the successfully bidding communities in combination with the current government's interests in evidence-based policy making. The initiative throws up the tension that has been ever present in urban policy through the 1990s of attempting to empower communities while getting those communities to demonstrate the value of what they plan to do within their neighbourhoods and communities through evaluation. Consequent to the complexity of the task and the multiplicity of government and governance levels implicated, the NDC initiative is subject to evaluation and monitoring activities at a number of institutionalised moments.

The question for us as evaluators and observers of evaluation in NDC is to make sense of this complexity and to ask the question of how do the different evaluation activities fit together. This chapter argues that the way evaluation activities have emerged has led to little evidence of learning in the early phases of these complex and fragile institutional structures. Our interest in how evaluation works within the NDC initiative needs to be located in the broader debate about understanding the utility of evaluation (or the apparent lack of it, see Patton, 1997). This work is our attempt to reflect upon our contribution to the National Evaluation of NDC and part of our ongoing commitment to work with partnerships to develop local evaluation frameworks.

Evaluation professionals have two potential and complementary strategies for developing the utility of evaluation practice. The first strategy prioritises epistemological enlightenment in order to better see the research subject (see, for example, Pawson and Tilley, 1997). The second research strategy stresses the better understanding of the socio-political context in which evaluation-based knowledge is constructed and employed. We place this chapter in this second storyline where evaluation is one process of knowledge generation that might inform policy development and implementation among others.

The chapter is divided into three sections. The first outlines a conceptual framework through which one might start to understand the knowledge-creating contexts in which evaluation activities are taking place. The second section considers some observations on how evaluation activities are emerging and framing programme development work in two case-study partnerships. The third section then discusses these empirical observations from the theoretical perspectives set out in the second section in order to set out a research agenda for the role of evaluation and knowledge generation in urban regeneration initiatives.

Conceptual frameworks for understanding the learning context

In this section, we present a number of ideas that give some purchase on understanding the politics of evaluation in the case of the NDC programme. We concentrate on three main issues: the first is how to understand the institutional context for understanding evaluation as a unit of analysis; the second draws on the organisational theory literature to consider organisational learning; and third, we want to consider the importance of discourses of evaluation as evidence of employing knowledge in institutional settings.

The NDC programme is a regeneration initiative that is formulated, delivered and evaluated through a complex network of organisations operating at various spatial levels (see later in this chapter). This complex network is what Hjern and Porter (1993) would refer to as an implementation structure and this forms the basic organisational unit of analysis in policy analysis. This can be a policy community or network that shapes the formulation and delivery of public policy. However, it is not enough to simply identify the presence of an implementation structure since we must also ask whether such structures are institutionalised (as opposed to a contingent coalition of individuals and organisations). The significance of institutionalisation is that one can pose the question as to the value added to the policy process by its organisational formulation. Under older interpretive notions of pluralism (as outlined by Stoker, 1991) an implementation structure is merely the sum of the interactions of individuals within the structure. However, under the new institutional perspective (as reviewed by Lowndes, 1996) implementation structures are more than the sum of the individuals/organisations that make up the structure since the process of institutionalisation adds value. Adopting the new institutionalist perspective allows us to mark a distinction between institutional learning and learning accomplished by individuals within organisations under conditions of pluralism.

Organisational theory helps flesh out the mechanisms by which institutions learn. Argyris and Schön (1996) have, over 20 years, conceptualised the idea of organisational learning based on their work with organisations. Broadly, their perspective starts with the notion of identifying where there is institutionalised organising or agency as opposed to ephemeral organisations (1996, pp 9-10). Where there is institutional agency, they consider the existence of organisational inquiry when individuals "function as agents of an organisation according to its prevailing roles and rules" (1996, p 11). Following on from the idea of organisational inquiry, "organisational learning occurs when individuals within an organisation experience a problematic situation and inquire into it on the organisation's behalf" (1996, p 16), stimulated by the mismatch that might occur between expected and actual results of action. This learning may result in two different organisational responses: the first implies single loop learning where the learning product is the revision of an organisation's strategies and action in response to a given situation, whereas the second learning product is double loop learning, where not only organisational strategies are modified but the underlying theories of action of the organisation are questioned and transformed.

This chapter poses two questions: first, do the evaluation activities identified in the case study NDC initiatives constitute a process of organisational inquiry? Second, we are interested in the nature of any learning responses that flow from evaluation activities.

We are interested in applying Argyris and Schön's ideas to these questions. However, in doing so we accept that their work has some limitations. First, Argyris and Schön were principally interested in how organisations learn rather than in how complex institutional settings (as networks of organisations) learn. Second, their work does not offer much in terms of explaining why organisations (or complex institutional settings) choose to learn the way they do. For Argyris and Schön learning occurs once agents within an organisation become aware of differences in expected and actual outcomes of organisational action. It is a rational response to a logical inconsistency. At one level, one might note that implementation structures for urban regeneration initiatives engage in evaluation (as organisational inquiry) because it is a condition of their funding, but there are many strategies for inquiry and many potential subjects for inquiry. Thus, next we must briefly consider explanations for why institutional settings engage in inquiry and the creation of knowledge.

In order to understand the interplay and motivations about why implementation structures might learn (either as single loop or double loop learning), we would consider two potential frameworks for understanding how organisations frame and value ways of knowing. The first framework is based on 'the communicative approach' to institutional policy formulation (outlined by Healey, 1997); the second that we have labelled 'the conflictual hegemonic approach' relates to the relationship between power and rationality (developed through the work of Flyvbjerg, 1998).

The communicative approach outlined by Healey presupposes the need for institutionalising a dialogue across the diverse range of actors engaged in public policy making. Healey's (1997) project is to bring together new institutionalism with the communicative approach understanding that knowledge is socially constructed and thus we must understand the social contexts by which knowledge is constructed and that communication of knowledge takes many forms (for further development, see Healey, 1997, p 29). Healey suggests that learning becomes transformative action understood in a broader project elaborated by Habermas, that brings together instrumental-technical reasoning, moral reasoning and emotive-aesthetic reasoning. Healey accepts the cumulative inequity of power relations within policy networks but stresses the need to develop better communication between parties with the underlying assumption that there is a unity to be constructed. Thus, this framework would see evaluation as one process of communication among others and as a process of knowledge creation that is informed both by the technical-rationalist reasoning of government but also by the moral and emotive-aesthetic reasoning of other lifeworlds. There is, however, an idea that all parties in an ideal world are striving for a single negotiated truth, although there is inherent to this the idea that cumulative inequity still exists within such an institutional framework.

Flyvbjerg (1998, p 27) offers a slightly different take on the evolution of policy and the use of knowledge within the context of defining policy when he states "power defines what counts as knowledge and rationality". For Flyvbjerg, rationality is one form of argument that is relatively open to those without influence such that those with the greatest power have least call on rationality. In this framework, evaluation as a learning activity becomes problematic for those who hold power within the implementation structures of the initiative. He draws a distinction between rationality and rationalisation: rationalisation is a strategy of justification while rationality is a way of knowing. For Flyvbjerg, rationalisation presented as rationality is a principal strategy in the exercise of power (1998, p 228). Under the Habermasian notion of communicative action, successful rhetoric that is not based on rationality is a distortion, whereas the work of Flyvbjerg shows that the power may choose to refashion rationality to its will as a deliberate strategy (1998, p 228).

Hence, we are left with two potential frameworks. The first implies that evaluation is one form of communicative action, where agents within implementation structures are attempting to converge on a single rationality that merges different forms of intellectual reasoning. This position accepts the cumulative inequity but separates power and rationality and the social researcher is placed as participant whose ethical position is to remove distortions in the communicative act of evaluation. The second position suggests the power within institutional structures defines rationality such that evaluation is either defined in order to reify the position of power or it is not taken into consideration. Here the position of the social researcher is to consider the ethics of different positions around evaluation without there being a single undistorted rationality. In both these positions we can consider the presence of institutionalisation and whether evaluation results in learning products. Figure 12.1 draws out the key issues arising from the conceptual discussion.

Figure 12.1: Key issues arising from evaluation as knowledge-generation and evaluation as learning

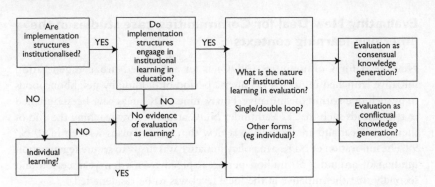

Research strategy

Having outlined some key ideas that inform our understanding of evaluation as a knowledge-generating process and as an element of institutional learning, this next section considers how we might investigate the processes we have outlined through our case study initiatives. The first point is to stress the importance of discourse expressed both in what stakeholders say but also in texts produced by institutional actors. Second, we want to explore the relevance of institutional 'level' expressed in terms of territorial scale (neighbourhood, local, regional and national). The institutional actors included in this analysis must have some a priori input into the local NDC programme and must have some control over evaluation activities. This leads us to a common-sense list of institutional actors within a programme locality: the professional officers supporting the NDC partnership, resident members of the NDC partnership, the local authority and the apparatus of central government (the Government Office and the NRU).

Our two case study areas are 'Pathfinder' or 'round 1' initiatives. Within each case study, we need to firstly map out the stakeholder engagement within the NDC localities. Second, we need to outline what the main evaluation positions of key stakeholders are and, third, we need to consider particular strategies of acquiring knowledge about regeneration in the context of evaluating New Deal for Communities initiatives. Evidence on these three issues will then inform our discussion on how best to understand and how best to intervene in the process of knowledge generation in the NDC programme. However, given the restrictions of a short chapter and the early stages of the overall evaluation framework, we will present the evidence in aggregated form. Our presentation of the evaluation discourses presented by the different stakeholders focuses on the perceived implementation structures for evaluation, on preferred sources of knowledge, on assumptions about the learning environments in which the actors operate, as well as on the geographic tactics for learning about regeneration.

Evaluating New Deal for Communities: case studies of the emerging learning contexts

New Deal for Communities (NDC) is an area-based urban regeneration initiative launched in April 1999 after a period of bidding by neighbourhoods to be included within the initiative. Thirty-nine NDC areas have been launched in two rounds such that 17 Pathfinder NDC areas are now reaching the end of their third year and are looking to review the delivery plans written in 1998/99. The innovation of NDC as a policy initiative was firstly to secure regeneration funding of around £50 million per area spread over a ten-year period and secondly that the initiative at the local level was to be resident-led.

New Deal for Communities was launched in the initial stages of the Labour government's crusade for 'evidence-based policy' at a time when its mantra of 'what matters is what works' formed the philosophy underpinning policy development. Consequently, government guidance for areas wishing to be considered for NDC status stressed that funding would be given to areas which demonstrated evidence of an analysis of problems and an understanding of "how change will be achieved, drawing on lessons learned elsewhere" (DETR, 1998; Social Exclusion Unit, 1998, para 4.6). Learning lessons was embedded into the NDC discourse at an early stage; the very concept of having a Pathfinder round seemed to indicate that the government was willing to learn lessons from practice (from successes and failures) and guidance supported this.

The multiple evaluations of NDC both within specific localities and across the programme as a whole are still in their very early stages. Thus, there are aspects raised in the conceptual section that it is currently too early to comment on. However, we have sketched out a broad set of categories by which we might define the processes of knowledge creation constituted by evaluation in NDC. The two dimensions we set out earlier in this chapter contrast institutional versus atomistic political learning and communicative versus hegemonic dialogue. At this stage, we can set out the emerging patterns of knowledge generation and learning within the two case study areas. We are unable to comment on the level to which implementation structures have become institutionalised in these localities at this time. What we offer here is an initial mapping of four stakeholders in creating knowledge about the initiative and then we construct four discourses of evaluation.

Discourses of evaluation

Table 12.1 outlines some key ideas that have emerged either through interviewing individuals implicated in evaluation within the two case study localities or through the analysis of documentary texts produced by organisations within the implementation structure. These ideas have been summarised under

Table 12.1: Evaluation discourses for stakeholders in NDC evaluation

	Resident-members of NDC	NDC officers	Local authority	Neighbourhood Renewal Unit
Implementation structure (for evaluation)	Currently un-institutionalised. Stress oppositional nature of local versus non-local evaluation activities	Community development preferred. Formalise through strategy. In-house versus external consultant expertise	Professional officers seconded to NDC. Own professional capacity for own engagement	National Evaluation, monitoring and performance management for all with local evaluation based on national guidance
Preferred forms of knowledge	Emotive aesthetic – holistic	Instrumental technical and emotive aesthetic – although relationship between the two not clear	Instrumental technical also emotive aesthetic (political)	Instrumental technical – tension in knowing 'spend' versus knowing 'impact'
Attitudes to institutional learning and change	Importance of making a difference. Want double loop learning but not necessarily see themselves as part of this	Importance of delivery. Tension between single and double loop	Importance of delivery. Single loop predominates	Importance of delivery. Evidence-based policy formulation – single loop
Geographic tactics for knowledge acquisition	Neighbourhood and project focus – some links to other areas in city and nationally	Neighbourhood in terms of immediate evaluation – professional practice via national bodies	Within local authority area – professional practice via national bodies	National focus and programme-wide

four headings dealing with the implementation structures for evaluation (as distinct from the implementation structures for the initiative as a whole), preferences for the types of intellectual reasoning, on attitudes to institutional learning produced through evaluation and finally the geographic tactics employed for learning about urban regeneration practice.

Implementation structure of evaluation

The four stakeholder constituencies have differing views on the nature of the emerging implementation structure of evaluation in their localities. The NRU's espoused implementation structure is based on a complex set of activities to be organised at the national, regional and neighbourhood level. At its simplest, the idea of evaluation, monitoring and review was to take place at three levels:

1. the NRU, as part of central government, would monitor activities via the Government Offices as its intermediary;
2. the NRU would fund an independent evaluation of the programme as a whole that would be let by competitive tender; and
3. local NDC partnerships would evaluate their own activities by whatever means they considered to be appropriate.

As one might expect, this three-point multi-level framework for evaluation becomes highly complex when applied to specific localities.

The view expressed by the local authority on how evaluation activities were to be organised was based on the notion that they would play an expert consultant role for the NDC partnerships and would be implicated in the evaluation of projects where the local authority played a role. Local authority officers have been active in the review of baseline statistics and have been involved in the measurement of mainstream service provision in regeneration areas.

In practice, NDC partnerships are still exploring how they might evaluate their respective programmes with two basic institutional frameworks emerging for the task. The first framework implies that local partnerships will evaluate themselves using in-house teams to interpret, commission or carry out evaluation work. The second model that is emerging involves subcontracting the complete evaluation task to external consultants often with the idea that the consultants will train partnership staff to take on the evaluation role in a few years' time. For the year 2001/02, local evaluation activities were poorly developed and fragmented within the individual NDC partnerships with many partnerships without an explicit evaluation strategy.

In both case study localities, a local evaluation group has been established. In each case, this body brings together officers within the partnership and 'experts' from outside of the partnership in order to frame and discuss evaluation issues as they are linked to the locality area. In both cases, interested resident members of the partnership have joined the group along with representatives of the local authority, regional bodies and members of the National Evaluation team. In case study area A, this group was formed to reduce duplication of surveys and other research. It was also a response by the partnership to respond to the demands placed on the partnership by the National Evaluation and a regional evaluation.

Neither of the local evaluation groups have terms of reference. Community involvement is very limited and it is not clear how the information from this group feeds into other structures within the NDC. In both cases, the local evaluation groups are seen as useful places for information exchange but in neither case did the output of the group appear to carry much weight within either partnership. The groups are not necessarily implementing an evaluation strategy but have the potential to do so once evaluation becomes higher on the agenda.

Again, neither case study area has a formal evaluation strategy encapsulated in a document and no one person has overall responsibility for evaluation at the moment. Thus, the responsibility is not institutionalised in a clearly identifiable role. Instead, the responsibility for evaluation is distributed and is not clearly outlined. In case study B, one NDC officer recorded that there had been ongoing debate about whether or not evaluation constituted a core management responsibility or whether it was an activity that would take place "at a distance" from core programme responsibilities. In case study A, there has been a very fragmented and ad hoc approach to evaluation so far. There have been recent developments and a person has recently been appointed to manage and coordinate evaluation within the partnership. A service-level agreement has been agreed with the local authority and there are plans to go out to tender for an external local evaluation (which will incorporate training to develop in-house evaluation capacity).

Preferred type of knowledge/approach to evaluation

The relationship between the monitoring activities of the NRU and the monitoring and evaluation activities of the local partnerships is outlined in guidance published by the NRU (DETR, 1999) for the preparation of delivery planning. This guidance stresses the need to adopt an evidence-based approach to planning and implementing NDC, associated with access to 'good information', references to research evidence, the monitoring of progress and the evaluation of impact. The guidance indicated what 'weapons' should be at the NDC's disposal, such as databases of good practice, hands-on expertise and "methods for accumulating experience in a structured way" (DETR, 1999, p 41). Guidance on monitoring, review and evaluation is also included, with the emphasis on monitoring, to keep track of progress towards outcomes and accountability for public money. The review process based on mid-year and annual cycles involves the partnership and Government Office and assesses the partnership's performance against milestones and outcomes.

Whereas there is guidance on the general framework for managing and describing implementation of the initiative in localities, specific guidance on 'evaluation' is limited to two short paragraphs and emphasises the need to collect baseline data and to regularly update it. Evaluation is viewed in terms of assessing impact and local NDC schemes are expected to evaluate their activities by whatever means they see fit. Evidently within this framework there are the tensions of evaluation being a tool for managing compliance (explored by Segerholm, 2001) as well as letting partnerships construct knowledge about and for themselves.

Despite this emphasis from central government on quantitative data, in our case studies local stakeholders were keen to incorporate qualitative measures within the evaluation programme and thus ensure that any evaluation was not solely concerned with quantitative outputs. However, local authority officers interviewed felt constrained by central government's requirements about what data they had to collect. Case study A drew particular attention to the prescriptive nature and excessive detail of the baseline information required for the Delivery Plan, referring to it as more 'rigid' than any other regeneration scheme and leaving little room to collect baseline data in line with local needs and decisions.

The government's approach to evaluation is as much about monitoring, accountability and value for money as learning. However, the government's vague guidance on local evaluation gives partnerships the possibility to develop their own approaches to evaluation.

Local residents tend to stress the importance of local knowledge, residents in case study area B stressed the importance of keeping evaluation 'as local as possible'. They focused on wanting to know whether programmes make an impact on the lifeworlds of residents, which is often expressed as "evaluation needs to be embedded in everything we do – it is part of action and reflection", whereas the instrumental technical reasoning is about constructing categories of things. Residents' views are often expressed in holistic visions (emotive-aesthetic reasoning). They emphasise that "evaluation is essentially qualitative not just number-crunching". They also felt that the key issue for residents was to put the scheme under the spotlight in contrast to a feeling that evaluation programmes were putting the residents themselves under the spotlight.

For NDC staff, evaluation comes in many forms, incorporating statistics, monitoring data, performance review, informal conversations about previous initiatives and experiences in other areas, action research, workshops, citizen's panels and focus groups. It is also seen in terms of learning about what has happened and why, as well as showing that targets have been met.

Assumptions about learning and change

These different levels of evaluation are being carried out in a complex environment where different stakeholders have both different understandings and expectations of evaluation. There is a lack of clarity among the different constituencies about evaluation, both what is meant by evaluation and what is happening on the ground at the different levels. At a local NDC level, evaluation is often very low down on the list of priorities, since the priority is to be seen to be delivering and implementing the programme. This means that, in terms of providing an evidence base which can be used to learn about 'what works', formal evaluation is often neglected.

There is a desire by NDC professionals to get the evidence to show how things are going and whether the programme is on target, making a difference and how things could be done better. But up until now, there has simply not been the commitment and time given to carry out evaluation to meet these desires. The drive for formal evaluation has not been timely: it is happening years into the programme rather than being built in at the beginning. The National Evaluation was presented in report form to both case studies' executive staff members and in case study A an away-day presentation was made. However, it is unclear how this information was used and what change resulted from the National Evaluation as opposed to staff and partnership changing structures and processes as a result of general reflections on day-to-day running of the programme and systematic reviews by central and regional governments.

However, it is not only important to consider how knowledge generated by evaluation is disseminated among New Deal officers, it is also important to see how this knowledge is communicated and debated with residents in the New Deal area. Here we are specifically interested in how active residents who sit on steering groups, theme groups and boards consider the value of knowledge generated through evaluation. On the whole, this small group of residents (estimated at around 40-50 individuals per area) see evaluation and the knowledge generated by evaluation as an add-on activity that is a requirement for funding. It is something that takes resources away from 'delivery' and is mainly directed at judging the success of a project by outsiders. They generally did not distinguish monitoring from evaluation. A smaller group of residents saw the importance of evaluation but were frustrated by the assumption that any learning that might result should only apply to the project workers rather than a wider constituency that would include the NRU.

The NRU commissions research on various aspects of regeneration projects that it funds, and this could contribute to learning across the full implementation structure. Early on in the NDC programme, the NRU commissioned an evaluation of Phase 1 NDC Pathfinders (the initial 17 partnerships) that provided some insight into the process of preparing a delivery plan. One aim of this exercise was to share lessons between Pathfinders and Round 2 partnerships within the NDC programme (DETR, 1999).

The NRU is the commissioning body for the National Evaluation, which is being carried out by a consortium of university research centres and consultants. The National Evaluation collects information about the activities of partnerships including both quantitative and qualitative data on both local programme inputs as well as secondary data on programme outcomes. This National Evaluation also makes assessments on issues such as the quality of community engagement, programme management and other process-related issues. Findings from the National Evaluation are disseminated through paper-based reports as well as through web-mediated formats. It also collates information on programme performance through the Government Offices in the form of monitoring data and performance management/self-assessment data. In total, this body of knowledge is constructed with the aim of justifying and aiding the continuation of the programme as a whole rather than addressing the underlying norms and values of the policy itself. Hence, it only constitutes a potential single learning loop.

Despite the history of regeneration initiatives in the UK, interviewees had conflicting opinions about the usefulness of the evidence base for regeneration practitioners. Interviewees in case study A thought there was more information and evaluation evidence around now than during other regeneration programmes. One interviewee thought that research evidence was now more accessible, with more links between theory and practice and looking at underlying causes to problems, and considering outcomes rather than outputs, as well as looking at issues comparatively. Another interviewee at the local authority was more sceptical, stating that there were plenty of evaluations around, all stating how projects and programmes were a success rather than looking at *why* things happened and what mistakes have been made as well as looking on a long-term, continuous basis. Evaluations do not necessarily form the basis for learning, and it was felt that learning had been done through practice in the local authority area in terms of processes such as how to bid for funds and organise partnerships. However, this still leaves the question of whether this translates into real change and impact on NDC neighbourhoods and the people living in them.

Learning in the context of NDC is not only about the NDC partnership's capacity to learn as an institution, but, because it is an experiment, it is expected to influence and enable others to learn and change. The concept of mainstreaming within the NDC rhetoric means that NDC partnerships are supposed to influence the way statutory agencies deliver their services. However, as a temporary ten-year programme, the NDC partnership does not always have the power to influence mainstream agencies.

Geographical scale of evaluation

New Deal for Communities is implemented in small neighbourhoods. The evaluation of such initiatives raises several questions about the scale of evaluation and this ranges from the impact on individuals to groups of people, to the effect on the neighbourhood as a whole. The impact of the NDC partnerships is also assessed in comparison to their wider city or locality and national indicators. Residents may be interested in the impact of the NDC solely on their neighbourhood, whereas the local authority is concerned with getting data which is comparable with other areas in the locality as well as the locality or city as a whole.

The evaluation focus on the NDC area often ignores questions of the wider context within which the NDC sits, for example wider locality or city-wide developments will inevitably have spillover effects on any given New Deal area. Other area-based initiatives at local or sub-regional level will also have an impact on the neighbourhood. All 39 NDC schemes are operating in wider urban contexts and evaluation work must take account of the impacts of the New Deal programme that fall outside of the strict geographic delimitation of the New Deal area. The challenge is not only how to measure results effectively at different geographical levels but also how to ensure coordination and use of the research. New Deal for Communities officers and the local authority stress the importance that any National Evaluation must provide contextual knowledge about NDC initiatives.

Geographic scale is also apparent in the tactics and strategies by which the stakeholders acquire knowledge about what works. Broadly, NRU takes on filtered knowledge from all over the country. It is assumed that this information is then trickled down to local partnerships. However, case study NDC partnerships (both residents and officers) have started to employ differing strategies for finding knowledge. In case study B, residents are setting up forums to discuss regeneration with other neighbourhoods within the city and have held an Urban Forum seminar for NDC residents across the country. New Deal for Communities officers in both case study areas sit on the local partnership reference group of the emerging National Evaluation with some, albeit limited, success in influencing the shape of National Evaluation activities. In case study A, residents have visited other neighbourhoods nationally with regeneration programmes. The chief executives and chairs in both case studies also sit on various locality/city-wide partnerships as well as sub-regional bodies. Networks across the various geographical scales are therefore an important context for learning.

Research agenda for understanding emerging institutionalised learning contexts

The evaluation framework for considering the NDC programme continues to develop. We are in the middle of our first summative evaluation round with our respective partnerships and each partnership is working through the development of a local evaluation framework. There is evident need to refine the methodological bases for carrying out evaluation activity but we must ask to what degree does our understanding of the evaluation discourses within our case study areas allow us to comment on the presence of institutional learning? This returns us to the initial question: learning what for whom?

In terms of identifying institutional learning in NDC localities, the early evidence is unclear. There would appear to be a number of fragments of an implementation structure and some of these fragments are institutionalised. However, the resident-led elements of the partnership appear at this stage to be the least institutionalised and this is problematic in the identification of institutional learning (although there is evidence of individuals learning).

In terms of identifying processes of institutional inquiry (that is, the process of creating knowledge), formal evaluation is only one part of the learning process. In addition to activities formally identified as 'evaluation', there are parallel processes of generating knowledge as performance management, formal acquisition of knowledge through NRU advisors as well as through national and regional NDC networking (visits of residents and meetings). Equally NDC officers often have career histories in regeneration schemes where they can draw on their own experience. There is clearly much information around, but the broader question is whether the processes of inquiry are institutionalised or whether they are linked to personal curiosity on the part of individuals associated with evaluation activities. Given the fragmented picture of organising associated with evaluation activities, it follows that there is patchy evidence in the case study localities of institutional inquiry. There is only weak evidence of evaluation as organisational knowledge embedded within the institutional implementation structures. What evidence is employed within the NDC locality implementation structures is clearly filtered through political ideology. This is particularly true of national government as it attempts to implement its guidance. As such, there is some suggestion that the NRU are using monitoring information as a form of governance especially with regards to spending targets. In addition, there have been attempts to make the National Evaluation exercise relate more closely to the performance management objectives of the NRU. We are left with the mantra of 'what works is what we want to work', with evidence being used for political purposes and unpalatable evidence is dismissed (Nutley and Webb, 2000). Within this frame, as long as NDC partnerships meet targets and yield results then the programme is likely to be labelled as successful.

There is a fear that the current implementation structures for evaluation in NDC are moving to become contractual schemes rather than genuine locally driven schemes. The traditional evaluation has been based on knowledge generated through nationally set indicators, performance management schemes, financial monitoring and continuation of Single Regeneration Budget (SRB) output-driven monitoring. These are all forms of instrumental technical reasoning. However, the knowledge that concerns residents in NDC areas is missing. This is the aesthetic-emotive knowledge encapsulated in the lifeworlds of residents and is crucial in knowing whether the programme 'made a difference'. Inevitably, this leads us back to questions about methodology, but these questions should be framed within the broader analysis of the competing discourses being evaluated.

New Deal for Communities is an ever-evolving programme and as such there is an ongoing development of evaluation structures and mechanisms providing the context for knowledge and learning. Technical fixes are being developed for the learning context, most notably the development of an NRU-sponsored 'knowledge management system' website. As with any ICT-mediated information service, this can only assist where there is an appropriate learning context in which to employ this tool. Contractual fixes for the learning context are already in place or are emerging in the form of formal protocols (for example between the National Evaluation team and their case study partnership).

Finally, if NDC partnerships are to develop the capacity for institutional learning then the National Evaluation should play a role in this. The National Evaluation is positioned between central government and the local NDC partnerships and as such finds itself in a position where it has to mediate between the two levels. Most importantly, the National Evaluation needs to address the 'crisis in utilisation' first raised in the introduction to this chapter and be able to effectively disseminate findings at all levels. It needs to be able to bring together differing sources of knowledge and address issues of power (in terms of access to knowledge, for example). It also has the difficult task of making more explicit whether the NDC programme is about teaching communities how to regenerate themselves, or if it is about all parties from neighbourhood to national levels learning how to formulate more effective regeneration initiatives.

Overview

- Questions were raised as to whether evaluation activities constitute organisational inquiry and around the nature of any learning responses that occur as a result.
- Case studies of two NDC partnerships have found weak evidence for institutional learning and knowledge generation through evaluation.
- Attention was drawn through the case studies to the demands of meeting the prescriptive and excessive nature of data required and the impact of this upon allowing the concerns of local people to be addressed.
- The body of knowledge constructed aimed to justify and sustain the programme rather than allow the underlying norms and values of the policy to be scrutinised.
- Interviewees voiced differences of opinion as to the usefulness of the evidence base for regeneration practitioners. For example, one felt this was increasing while another claimed that learning had been acquired through practice rather than evaluation.
- The National Evaluation is needed to play a role in developing the capacity for institutional learning.

Note

[1] The discussion in this chapter is drawn from work undertaken in conjunction with research commissioned by the NRU. The analysis and conclusions are personal to the authors and represent neither the project findings nor the views of the NRU.

References

Argyris, C. and Schön, D.A. (1996) *Organisational learning II: Theory, method and practice*, Wokingham: Addison Wesley Publishing Company.

DETR (Department of the Environment, Transport and the Regions) (1998) *New Deal for Communities. Phase 1 proposals: Guidance for pathfinder applicants*, London: DETR.

DETR (1999) *New Deal for Communities. Developing delivery plans*, London: DETR.

Flyvbjerg, B. (1998) *Rationality and power: Democracy in practice*, Chicago, IL: Chicago University Press.

Healey, P. (1997) *Collaborative planning: Shaping places in fragmented societies*, London: Macmillan Press.

Hjern, B. and Porter, D.O. (1993) 'Implementation structures: a new unit of administrative analysis', in M. Hill (ed) *The policy process: A reader*, London: Harvester Wheatsheaf, pp 248-65.

Lowndes, V. (1996) 'Varieties of new institutionalism: a critical appraisal', *Public Administration*, vol 74, pp 181-97.

Nutley, S. and Webb, J. (2000) 'Evidence and the policy process', in H. Davies, S.M. Nutley and P.C. Smith (eds) *What works? Evidence-based policy and practice in public services*, Bristol: The Policy Press, pp 13-42.

Patton, M.Q. (1997) *Utilization-focused evaluation: The new century text*, London: Sage Publications.

Pawson, R. and Tilley, N. (1997) *Realistic evaluation*, Newbury Park: Sage Publications.

Segerholm, C. (2001) 'National evaluations as governing instruments: How do they govern?', *Evaluation*, vol 7, no 4, pp 427-36.

Social Exclusion Unit (1998) 'Bringing Britain together: a rational strategy for neighbourhood renewal', Cm 4045 (www.socialexclusion.gov.uk/downloaddoc.asp?1d=113) [September 2004].

Stoker, G. (1991) *The politics of local government* (2nd edn), London: Macmillan Education.

THIRTEEN

Community-led regeneration: learning loops or reinvented wheels?

Mike Rowe and Marilyn Taylor

Introduction

Area-based initiatives are, perhaps, one of the most monitored and evaluated policy arenas today. National and local evaluations have been commissioned of Health Action Zones, Single Regeneration Budget (SRB) funding, Neighbourhood Management Pathfinders, Sure Start, New Deal for Communities (NDC) and of the Neighbourhood Renewal Fund, among others. While each is different in terms of geographical areas, objectives and of funding rules, evaluators confront the same problems. There is substantial evidence and learning to draw upon from past evaluations, both locally and nationally, yet there is little evidence that these lessons have been learnt. Indeed, many practitioners appear to set out with a clean sheet, a new and unique political context and priorities or agendas of their own. Drawing upon research on two EU-funded URBAN programmes, both the subject of national and local evaluations, this chapter will seek to understand the problems and possibilities of learning from past evaluations.

The role of evaluation

Evaluation makes little sense unless it is understood as part of a learning process. Learning distinguishes it from audit, performance management and reporting. Indeed, for some, evaluations should be explicitly framed to ensure their use by policy makers and other stakeholders, including practitioners (Patton, 1997). Without wishing to engage in the methodological implications of such an approach, it is common to assume that evaluations of public services will, in some way, contribute to a body of knowledge and understanding, leading to improved policy making and practice. Weiss (1998, pp 25-8) identifies a number of ways in which evaluation might contribute to decision-making:

- midcourse corrections to programmes;
- continuing, expanding, cutting or ending a programme;

- testing new ideas; and
- selecting the best of several alternatives.

Evaluations undertaken with such objectives might contribute to organisational learning by:

- providing a record of a programme;
- giving feedback to practitioners;
- highlighting programme goals;
- providing a measure of accountability; and
- contributing to understanding of social interventions.

As such, evaluation plays an important role in developing organisations and improving interventions in the future.

However, experience suggests that there are, in fact, many other roles that evaluation might play. Weiss (1998, p 22) suggests that evaluation might act as a form of subterfuge, for example:

- postponing difficult decisions pending an evaluation;
- ducking responsibility by relying on the 'independent' findings of a study;
- as window dressing for decisions that have already been made; and
- as a public relations exercise to draw attention to positive aspects.

In other circumstances, evaluations might simply be undertaken to fulfil grant requirements, satisfying funders and policy makers but with little other purpose. As such, evaluation is "a rational enterprise often undertaken for non-rational, or at least non-informational reasons" (Weiss, 1998, p 23).

Under the New Labour government, the profile of evaluation has been raised. The language of 'evidence-based policy' permeates documents. The mantra of public services has become 'what works is what counts' (Cabinet Office, 1999; SEU, 2001). As such, the language suggests that there is a clear intention to replicate good practice and, by doing so, to improve public services for all. In some senses, this might be seen as part of the 'third way' and of a post-ideological emphasis on pragmatism (Newman, 2001).

However, in the context of community-led regeneration, evaluation is particularly problematic. Resources are allocated on broad indicators of deprivation and need but, while there are a growing number of examples of successful practice cited in the literature and on the websites, there is still, as yet, little systematic evidence of what might work at a local level let alone how 'good practice' might be replicated and the lessons transferred. Recent interim research reports, conducted as part of the NDC programme, make clear the gaps that are to be found in the evaluation evidence. For example, reviewing evidence on education, one report comments:

that there was no single model of effective intervention across all the educational policies and initiatives examined. Evaluations concluded that there was no simple recipe for success and indicated that successful interventions were grounded in, and responded to, local context and circumstances. (Sims and Stoney, 2002, p 2)

At the heart of the problem of evaluating community-led interventions at a local level are the nature of the community, its capacity and the processes of engaging with and developing that community (Harrison, 2000). The concepts of 'community' and empowerment are much more complex than the rhetoric implies and associated concepts, which have been imported into the policy discourse, such as 'social capital' and 'civil society' are contested, with a number of interpretations even at a theoretical level (PIU, 2002, p 2; Taylor, 2003). Developing a robust analysis of how these have developed during a programme like URBAN is fraught with difficulties. Attributing any change to a particular intervention only magnifies these difficulties, especially in the current policy environment, where the sheer pace of change in the regeneration (or neighbourhood renewal) field threatens to overwhelm key players in both the community and the statutory sectors.

The 'evidence-based policy' discourse assumes that there can be clear and uncontested outcomes from any intervention that will then inform the design of later programmes. However, commenting on a much earlier regeneration programme – the 'War on Poverty' in the US – Peter Marris and Martin Rein (1967) counsel against too much dependence on rational scientific method. Describing the original intention of the programme as "a blueprint of planned intervention" (p 207), they found that:

> The final outcome cannot simply be related to the initial aim and method, since these have undergone continual revision. The whole process – the false starts, frustrations, adaptations, the successive recasting of intentions, the detours and conflicts – needs to be comprehended. Only then can we understand what has been achieved, and learn from the experience. (p 207)

However, the growth in uncertainty and the complexity of decision making in today's world intensifies the search for ways of understanding and pinning down the key components of change. Viewing the policy process as a rational, scientific exercise appears to offer a way of controlling this uncertainty. In this view, policy goes through a cyclical process, where the assessment of needs is followed by the identification of objectives, by the development and implementation of plans to meet these objectives and by systematic monitoring and evaluation, which feeds back into the development of future plans. Evaluation is a crucial link in this chain (Jenkins, 1978; Hogwood and Gunn, 1984).

This chapter explores the extent to which this rational process was achieved in two local regeneration programmes, established as part of the URBAN programme. Launched by the EU in 1994, the URBAN aimed at fostering a community-led approach to regeneration in the most disadvantaged areas in Europe, and providing a comprehensive and integrated response to economic, social and environmental needs. An interim national evaluation was commissioned to learn the lessons from the early stages of the programme and, in some areas, evaluation was also built in from an early stage of the local programmes. Each local programme developed an action plan with specific actions under which projects were funded. Specific outputs were identified for each project and a quarterly monitoring process charted progress both on spending and on outputs targets. A report was compiled at the end of each of the two funding streams involved in URBAN (see later in this chapter), detailing the actual against planned outputs.

This process provided some of Carol Weiss's contributions. Monitoring allowed for some modifications to be made during the course of the programmes – in one case, to close down a project which was not achieving and divert the funds elsewhere. In the same locality, the fact that the programme exceeded its outputs and made contact with a significant proportion of the population, also vindicated an intervention that had been viewed as problematic for much of its life.

However, in an earlier paper, we suggested that there were significant costs to the monitoring process as it was applied in URBAN (Rowe and Taylor, 2002). Viewed by many participants more as a process of risk and expenditure control than one to allow learning, the process imposed a significant burden, particularly on the smaller, community-based projects and was thought to have excluded some from engaging at all. It is possible to argue that a 'lighter-touch' monitoring process could have achieved similar promotional and management outcomes. However, so far as we know, there are no plans for a longer-term follow-up, which would establish whether the outputs led to the desired outcomes and how far these outcomes have been sustained. Even if there were, without some sort of control population, it is impossible to say how far improvements could be attributed to particular interventions.

In URBAN, monitoring was never intended to fulfil the evaluation role, although it made a useful contribution. The two local programmes that we report on here were also subject to a qualitative process evaluation. These evaluations had an explicit learning agenda, feeding back into the URBAN programme groups throughout the process. An overall interim evaluation was also commissioned at a relatively early stage in the programme, covering all UK programmes, which explored the processes of action planning and the early experience of appraisal (EKOS, 1999).

Carol Weiss's contributions apply more to programmes as a whole than individual local elements. However, by the time the EKOS report (1999) was written, the programme had moved on. It would be interesting to know how far their evaluation influenced the design of URBAN II. Meanwhile, as we shall argue later in this chapter, the extent to which the lessons of evaluation have, in the past, been heard and acted on by government funders or even local regeneration partnerships is limited, compared with new policy trends and the political need to rebrand new programmes.

The URBAN initiatives

The national interim evaluation of URBAN in 1999 described its 'unique feature' at the time as:

> the emphasis on community-led regeneration, involving significant capacity building at the development stage to ensure meaningful involvement of the local community both in the development of the Action Plan and its implementation. (EKOS, 1999, p 12)

Funding was derived from two sources: the European Social Fund (ESF) and the European Regional Development Fund (ERDF).

The two initiatives studied here were both approached to make bids in the first round of URBAN, announced in 1994. One (the Partnership Council in Nottingham) was immediately successful and funded to the tune of £5.4 million; the other (in Brighton) was not successful but was invited to bid again in 1996, when additional funds were made available, and it was awarded £3 million. Both awards were subject to matched funding. The overall programme was funded over seven years to the end of 2000 (in the case of ESF funding) and 2001 in the case of ERDF funding. A second complete round is now underway. The EU required each successful site to form an URBAN programme group with significant community representation for decision-making purposes. Funding was managed through an accountable body, and grants awarded within the framework of an action plan, grouped under 'actions', which was to be developed with active participation from the community. The action plan was required in late 1997, although in Brighton this period was extended to the following spring; outputs had to be specified within the action plan and all monies had to be committed by the end of 1999. European Social Fund money had to be spent by the end of 2000, and ERDF money by the end of 2001, leaving little time to achieve outputs.

The whole process was delayed by disagreements between the then Conservative government and the EU over the terms of the programme. In 1994, the participatory approach outlined for URBAN contrasted with the British government's business-led approach to urban regeneration. Initial negotiations between the local partners and the EU over the terms and conditions of the funding also delayed the development of action plans. This meant that the length of the programme and the time for community participation was severely truncated. In Brighton, the delays meant that application timescales were extremely tight.

Although this model of funding is by now quite familiar, the level of community involvement, particularly at a decision-making level, was unusual at the time. The complexity of the processes and the level of monitoring required were also new to many of those involved. Joining together ESF and ERDF within one programme was intended to allow a holistic response to locally defined needs and ease access to European funding. However, URBAN came with all the rules associated with each funding stream. The systems of monitoring and of output reporting which were required tell little of the process elements of partnership working and of community-led regeneration – that is, processes at the heart of URBAN.

A number of external evaluations at national and local level offered an opportunity to understand more fully the different approaches taken in each location and to draw lessons from this experience. A national interim evaluation was commissioned by the UK government and conducted by EKOS (1999). This was intended to allow for corrections and learning during the life of the programme. Both Brighton and Nottingham commissioned their own qualitative evaluations of the programme at an early stage. The focus in Brighton was on the programme as a whole and, specifically, the effectiveness of the capacity building that took place (Taylor, 2002). In Nottingham, the evaluation focused on the projects developed through its process of action planning, working groups and of tendering (Rowe and Devanney, 2002). These evaluations were intended both to feed learning back into the existing programme and to benefit later programmes, learning lessons of benefit to practitioners and policy makers. Additionally, in Nottingham, local partner organisations, including the city council and a long-standing conurbation-wide partnership, commissioned a further external evaluation conducted by Enterprise Plc. (Enterprise, 1999, 2000). As we will discuss later in this chapter, the focus of this evaluation was unclear. It quickly became a three-stage process, involving negotiations to sustain the Nottingham URBAN partnership beyond the life of the EU funding.

Evaluating URBAN

National interim evaluation

The remit of the EKOS evaluation (1999) was both to assess progress and to disseminate evidence of good practice (EKOS, 2000). While this represents an attempt to learn, the approach taken was a remote one. Evaluators examined documentation, evidence of participation and reports of outputs from projects. Contact with the programmes was limited, in the case of Nottingham, for example, to attending one partnership board meeting and interviewing the project coordinator. As such, it was experienced more as an audit than a thorough evaluation. On this limited evidence, the partnership was praised for its approach, its record of committing funding and for the way in which it engaged people. Judgements were similarly reached about other URBAN programmes, presumably on the back of similar evidence (EKOS, 1999). Nonetheless, it had a number of criticisms of the programme as a whole, which are reported later in this chapter.

The evaluation described the differences in the approaches taken by each

URBAN programme. From this, a good practice handbook was produced (EKOS, 2000). However, by the time the evaluation report was published, the processes of establishing URBAN and appraising projects that had been the focus of the report were almost at an end. The good practice handbook was published in the last year of ESF funding and ERDF had little more than a year to run. As such, the evaluation produced little learning within the programme and there were no real attempts to disseminate the learning more widely (through workshops, for example). Nor is there evidence that the reports have informed later policy initiatives, such as NDC. This is perhaps due in part to the lack of coordination, nationally and regionally, between officers concerned with EU funding and those dealing with national programmes.

Local evaluations

The local evaluations offered a much greater opportunity to tailor the criteria to local conditions, to involve all the stakeholders and to get under the skin of the programmes. Before looking at the form that evaluation took at a local level, however, we need to acknowledge the different roles played by ourselves, the authors, in the process. In the case of Brighton, the evaluation was commissioned at the outset and carried out by the University of Brighton, an organisation with no other active involvement in the URBAN programme. As such, the evaluation was undertaken by external and impartial sources with no direct interest in the outcome. In the case of Nottingham, the evaluation of projects was tendered twice with no interest being expressed, largely because of the need for matched funding. Negotiations were then initiated, through a resident director who also worked for Nottingham Trent University, and an agreement reached with the business school to undertake the work. Thus one of the evaluators was engaged in the partnership process as well as in the evaluation of some of the projects. While not strictly a form of action research, since neither evaluator was involved in the projects evaluated, the researchers did have a closer link with the partnership than was the case in Brighton. With these differences in mind, we shall look at the evaluations of the two programmes.

Brighton

The Brighton evaluation was designed from an early stage and did not have to go through a tendering or bidding process. It involved interviews at regular intervals throughout the process with all URBAN Partnership Group (UPG) members, interviews and focus groups with project managers and a sample of rejected applicants, annual evaluation workshops and a small number of interviews with users of the two community centres supported by URBAN. The UPG and the accountable body were very accessible and took the evaluation seriously, giving it space on agendas and making time available for interviews and workshops.

The intention was to make it a fully participatory process, with people from local communities themselves agreeing the criteria for the evaluation. However, the lack of community development support to local communities at the outset made this impossible. Without that foundation, there was little prospect of getting people involved beyond the UPG. Instead, criteria were derived from a visioning exercise for the UPG, which was attended by about half of the membership and revisited at a later workshop. The UPG was involved throughout in what aimed to be an action-research process, with regular annual reports: on the setting up process; on the appraisal process; on the early stages of implementation; and at the end. Annual workshops allowed the UPG to revisit the criteria and, at the end, to identify their own learning from the process.

The final report made some 40 recommendations. It echoed the EKOS criticisms of the delays and moving goalposts at the outset and made a number of suggestions about the 'infrastructure' that should be in place at the beginning of programmes of this kind and not subject to the tendering process. It was critical of the lack of resources for community development at the outset and the opportunities that had been lost to engage people more fully in an area that, unlike the Nottingham area, did not have a history of support of this kind. This meant that URBAN had not engaged as many people in the community in its running and management and that sustainability was likely to be limited. The report explored the tensions between accountability and flexibility that bedevilled the programme, recognising that projects had different experiences, some feeling that they had been helped enormously by the accountable body in handling this, but others feeling that the demands had been unfair and onerous. Certainly the complexity of the applications process had made it difficult for less experienced community groups to apply and the recommendation was made that support with applications should be built into the process. The report acknowledged the distance travelled by a UPG that had left 'blood on the carpet' in its early stages, but had learnt to work effectively and delivered on its outputs. It regretted, however, that there was little prospect of formal sustainability beyond those projects that had found further funding, and that the experience of the UPG might well be lost. It also regretted the absence of links between URBAN and the mainstream local authority.

Carrying out an ongoing evaluation poses a number of challenges. One is the challenge *to produce reports that reflect honestly what people have said and provide a critical assessment of progress*, yet do not undermine progress or appear to be targeting individuals. Efforts were made to depersonalise criticism by expressing problems as tensions and occasionally reminding people that problems experienced were not just confined to their programme, but had been experienced in many regeneration schemes. It was important to ensure that the report did not fall into the trap of making judgements on individuals. However, there were times when criticisms were taken personally.

A second challenge is *to allow UPG members the opportunity to feed back and suggest changes without destroying the independence of the evaluation*. Redrafts of each report were generally based on the spirit of the discussion at the meetings and allowed the researchers to add further insights or perspectives. However, most of the more specific changes were suggested by the accountable body participants in the UPG, who were more easily identifiable and as a result were, probably inevitably, more sensitive to criticism. They sometimes felt their perspective was not given enough weight. Nonetheless, they remained committed to and supportive of the evaluation.

This relates to a third challenge which was *to make sure that everyone felt that their views had been given space in the report*. To present a balanced view was quite difficult, especially given real and perceived power differentials on the UPG.

A fourth challenge was *to deal constructively with criticism*. The early days of URBAN in Brighton were marked by conflict and it was seen as a problem programme (until the outputs showed otherwise). It was important to acknowledge the positives at times when things were not going too well, rather than just focusing on the acknowledged difficulties. And it was important not to give ammunition to the denigrators of URBAN. In all the reports to the partnership, some assessment was made of the achievements against the UPG's evaluation criteria. However, the reports also explored the processes involved in developing URBAN, saying what could have usefully been different, what had been learnt, but also highlighting the inevitable tensions involved in developing a community-led programme and how they both had been and could be addressed. These provided the material for the workshops and were explicitly intended as points of learning throughout the course of the programme.

So what did the evaluation achieve? It provided a sense of legitimacy to URBAN in Brighton, especially given the difficulties at the outset. Having an evaluation also gave URBAN some status in the eyes of those involved and made them feel it was being taken seriously. The evaluation was something that could be quoted in other settings. At the same time, it endorsed the lessons that people felt they were learning and gave people an opportunity to challenge views that they disagreed with in a neutral setting. As such, it provided an account of the distance travelled and a way of understanding what had happened and of celebrating successful delivery against outputs.

Whether the learning was spread more broadly is less clear. The UPG reported to an URBAN Management Group (UMG), made up of members of the Brighton Regeneration Partnership. However, participants in URBAN did not feel that the UMG had a strong identity with URBAN or that it worked as a mechanism for taking the lessons from URBAN into a wider arena. Equally frustrating for UPG members was the fact that their perception that the new high-profile NDC (that had been established in part of the URBAN area) did not appear to acknowledge that there might be something to learn from URBAN. There are a number of reasons for this. The NDC covered a part of the URBAN area that some people felt had got a raw deal from URBAN. There had been a lot of controversy about URBAN in the early days in this neighbourhood, and the local MP had been particularly critical. Despite the fact that URBAN money went into this neighbourhood, community activists there felt that their bids had been scrutinised more closely than others and that they had not got as much money as they should have (others dispute this). However, the 'Not Invented Here' factor may also have been at work – the NDC was a flagship government programme, which wanted to develop its own approach. The first director did suggest a meeting between the two programmes and a group was set up for cross-fertilisation. It only met once, however, and the NDC did not field any residents. This led to considerable frustration among UPG members, including those from the neighbourhood concerned, who definitely felt that the wheel was being reinvented – especially in relation to excessive bureaucracy. They also felt that their experience was being ignored and therefore undervalued.

Towards the end of the programme, there appeared to be a greater willingness to share the learning from Brighton URBAN more widely, both within the locality and beyond. At the suggestion of the Government Office for the region, a team developing an URBAN II programme elsewhere in the region was invited to the Brighton URBAN's final evaluation workshop, so that experience could be passed on to the second generation of programmes. More locally, a meeting of the UMG – which was a subgroup of the Brighton Regeneration Partnership, recommended that an event should be set up to share the learning. This resulted in a conference where URBAN and a Single Regeneration Budget (SRB) project that had also been evaluated shared their findings more broadly. The day allowed for discussion around the tensions that the reports had discussed: representation; dealing with conflict; and accountability. As a result recommendations were made to the new local strategic partnership for taking forward the lessons from URBAN and elsewhere. We now have to wait and see what comes of this.

Nottingham

In Nottingham, two evaluations were undertaken, each with a different focus. The need for the first of these evaluations arose at an early stage in Nottingham. Part of the criticism residents made of current public services, notably education and training, was that they were obsessed more with numbers – 'bums-on-seats' – than with the quality of the provision. Were URBAN to deliver in the spirit of the action plan developed by local people, quality would be as important as the quantitative outputs achieved. Thus, the need for a qualitative evaluation was identified in the action plan. It was intended that this would be up and running at an early stage and able to inform and influence project management and monitoring during the life of the programme. However, understandably, the focus of working groups was to negotiate and agree the service delivery projects rather than that concerned with evaluation. However, by the time the Qualitative Evaluation Project (QEP) was negotiated and agreed, and after negotiations over funding, only eight months of the programme remained. Indeed, at this stage, all projects funded through ESF had finished. Furthermore, the original idea of a facilitated participatory evaluation of all projects (some 60 in total) had to be curtailed. Instead, six projects, representing a spread from capacity building to capital investment, were chosen for evaluation. Through this evaluation, some light was also shed upon the processes of the partnership itself and the structures it had developed to implement the original action plan. Nevertheless, the focus was a quite limited one. Having said that, the evaluation raised some key themes that build upon those in the others already discussed. In focusing upon the design, management and delivery of projects, it also touches on issues not directly confronted in other evaluations.

The purpose of the QEP, set out in the action plan, was to satisfy the local community that the ideas and projects they had developed were being implemented in the spirit of the original ideas. As such, it might have played a part, in addition to project monitoring and audit inspections, in steering and correcting projects during their lifespan. By talking to beneficiaries and intended beneficiaries, the QEP was to reflect their experience in order to improve projects and to ensure their effectiveness. Given the late start of the evaluation (two of the six projects evaluated had finished by the time the QEP started), little in-process feedback and correction was possible. Nevertheless, the QEP retained features that reflect this original intent. In its approach, the QEP sought to tell the story of each project, from ideas, through service specification to delivery. It did so by drawing upon the experiences of those involved in specifying the project, of those managing it and of the beneficiaries. The audience was intended to include local people and participants, projects, their workers and beneficiaries, practitioners and, ultimately, policy makers at local, regional and national levels.

The key lessons from the projects that emerged from the evaluation confirmed those identified in the national interim evaluation (EKOS, 1999). The attempt to engage participants throughout the process in actively developing projects, rather than passively in consultation or on a board, succeeded while not jeopardising spending. Indeed, Nottingham managed to maintain participation throughout the URBAN programme and achieve a 97% spend. However, a number of key lessons were drawn out (Box 13.1).

Box 13.1: Key lessons from the projects

- The process of forming an action plan, engaging a wide range of local residents and workers, developed a range of challenging ideas and issues for the URBAN programme to address. These were turned into service specifications by working groups, composed of local residents, workers and professionals. This process was funded, supported and removed the burden of interpreting EU regulations and rules away from project deliverers. That some of the projects subsequently proved difficult to implement reflects both the problematic nature of the issues they sought to address, such as exclusion among young people and ex-offenders, and the unwillingness of some local agencies to change.
- Projects were hindered by delays, changing rules and a lack of investment in start-up costs. Not least of all, the QEP itself suffered from this.

- Asking local agencies to work in partnership to jointly resolve complex problems requires clarity of purpose and sound communication.
- Despite the problems and barriers imposed by funding regimes, projects and project workers managed to find new and flexible ways of addressing difficult social issues. This was particularly the case where projects were effectively supported by working groups reflecting the interests and needs of the wider community.
- Although funding rules were highly restrictive, with effective support and evidence derived from consultation, some flexibility could be achieved. (Rowe and Devanney, 2002, pp 68-71).

It has already been noted that some of these lessons were learned late in the programme. However, a number were recognised by participants in both the Partnership Council (PC) and the projects themselves and steps were taken to change practices during the course of the projects. Emerging conclusions and early drafts informed discussions and project bids for further resources to the subsequent Nottingham NDC and other funding programmes. Delays in dissemination and publication have also limited its impact to date on a wider audience. These delays are, however, closely connected with the final evaluation we shall review in this chapter.

Commissioned by local partner organisations, including the city council and the Greater Nottingham Partnership (GNP), Enterprise Plc. was asked to evaluate the PC, Nottingham's URBAN partnership organisation. The expressed aims of this evaluation were:

> to objectively identify the good practice developed by the Partnership Council in its stewardship of the URBAN Community Initiative and to provide a succinct summary of learning, actions and recommendations directed to:
>
> - the Partnership Council Board
> - New Deal for Communities
> - Nottingham City Council
> - other private and public sector partners. (Enterprise, 2000, p 1)

As such, it was explicitly concerned with spreading the learning identified in the EKOS evaluation (1999) within the city and, specifically, to the successor NDC, announced in 1999. However, the team of evaluators brought experience of the private sector and of physical regeneration initiatives. The team had little shared understanding of concepts like social capital or capacity building. Using documents and interviews, the evaluators sought to understand the structures and processes behind the URBAN programme, seeking to triangulate wherever possible. However, each member of the team took charge of particular elements of the evaluation, with few evident connections made between them.

Partly as a consequence, the initial report (Enterprise, 1999) was very descriptive and confused, each section having a different thrust. It was difficult to draw conclusions from often contradictory messages. Furthermore, and particularly in discussion with the evaluators, there was an almost obsessive interest in minutiae. For example, filing cabinets, some with string drawer handles, had been donated or borrowed as a way of saving on overheads. At the same time, this had the advantage of making the PC's offices look less like a public sector organisation and so less intimidating and hostile to the local community. However, the evaluators saw this as a sign of a lack of professionalism. While this is a small point to make, it highlights the lack of understanding of the environment in which the PC was working. This lack of understanding was more evident in the assessment of resident participation. While the report praised the participatory structures as being genuinely open throughout, giving residents a key role in setting the agenda, designing projects and selecting deliverers, other parts of the work questioned the numbers involved. From a population of approximately 21,000, about 900 engaged with the consultation processes and more than 70 were actively involved in developing service specifications and selecting the service deliverers. While this may seem a small proportion in capacity-building terms, the learning and skills development gained from participation appears more significant. Indeed, the numbers alone compare favourably with other similar programmes (EKOS, 1999).

Nevertheless, after some lengthy discussion, a final report was produced that drew together some key findings (EKOS, 2000). Principally, the report concluded that partnership working requires an investment of time and resources to deliver benefits over the longer term. In this respect, the report suggested that Nottingham's NDC had a lot to learn from the PC's experience. However, these conclusions and associated recommendations proved highly contentious. Despite this locally commissioned work and some national recognition of the PC's successes, the partner organisations did not appear to value the experience gained through URBAN. At the time of the report, Nottingham's bid for NDC funds had been recently approved. An embryonic partnership and delivery structure was being created. Yet, neither the city council nor the Greater Nottingham Partnership seemed to want to build on the experience of the PC. Indeed, some senior officers deliberately sidelined the PC. The reasons for this refusal to learn echo those in Brighton and must lead to some reflection on the seriousness with which learning from evaluations is taken in these contexts.

Evaluating community-led regeneration

Returning to Carol Weiss's lists of the uses to which evaluations are put, we can find some evidence of many of them within the evaluations discussed in this chapter. Those associated with contributing to decision making, while more clearly concerned with monitoring and output reports, can be seen in both the EKOS work and the local evaluations conducted in Brighton and Nottingham. Certainly, the intention was that each would, in some way, contribute to mid-course corrections and to testing what was, in the context of the time, a new approach to regeneration. That there is little evidence that this intent was realised is, perhaps, a matter of timing – a problem common to many evaluations. Too often, lessons are learnt when it is already too late. One clear lesson from the experience reported here is the value of building evaluation in from the start and separately from the project appraisal process and the delays that this inevitably engenders (although obviously there is a balance to be struck here with ensuring community ownership).

Of more concern for this chapter is the extent to which any sense of learning can be discerned in the evaluation of URBAN. Certainly, the local evaluations provide a record of different aspects of each programme. As such, they have proved a source of learning within the partnerships. One latecomer to the Brighton partnership who eventually came to chair it said she found the early reports extremely useful in giving her an understanding of the UPG, its history and the context in which current discussions were set. In Nottingham, detailing the story of six projects provided partnership members with a sense of what it was they had created, a sense that was otherwise a remote one. However, in neither locality did those involved in the delivery of URBAN feel that the UMG showed any clear understanding of or interest in the outcomes of the evaluations during the life of the programme. This changed in Brighton towards the end, however, when Brighton's UMG did take action to disseminate the findings more widely.

The local evaluation of Brighton's programme also provided a constant reminder of the UPG's criteria. Each report offered an opportunity to reflect on 'distance travelled'. Three workshops were run – a visioning one in Year One, a stocktake in Year Two and a lessons learned workshop in the final year – which gave people an opportunity to develop and revisit the evaluation criteria. In this sense, it also provided a measure of accountability. Some people did read reports thoroughly: especially the accountable body, the one councillor who stayed involved, the chairs of the UPG and one or two others. The final report was presented to the UMG and in summary, as we have mentioned, to a larger workshop attended by many active in the regeneration field. The same was not true of Nottingham's evaluation of projects, largely because of timing and the different focus of the evaluation. Its concern was much more with Weiss's point of contributing to understanding interventions. By focusing on the detail of individual projects and the experience of beneficiaries, the evaluation was pitched at this level. Only time can tell whether any learning will come from it or not.

What is clear is that the learning gleaned from all the evaluations has been limited largely to those directly involved. Although moves were made to disseminate the Brighton URBAN experience in the later stages, there was still considerable disappointment among participants that, as they saw it, the learning from URBAN had not been taken on board in NDC. To an extent, this was inevitable. The URBAN programme's reputation in the NDC area never really recovered from its poor start, despite the fact that it did fund community-based projects there. In addition, NDC nationally has prided itself on its ability to learn from the mistakes of the past, putting in longer lead-in times, and providing for capacity building, for example. The NDC in this neighbourhood involved many new people and there would have seemed little incentive to look back to URBAN.

In Nottingham, there have been a number of high-profile efforts to transfer learning from the PC to NDC. But these efforts demonstrate some of Weiss's elements of subterfuge. A number of reports and studies, including those from Neighbourhood Renewal Advisors, have questioned and criticised the programme, but the programme remained unchanged. While there have been many concerns about the course being taken by NDC, only recent press coverage of financial management problems following the leak of two audit reports has prompted serious action (*Nottingham Evening Post*, 21 June 2003, pp 12-14). The deliberate refusal to learn from the PC and its experiences, both good and bad, has led to NDC replicating some of the problems to be found in the city's past.

Was there anything to learn? Some of the people who have been involved in both URBAN and NDC feel more dialogue would have been useful and more than one project leader agreed:

> All the things that came out of URBAN that were difficult are now being repeated in the NDC. People didn't learn. The process is just as difficult.

Some of the legacy of URBAN, however, is being fed into the NDC through people who participated in both – one of the Brighton partnership members is now an elected member of the Community Partnership – but there is not much likelihood that any formal sharing of experience would be useful or appreciated at this stage.

What, then, is the barrier to learning in a community-led regeneration context? Are the barriers specific to the field, or do they afflict all policy arenas? Certainly, some of the failings of the evaluations discussed in this chapter have been mirrored elsewhere: produced too late to effect change; little read; and difficult to assimilate in later programmes. Nevertheless, there does seem to be something specific and deliberate about the failure to learn from URBAN that is particular to the community-led context. In both Brighton and Nottingham, URBAN was succeeded by an NDC programme in a smaller part of the area of benefit. But the respective UPGs felt very much like the 'poor relation' to the new flagship initiative. In neither locality did the evidence suggest that the NDC wished to learn from URBAN. In engaging communities in shaping services, participatory organisations and partnerships will bring new people around the table. In this chapter, we have discussed evidence of the determination of NDC partnerships to start afresh and to plough their own furrow. Whether they end up reinventing wheels seems to be of less concern. However, there is also something specific about the politics of local communities. In Brighton, the perception (justified or not) that URBAN had disadvantaged the NDC area aggravated the tendency to begin anew. In Nottingham, the capture of NDC by particular interests, ones that URBAN had challenged (Rowe and Devanney, 2003), meant that the experience of URBAN was not one to learn from but one to reject outright. Indeed, there was no evidence of a genuine climate for learning, at least from URBAN, in either location, although there were signs that this had changed towards the end in Brighton and it will be interesting to see whether this is sustained. But the danger remains that those who feel that they have nothing to learn from the past run the risk of repeating at least some of its failures – a danger that has been evident for over 30 years of regeneration programmes in the UK.

Overview

- There are a number of ways in which evaluation can contribute to organisational learning and decision making.
- New Labour's use of 'what works'-type language suggested a clear intention to learn from evaluation in order to replicate good practice and thus improve public services.
- Evaluation might play other roles. It could for example act as a form of subterfuge.
- In evaluations of community-led regeneration initiatives, there are difficulties with identifying 'what works' and transferring this learning from one locality to another. Change cannot be simply attributed to a particular intervention but must be considered in context.
- Barriers to learning in the Brighton and Nottingham URBAN evaluation case studies were identified. These included inadequate timely dissemination and a lack of willingness to learn on the part of the NDC.

References

Cabinet Office (1999) *Modernising government*, London: The Stationery Office.

EKOS (1999) *URBAN interim evaluation report*, London: DETR.

EKOS (2000) *UK URBAN community initiative best practice handbook*, London: DETR.

Enterprise (1999) 'Evaluation of the Nottingham Partnership Council', Unpublished evaluation report, Preston: Enterprise Plc.

Enterprise (2000) 'Evaluation summary report', Unpublished evaluation report, Preston: Enterprise Plc.

Harrison, T. (2000) 'Urban policy: addressing wicked problems', in H. Davies, S. Nutley and P. Smith (eds) *What works? Evidence-based policy and practice in public services*, Bristol: The Policy Press, pp 207-28.

Hogwood, B. and Gunn, L. (1984) *Policy analysis for the real world*, Oxford: Oxford University Press.

Jenkins, W. (1978) *Policy analysis: A political and organisational perspective*, Oxford: Martin Robertson.

Marris, P. and Rein, M. (1967) *Dilemmas of social reform*, New York, NY: Atherton Press.

Newman, J. (2001) *Modernising governance: New Labour, policy and society*, London: Sage Publications.

Patton, M. (1997) *Utilization-focused evaluation: The new century text* (3rd edn), London: Sage Publications.

PIU (Performance and Innovation Unit) (2002) *Social capital: A discussion paper*, London: PIU.

Rowe, M. and Devanney, C. (2002) *Nottingham's URBAN programme. A qualitative evaluation of projects*, Nottingham: Nottingham Business School.

Rowe, M. and Devanney, C. (2003) 'Partnership and the governance of regeneration', *Critical Social Policy*, vol 23, no 3, pp 375-97.

Rowe, M. and Taylor, M. (2002) 'Auditing local area programmes: exploring the tension between accountability and participation', Paper presented at Social Policy Association Conference, Teeside, July.

Sims, D. and Stoney, S. (2002) *Domain review of major policy developments in education and the evidence base*, London: Neighbourhood Renewal Unit (www.neighbourhood.gov.uk/formatteddoc.asp?id=127).

SEU (Social Exclusion Unit) (2001) *A new commitment to neighbourhood renewal*, London: SEU.

Taylor, M. (2002) *Brighton URBAN: The evaluation summary report*, Brighton: Brighton University.

Taylor, M. (2003) *Public policy in the community*, London: Palgrave.

Weiss, C. (1998) *Evaluation* (2nd edn), New Jersey: Prentice Hall.

FOURTEEN

Can social capital be a framework for participative evaluation of community health work?

Jennie Fleming and Thilo Boeck

Introduction

This chapter explores how the concept of social capital can be adapted and used as a tool for participative evaluation of community-based work. The chapter draws on our experience of working with the Nottingham Social Action Research Project (SARP) as an example. (Parts of this chapter draw on material published recently; see Boeck and Fleming, 2002.) Within SARP, we facilitated a process of learning and the development of ideas and concepts. We worked with the local workers and community members to increase their capacity to evaluate their work, particularly around social capital enhancement.

This chapter briefly sets out some of the criticisms of the social capital framework as a neoliberal concept. However, its main focus is presenting how, when informed by the principles and processes of social action, it can be adapted and used for evaluation in a way that people can find meaningful and empowering. It is our experience that the projects found social capital an excellent framework for evaluation: in addition to quantifiable information, it allowed people to demonstrate the wide impact of their work with communities and inform their own practice and project development.

The Nottingham Social Action Research Project (SARP)

The Social Action Research Project (SARP) was an action research project that aimed to explore if social capital can be built within communities. The SARP was funded by the Health Development Agency (HDA) for three years to consider the relationship between inequalities, social capital and health. Two areas were chosen for detailed study – Nottingham and Salford. The Nottingham SARP was managed by a Partnership Board made up of representatives from the funding bodies, the Assistant Chief Executive of the City Council, the Director of Public Health and representatives from the HDA. The Nottingham

SARP worked with groups made up of local workers and people in the two localities chosen to be the focus of work in Nottingham.

In 1999, a baseline survey was carried out to identify levels of social capital in each area. Following the survey, SARP worked with local partners who wanted to explore how their work could contribute to the building of social capital in their communities. The SARP provided funds for groups who wanted to increase social capital as part of the work that they were doing and SARP staff offered consultation and practical support.

One person from a mental health project summed up the purpose of the Nottingham SARP as:

> a response to the decline experienced by hundreds of communities, brought about by, among other things, lack of job opportunities, crime and poor housing. It focuses on the extent to which local people trust and feel safe with one another, the influence and power they have over their lives, the help they can expect from family, friends or neighbours and the quality of the social networks they can develop. (Boeck and Fleming, 2002, p 6)

What is social capital?

Putnam is one of the most well known writers on social capital (Campbell, 1999, p 7). Despite his notoriety, there are many other writers on the topic who offer a number of slightly different models of social capital, based on different theoretical positions (see, for example, Coleman 1990; Bourdieu, 1997). However, there are some common themes in all models: networks, social bonds and civic engagement in some form.

Rather than stressing the negatives, the sociological analysis of the concept of social capital looks at the quality of social relations and their impact on the lives of their participants. Social capital is created from the complexity of everyday interactions between people. Thus, the evaluation of 'social capital building' should not be used to stigmatise individuals, or make judgements about their lives, but should refer to the relationships between people, institutions, structures and organisations in communities:

> Social capital originates with people forming connections and networks based on principles of trust, mutual reciprocity and norms of action. It depends on a propensity for sociability, a capacity to form new associations and networks. (Boeck et al, 2001, p 90)

Social capital is a contested concept (Morrow, 2002, p 10). There is a concern expressed by some writers (Muntaner et al, 2000; Forbes et al, 2001) who believe the concept of social capital has been introduced within a neoliberal agenda. As such, they claim that it is imposed by policy makers to address the 'ills of society' with the effect once again of blaming individuals and communities for their problems. Others also believe that the concept of social capital does not recognise the issues of power and most importantly power imbalances, between and within communities (Erben et al, 2000).

Morrow (writing specifically about children and young people) points out that by focusing on such specific elements of individual and neighbourhood quality of life there is a danger that "broader questions of social justice will be overlooked. The wider responsibilities of central and local government to ensure a good quality of life for children in environmental terms – whether in their institutions or neighbourhoods – also need to be addressed" (Morrow, 2001, p 46). She also makes the extremely valuable point that, as constructed by Putnam, social capital is not intended to include children and young people (2001, p 8). However, she and a number of the Nottingham SARP projects have explored the relevance of social capital with young people.

Obviously, with HDA funding, SARP was concerned about the link between social capital development and the health and well-being of people in the areas where it was based:

> Much interest is currently being devoted to the hypothesis that people might
> be healthier in communities characterised by high levels of social capital.
> (Campbell and McLean, 2002, p 31)

While this hypothesis was a theme throughout the projects, in reality the timescale of SARP made it very difficult to make any assessment of the health and well-being improvements.

Through exploration and application of the concept of social capital in both research and evaluation, we have come to understand that social capital can be understood as a private and public good (Coleman, 1990; Portes, 1998; Putnam, 2000) and thus provides a framework for exploring community development in greater depth. Social capital allows for the consideration of the processes by which formal and informal social connections work through networks and communities to act as a buffer against the effects of deprivation:

> Theoretically, social capital ... attempts to link micro-social individual behaviour
> and macro-social structural factors. It attempts to set social relationships, social
> interactions and social networks within the context of wider structural factors.
> (Morrow, 2002, p 10)

Social capital is relevant to community development. It provides us with a tool to help gain insight and understanding into what is happening in communities. Kilpatrick et al (2003, p 431) write that they are led to conclude:

> that social capital resources are useful in the process of community development
> and that the process of building social capital can be part of a community
> development process.

Within the range of ideological, epistemological and methodological debates on social capital (Mutaner et al, 2000; Forbes and Wainwright, 2001) we would follow Woolcock's (1998) argument that there are different types, levels or dimensions of social capital and different performance outcomes associated with varying combinations of these dimensions. Originating with people forming connections and networks based on the principles of trust, mutual reciprocity and norms of action, social capital is created from the complexity of social relations and their impact on the lives of the people in them.

The Action Research Development Team (ARDT) had previous experience of using a model of social capital that included the concepts of value of life and diversity (Boeck et al, 2001). After discussion in the workshops run by the ARDT, people from the Nottingham SARP projects felt that these two categories should be included, as they were seen as fundamental to their understanding of social capital in their communities. These were integrated into the model and most projects used these eight categories of social capital to plan and evaluate their work.

Figure 14.1 illustrates the multidimensional model of social capital used by SARP in Nottingham.

In our work, we have developed and use this definition of social capital:

> Social capital is the bulk of social interactions, networks and network opportunities that either people or communities have within a specific environment of mutual trust and reciprocity informed by specific norms and values.

Figure 14.1: The social capital framework

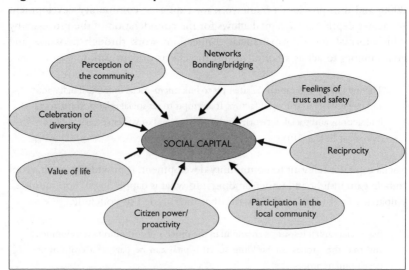

Source: Boeck (2002)

The different types of social capital are shaped by and depend on the different components; that is, the types of networks (bridging, bonding and linking); openness and diversity (outward or inward-looking); norms and values; type of community (location, interest, faith, common experience); and power. These types of social capital have different types of social, political and economic outcomes.

The work of the Action Research Development Team (ARDT)

The SARP board felt it was important to provide the initiatives they funded with support on how to evaluate their impact on the building of social capital in the communities in which they worked. To do this, they advertised for an outside agency to work as the Action Research Development Team (ARDT). The purpose of the ARDT was to work with the projects to increase their capacity to evaluate their own work, particularly around social capital building. We, the authors of this chapter, working at the Centre for Social Action at De Montfort University, were appointed as the ARDT. We worked with the projects "to develop tools appropriate for grassroots, operational and strategic work that will enable local people, staff and managers to record, plan and evaluate their objectives and performance using social capital indicators" (quoted from the invitation to tender document produced by the SARP board). Our role was to contribute to the process of social capital development, by providing a programme of action research consultations and workshops, to enable local people and workers to plan and undertake the evaluation of their projects.

The brief developed by SARP fitted well with the Centre for Social Action's philosophy and approach. The centre has considerable experience of practical work with communities and is committed to activities that encourage the participation of community members in all aspects of projects, to build and develop their skills and experience. Social action is an approach that starts from the issues, ideas and understandings of community members. Its emphasis is on facilitating a process of learning, development and change. This involves specific skills and knowledge, which is not the province of any one group or profession but should be available and accessible to all (Mullander and Ward, 1991).

Given the Centre for Social Action's value position (see www.dmu.ac.uk/dmucsa), our research and evaluation are not isolated from practice. Our experience shows that a qualitative focus, rather than a purely quantitative approach to evaluation, offers more opportunities for developing the research as a collaborative joint venture with community members:

> A qualitative evaluation is better for assessing a dynamic change rather than a static impact. The evaluator does not attempt to manipulate the project for the purpose of the evaluation.... It is based on inductive analysis in which the evaluator seeks to understand the process rather than imposing predetermined

expectations. Finally, it implies a continuous and close contact with project participants in their own setting. (Oakley, 1990)

At the core of our evaluation activities are three main points. First, the agenda is as far as is possible defined by the service users. Second, that all work should be based on partnership with the users of the services or members of the community group. Finally, there is recognition that all of the people involved have the capacity to be creative (see Fleming and Ward, 1999). The social action model of research starts by asking the question *what* has happened, then goes on to explore *why* it has happened and *how* the positive effects can be maximised or duplicated elsewhere.

The social action approach to evaluation keeps in balance the need for substantive information with a particular emphasis on working in partnership with people on the issues, concerns and problems that they identify, so promoting local democracy. This resonated with SARP, as being very much in harmony with their understanding of the concept of social capital building itself.

Our work indicates that when informed by the principles and process of social action, social capital can be a useful concept to help communities and those who work with them, to plan and evaluate their work (see also Boeck et al, 2001, p 102):

> The social capital part of the project is the added value, I am not sure we would have captured it if we had just been reporting to the HAZ [Health Action Zone]. Having the social capital framework focused the evaluation and helped us be clear what we were looking for beyond numbers. (a worker, quoted in Fleming and Boeck, 2002a, p 4)

Exploring social capital evaluation

Initially, time was spent with SARP projects finding out what they were doing and what support they might need. As a result of these discussions, two workshops were put on for local people and workers to explore the issues involved in the evaluation of the building of social capital. The sessions gave participants the opportunity to explore the concept of social capital and consider the meaning of it within their professional practice. They created the space for the different projects to share their ideas and develop evaluation strategies. The projects were very active in developing the meaning of social capital within the Nottingham SARP.

The reporting requirements of SARP were made clear during the sessions. Many projects had funding from more than one source and so consideration was given to how to minimise the burden of reporting to a number of different agencies. In their evaluation, participants said they had found the workshops helpful in increasing their understanding of social capital and in helping them consider a range of evaluation methods. Another aspect highlighted was the informal and stimulating way the workshops were delivered, with the stress on group discussions. They appreciated the fact that highly theoretical concepts were made accessible for their practice.

After these workshops, all the projects were visited by one of the ARDT with the aim of drawing up evaluation action plans which would outline what the project was doing, what they were looking to evaluate, their size, how much support they thought they would need, methods of information collection and timescales.

At that time many projects had not yet appointed their workers, or only one or two people from the project had attended the workshop, and they realised the importance of everyone involved having the opportunity to consider social capital and how it related to their work. We also ran 'mini-sessions' for all these projects, which reported they found these sessions looking at how social capital development applied to their specific initiatives very useful. This highlights the need for consultancy and support for projects to facilitate the process of reflection on how to apply theoretical concepts to practice, and then evaluate the impact of them.

Each project used the ARDT in different ways, so a very flexible approach was needed. Some projects were very clear they wanted to do the evaluation themselves; others wanted more support.

Developing the social capital framework

A major contribution of the ARDT was enabling people to consider what social capital meant and looked like for their project and communities. This process was started in the workshops where people, both workers and community members, had lengthy debates about the meaning and value of social capital. This contributed to the development of the social capital framework that was used by the Nottingham SARP. For example, the ARDT initially proposed a model of social capital that named one of the categories 'tolerance of diversity'. Participants objected to this term and chose to rename it 'celebration of diversity', and this became the category used.

This process of developing the meaning of social capital continued within the projects. The ARDT spent a considerable amount of time with the projects facilitating their exploration of the different types, levels or dimensions of social capital and different performance outcomes associated with varying combinations of these dimensions within their specific project. The practical application of the social capital framework was different for each project and they had to identify how each category could relate to their specific context, so that they could build their practice around these and hence, know what the focus of their evaluation would be. Initially, the complexity of social capital was daunting for people, but through this explorative process, it became a meaningful and useful concept to most projects.

The ARDT produced handouts about evaluation[1]. It also produced leaflets about social capital and wrote up the notes from the workshops. All projects and other interested organisations were given these and they were well used and often referred to later.

Both the SARP workers and the ARDT encouraged people to use the social capital framework to inform the development of their projects. The social capital categories were used in the service level agreements between SARP and the groups that received funding. They were asked how the projects would relate to the social capital indicators and how this would be demonstrated and evaluated. The ARDT also encouraged the projects to consider how they would create an impact on social capital in their work. Many projects were proposing to concentrate on just one or two social capital categories, but the ARDT gave special emphasis to the consideration of how each project would impact on them all.

Developing evaluation methods

When considering social capital as a framework for evaluation, it is necessary to ensure that it is built into the aims and objectives of the projects from the very beginning. It is clearly not good practice to tack the evaluation criteria on at the end, but rather have them integral to the work from the beginning. The next step is to work with the projects to develop methods for assessing their impact on the building of social capital. Methods need to be consistent with their style of work and understandable to the people with whom they work. Attention ought to be given, in partnership with the projects, to what evaluation tools might be most appropriate for this task, also taking into consideration the time and resources that are available.

As the ARDT, we worked with people to devise methods for evaluating their work. Each group developed their own methods. However, all those involved agreed that qualitative methods were most likely to capture the complexity and processes involved in the building of social capital.

Projects chose informal and reflective methods. Many favoured discussion (both formal and informal) with service users or community members as a method of collecting information. Another favoured method was the use of record or debrief sheets and workers' diaries to frame recording of discussions, anecdotes and observations of sessions:

> As a result of regular input and support about social capital, the team became competent at analysing certain behaviour and achievements and then correlating them with the social capital indicators. (Fleming and Boeck, 2002b, p 4)

Others devised questionnaires, using pictures as well as ranking measures and open-ended questions, all based on the understanding of social capital they had developed. Some groups explored issues raised in questionnaires in more depth via focus groups, which were deemed "the richest source of contextual information, and were an excellent way of discovering effective practice and the groups' perspectives on ways forward" (Fleming and Boeck, 2002b, p 4).

The ARDT encouraged people to consider a variety of methods; some projects used session recording sheets, specially designed questionnaires, workers' diaries, team discussions, photos and video and report writing to evaluate their work:

> We intend to use case studies, record people's experiences, questionnaires, photo stories and video to evaluate our work.

Through the work with different groups we devised a planning chart that some of the projects used to help them think all of this through. A Youth Work Forum organised a trip to a Carnival in another city and Table 14.1 is an example of how they could have used this chart to help plan the event.

In this type of work, it is crucial for the support to projects to be flexible and tailored to the specific needs of each project. This meant that the exact role and level of advice and guidance given by the ARDT varied. For some projects, the ARDT helped frame the questions to find out the things they wanted. We spoke with service users directly in other projects. Sometimes we were asked to check that questions would lead to the information wanted, or we might draft some questions that the project would then adapt and make their own, based on discussions with workers and volunteers in projects. We attended planning, review, evaluation and team meetings and, occasionally, events or sessions. To all we offered encouragement and reassurance.

For the whole of the SARP project, sharing learning was an important element. The ARDT often had a key role in letting projects know what others were doing and what was proving to be successful in both the building of social capital and its evaluation. Throughout the project there has been an ongoing exploration of description, explanation, analysis and critique of the building of social capital, and the role of the ARDT has contributed significantly to this.

The SARP also contracted a photographer who was available to projects to help them use photography as a means of evaluation. Single use cameras and a digital camera were also provided.

Incorporating social capital perspectives into project work

The projects approached the concept of social capital building and its evaluation in three distinctive ways. One group has seen it as a new addition to their work and viewed their involvement with SARP as a conscious process of adding the building of social capital into their practice. They committed themselves to the challenge of using the framework and all the categories, to plan their work and its evaluation.:

Table 14.1: Planning chart

Categories of social capital	Project activity that will contribute to building that category	Indicators – how will we know?	Measurement – evaluation tools or methods
Networking – Consolidating and building bridging and bonding networks.	The whole trip but specifically: Visiting a new place. The questionnaire about the carnival Picnic altogether.	Young people meeting and talking to people from Leicester. Young people meeting new people, and maybe staying in contact with them. Closer links within the Nottingham group. Young people staying together, being happy to do things with workers.	Workers' observations. Questionnaires. Group discussion. Informal chats.
Trust and safety	Workers checking the young people are OK. Sorting out expectations of each other. Arranging emergency meeting place. Encouraging young people to look out for each other. Workers being part of the group.	Group being confident outside their own area. Joining in with activities in unfamiliar situations. Young people looking out for each other.	Chatting with the young people. Group discussions. Observations. Questionnaires. Photos.

> How can I ensure that the work I am involved with sets out to build social
> capital and actually maximises its impact on all the categories of social capital?
> (quoted in Fleming and Boeck, 2002b, p 4)

The second group saw social capital as a new way of talking about what they
had already been doing and looked to fit their existing and current activities
into a social capital evaluation framework:

> I think we have always been doing this. Social capital has just highlighted what
> we already do. (Fleming and Boeck, 2002b, p 4)

A third group has taken one aspect of social capital and focused on developing
it. In the SARP these projects concentrated primarily on the building of
networks, such as the facilitation of both bonding and bridging links in groups
and communities.

In a pilot project like SARP, which aims to explore the contribution
organisations and individuals can make to the building of social capital, all are
equally valid approaches. Each of them takes the debate and discussion about
enhancing social capital further and raises questions for future investigation.
However, they do lead to different emphases in their evaluations and contribution
to learning outcomes, as can be seen in their reports and the project reports
complied by the ARDT (www.social-action.org.uk/sarp/advancedsearch.asp).

Sharing findings

Within the social capital framework for evaluation, it is crucial that findings
are shared. The model of social capital building used in Nottingham was based
on involvement, collaboration and participation. So, the final stage of the ARDT's
role was encouraging the projects to find some way of producing their findings
in a sharable form. Some people wrote comprehensive evaluation reports of
their overall projects and the special events they held. Others wrote brief accounts
of what they had done, some of which have been published (for example,
Green, 2003). A few projects used video and most have some photographic
record of their work. For a few projects, members of the ARDT have interviewed
workers, both individually and as teams, to enable written outputs to be
produced, for others a combination of all these methods has been used. However,
all have reflected on the impact of their project on the building of social capital.
Once again, it was crucial for the ARDT to be flexible and work with the
projects in a way that best suited them.

Other than for the workshops, no formal evaluation of the ARDT's role
with the projects has been undertaken. It must be said that some workers
found the burden of evaluation heavy. A few resented the requirements to
evaluate their work in terms of the building of social capital and found it very
time consuming. However, most projects have clearly appreciated the role, finding

that it has facilitated their understanding of social capital and enabled them to capture the learning from their project using appropriate methods:

> Methods were built into the consultation with local young people to ensure that the evaluation methods were appropriate for the local community. (quoted in Fleming and Boeck, 2002b, p 6)

> Your approach to working with us is really down to earth, and you understand the issues we face as workers. You have made good links between the formal requirements of SARP and the reality of our work. (Fleming and Boeck, 2002b, p 6)

Conclusion

It is our experience that, despite its critics, social capital can be fruitfully combined with social action to give a useful insight into the impact and effect of work within communities. Social capital provides the possibility of being specific about the outcomes one is looking to achieve in work with communities and also encourages people to consider the processes by which they achieve change or deliver services (Jochum, 2003, p 33). However, we have also found that project workers and community members require support in this process. The process of negotiating the relevance and meaning of social capital to specific situations can be complex. The SARP project in Nottingham also showed the importance of sharing knowledge, understanding and experience within and between projects using the concept of social capital to inform the development and evaluation of their practice.

In spite of this positive experience, our work has not been able to address issues of how sustainable this approach is. Like most current initiatives, the SARP funding was short term and the Centre's contract was just for 18 months. It is the nature of such contract work that it is hard to get a long-term view of change. In Nottingham, a group of people from the SARP board continue to meet: the After-SARP Group looks at how to build on the work of the SARP and promote discussion and debate about social capital with the local and health authorities[2].

However, in conclusion the authors can offer some recommendations, drawn from the people involved in this project, of how to encourage sustainability:

* Offer training to local people, community members and workers about social capital.
* Employ local people or community members as workers.
* Adopt a flexible and responsive management style.
* Work with funders to help them see the relevance of qualitative information and analysis of processes as well as quantitative data.
* Provide long-term funding for community initiatives.

Overview

- The concept of social capital informed by the principles and processes of social action can be a useful tool for participative evaluation of community-based projects.
- Social capital enables communities to formulate aims and consider processes through which these might be achieved.
- Community evaluators often require support with the complex processes of applying the relevance of social capital to specific situations.
- The Social Action Research Project (SARP) in Nottingham highlighted the need to share information between projects using the concept of social capital.
- More long-term investment is needed to explore the usefulness of our social capital framework with communities. A participative evaluation approach is a necessary part of this process.

Notes

[1] These handouts were informed by the work of Feurstein (1986), The Voluntary Action Unit, Northern Ireland (1997) and the work of Kirby (1999) and Ward (1997) for the Joseph Rowntree Foundation, for example. All these publications offer insights into how to undertake participative evaluation.

[2] The SARP was funded by the Health Development Agency (HDA) until March 2002. There are a number of written and visual outputs produced by the Nottingham projects themselves, the ARDT and others commissioned by Nottingham SARP to write on specific aspects of social capital development. All are available from the HDA website (www.social-action.org.uk/sarp/advancedsearch.asp) or from the Centre for Social Action, De Montfort University, Leicester LE1 9BH.

References

Boeck, T. and Fleming, J. (2002) *Social capital and the Nottingham Social Action Research Project*, Nottingham: Nottingham Primary Care Trust, SARP.

Boeck, T., McCullough, P. and Ward, D. (2001) 'Increasing social capital to combat social exclusion. The social action contribution', in A. Matthies, K. Narhi and D. Ward (eds) *The eco-social approach in social work*, Jyvaskyla: Sophi, pp 84-107

Bourdieu, P. (1997) 'The forms of capital', in A. Halsey, H. Lauder, P. Brown and A. Stuart Wells (eds) *Education, culture, economy and society*, Oxford: Oxford University Press, pp 46-58.

Campbell, C. (1999) *Social capital and health*, London: HEA.

Campbell, C. and McLean, C. (2002) 'Social capital, social exclusions and health: factors shaping African–Caribbean participation in local community networks', in C. Swann and A. Morgan (eds) *Social capital and health: Insights from qualitative research*, London: Health Development Agency, pp 29-46.

Coleman, J. (1990) *Foundations of social theory*, Cambridge: Belknap Press.

Erben, R., Franzkowiak, P. and Wenzel, E. (2000) 'People empowerment vs. social capital. From health promotion to social marketing', *Health Promotion Journal of Australia*, vol 9, no 3, pp 79-82.

Feurstein, M. (1986) *Evaluating development and community programmes with participants*, London: Macmillan.

Fleming, J. and Boeck, T. (2002a) *KISS: Knowledge and information on sexual health and sexuality*, Nottingham: Nottingham Primary Care Trust, SARP.

Fleming, J. and Boeck, T. (2002b) *The work of the Action Research Development Team*, Nottingham: Nottingham City Primary Care Trust, SARP.

Fleming, J. and Ward, D. (1999) 'Research as empowerment', in W. Shera and L. Wells (eds) *Empowerment practice in social work: Developing richer conceptual foundations*, Toronto: Canadian Scholars Press, pp 370-90.

Forbes, A. and Wainwright, S. (2001) 'On the methodological, theoretical and philosophical context of health inequalities research: a critique', *Social Science & Medicine*, vol 53, pp 801-16.

Green, J. (2003) 'Sexual health, social capital and social action', *Youth Action*, no 79, pp 12-13.

Jochum, V. (2003) *Social capital: Beyond the theory*, London: NCVO.

Kilpatrick, S., Field, J. and Falk, I. (2003) 'Social capital: an analytical tool for exploring lifelong learning and community development', *British Educational Journal*, vol 29, no 3, pp 417-33.

Kirby, P. (1999) *Involving young researchers: How to enable young people to design and conduct research*, York: Joseph Rowntree Foundation.

Morrow, V. (2001) *Networks and neighbourhoods: Children's and young people's perspectives*, London: Health Development Agency.

Morrow, V. (2002) 'Children's experiences of "community" implications of social capital discourses', in C. Swann and A. Morgan (eds) *Social capital and health: Insights from qualitative research*, London: Health Development Agency, pp 9-28.

Mullander, A. and Ward, D. (1991) *Self directed groupwork: Users take action for empowerment*, London: Whiting and Birch.

Muntaner, C., Lynch, J. and Davey Smith, G. (2000) 'Social capital and the third way in public health', *Critical Public Health*, vol 10, no 2, pp 107-24.

Oakley, P. (1990) 'The evaluation of social development', in D. Marsden and P. Oakley (eds) *Evaluating social development projects*, Oxford: Oxfam.

Portes, A. (1998) 'Social capital: its origins and applications in modern sociology', *American Sociological Review*, vol 24, pp 1-24.

Putnam, R. (2000) *Bowling alone: Collapse and revival of American communities*, New York: Simon and Schuster.

Voluntary Activity Unit (1997a) *Monitoring and evaluation of community development in Northern Ireland*, Belfast: Department of Health and Social Services.

Voluntary Activity Unit (1997b) *Measuring community development in Northern Ireland: A handbook for practitioners*, Belfast: Department of Health and Social Services.

Ward, L. (1997) *Seen and heard – Involving disabled children and young people in research and development projects*, York: Joseph Rowntree Foundation.

Woolcock, M. (1998) 'Social capital and economic development: towards a theoretical synthesis and policy framework', *Theory and Society*, vol 27, pp 151–208.

FIFTEEN

Learning the art of evaluation: presume the presence of politics

Georgie Parry-Crooke and Cathy Sullivan

Introduction

In tandem with the expansion of evaluation activity across all sectors has come an increased demand for teaching and training which involves those who will become 'external' evaluators and those whose main interest is in participatory and self-evaluation within organisations. In the development of academic courses, as well as a wide range of other courses, which aim to convey succinctly the essence of evaluation as both theory and practice, the characteristics associated with evaluation activities may be seen as central to achieving agreed learning objectives. The nature of the interactions and contributions of evaluators and other social actors within individual settings and contexts (from inception and design to execution and emergence of any evaluation outcomes) are important to an understanding of evaluation. Within the experience of evaluators, attempts to elucidate praxis therefore take their place alongside consideration of evaluation principles and theory in addressing the challenge of how to develop effective learning and teaching on this topic.

The discussion presented here is concerned with reflections on learning and teaching about one specific dimension of theory and practice that holds a key to understanding evaluation – that is, *the political*. It does not describe the political effects of the process or findings from a 'real' evaluation, nor does it discuss the substantive political implications of different types of evaluation outcome. Its focus is how the politics of evaluation feature in learning and teaching. Where and how do the politics of evaluation come to the fore? The politics of evaluation in this context operate at macro- and micro-levels and need to be understood as the "plurality of perspectives and the existence of competing interest groups" (Clarke, 1999, p 19), or as Alkin (1990, p 51) states, "every evaluation is a political act, political in the sense that there is continuing competition for stakes among the clients of an evaluation".

If evaluation is agreed to be an inherently political activity (through a commitment to change, by making judgements or providing the information on which judgements about policies, programmes and projects will be made) as argued by Pawson and Tilley among others (1997), where do politics find expression in the learning environment? If it is further assumed that politics do have a bearing on how those new to evaluation learn about the process and practices involved, we would argue there are a number of different possible routes by which this takes place.

First, those who participate in courses will frequently come from politicised environments, including health, social welfare and education. Second, the range of material presented to them is likely to contain some explicit description of individual and collective experience of situations where politics have been highlighted as influential in the process and outcome of evaluation. Third, participants will often be aware of the institutional processes in place within their learning or work environments that may be useful and successful or equally be undermined by the politics of the environment. This third route for the entry of the political also points to a distinctive issue for evaluation courses delivered in contemporary higher education institutions in the context of, what could be described as, predominantly 'performance cultures'. In addition to student satisfaction surveys and the use made of their findings, other educational quality assurance procedures or one-off evaluations may surface directly or indirectly within the students' course experience, together with their associated local institutional political contexts. This often leads to a particular way in which the institutional environment where teaching and learning takes place affects how students make sense of the politics of evaluation.

This chapter, through an exploration of key interrelated areas, examines some of the issues which have emerged from discussions we have held to review the way in which evaluation is taught at London Metropolitan University (North Campus). One such issue has been to determine how the politics of evaluation are threaded through while underpinning the courses and supervision provided to students undertaking a Master's degree in evaluation and social research (and other participants attending stand-alone courses). The areas are as follows:

- *student expectations* (the extent to which they are met by course design and content);
- *incorporating the political* (examples of our current strategies for addressing micro- and macro-politics); and
- *aspects of politics* (those we have yet to capture).

Student expectations

In order to make sense of student expectations, it is useful to acknowledge that, in our experience, those who consider embarking on a full Master's programme or who wish to attend short courses in evaluation are most usually in paid work within statutory and non-statutory organisations. Many are already involved in evaluation in some way, either through commissioning services or using evaluation in policy development. However, some arrive with the perception that policy development and its implementation is a simple and transparent process of change influenced by evaluation findings. Others may come to evaluation without the language or skills of research methodology yet wanting a 'takeaway toolkit' to be provided despite the recognition that "evaluation research is more than the application of methods. It is also a political and managerial activity" (Rossi and Freeman, 1993, p 15). Still others may resist the possibility that evaluation itself is subject to the same influences and vagaries of policy, programme and project development.

Do these students get what they hoped for? To date, module evaluations suggest that they get both less and more. The less is the perceived absence of research methods teaching within evaluation modules. This is deliberate on our part. Within an emerging discipline or trans-discipline of evaluation (Scriven, 1991), there are many models or approaches including goal-free, goal-focused, participatory and realistic among others too many to list here. Each of these could make use of the full range of research 'tools' or techniques available and some will inevitably adopt a multi-method design. However, when working towards achieving an understanding of the principles and practice of evaluation, the emphasis must be placed on unpacking what these are, rather than concentrating on the tools of data collection and analysis. A student who designs an excellent questionnaire does not, through this, demonstrate an understanding of evaluation.

Providing students with more than they hoped for, however, relates to the contexts covered. These include the opportunity to meet with evaluators, discuss live examples and give thought to issues of politics and ethics in the evaluation process. Some of the ways we work are described later in this chapter.

Incorporating the political: examples of our current strategies

To successfully convey the message, providers of courses and teaching in evaluation may need to explicitly address the political dimensions. Published evaluation findings are rarely presented in such a way that the politics surface in reports, although the use of case studies goes some way to circumventing or uncovering the 'real story'. This, however, may have implications in terms of confidentiality and other ethical issues. In addition, offering description and discussion of the range of evaluation approaches available and their appropriate use is important thereby avoiding or, better, making explicit any methodological or political bias on the part of course facilitators. Here we give three examples of how we have attempted to address these issues.

The first is through constant and repetitious reference to values, politics and ethics throughout the formal content of modules. This ethos underpins the whole approach to modules, yet it can still remain implicit, or seemingly so, rather than explicit through sessions which address these specific topics. The following examples illustrate our attempts to elaborate on such general referencing with more focused pedagogic strategies, drawing out the political texture of both the practical and structural features of evaluation practice.

Thus our next example is to work with groups of students to create person specifications ('Who is the evaluator?') and job descriptions ('What will the evaluator do?'). The purpose of this type of exercise is to think beyond the application of methods or toolkit approaches to a discussion which often leads to the identification of key qualities including negotiation skills; interpersonal skills; comprehension of organisational strategy and planning, and so on. Developing a job description leads to a consideration of tasks which will usually include defining evaluation boundaries, making sense of sometimes competing perspectives and an acknowledgement of the need to go below the surface.

A further example is an attempt to facilitate a broader discussion of values within evaluation practice such as an examination of 'performativity' within public services and policy review frameworks. This is an important dimension often embedded within introductions to and development of models of evaluation and associated activities aspiring to or claiming to provide evaluative statements about programmes and services within the public sector. In examining the range of such contemporary approaches characterised by more continuous, integrated assessment of programmes and services, the notion of performance is discussed explicitly in teaching and located in context. This hopefully serves to illustrate the importance of analysing performance assessment as more than a set of objective tools, techniques and procedures and identifying it as a social construct. The specific issue of performance and performativity is developed when examining the range of models and frameworks in use and considering their status as evaluation, and their relationship to evaluative activities. As part of this strategy conceptual linkages to a wider socio-political context are explored.

Box 15.1: Examples of issues discussed on the Master's programme

- *Policy origins of evaluation* (is this primarily concerned with quality agendas and economic conditions?)
- *Underlying assumptions and perspectives* (for example, quasi-market approaches and public choice theory, or theories around new managerialism and governance)
- *Pursuit of 'standards'* (thereby viewing evaluation in the context of enhancing measurability and comparability)
- *Purposes of evaluation* (including different meanings of accountability, and forms of legitimacy)
- *Grounds and criteria in operation* (what are the determinants of success and, indeed, whose success is it?)
- *Potential alternative aspects of performance* (would this need to include values, local knowledge and continuity?)
- *The utility of evaluation* (with consideration of performance assessment in use)

But what does it all mean if not located within specific case examples, which in turn leads to concerns about confidentiality? It may be that these broader evaluation issues can be transformed using 'real' evaluation. One example of this was a specific evaluation study in which an issue emerged that related to the context for the evaluation: a change in the staffing and management arrangements of an organisation which raised questions about how two post-holders worked together. This shift generated changes in the extent to which they linked their work programmes, and in turn had implications for an evaluation plan being developed around certain areas of the work. There was a division of work between the two post-holders, which had some basis in service need and different ethnic communities, but it was also historical: a permanent post and then a new short-contract, separately funded post. The latter post was part of a demand for more coordinated approaches to working with communities and so implied close working with the other similar post anyway. But funding boundaries, and experience of previous evaluation activities, restricted evaluation planning to specific areas of the work. The temporary shift of the permanent post to be managed by the second post-holder's line manager while a vacancy was filled resulted in closer planning of programmes.

A second issue that emerged from this in thinking about evaluation was that both post-holders identified the evaluation with the evaluation of posts, and not with the evaluation of a programme of work. They reported concern at this, and given that at this point they were now planning a specific coordinated project together, they wanted the evaluation of this project to be undertaken separately to other aspects of the evaluation already anticipated. If this did not happen, the permanent post-holder was concerned that his or her own input to any activity would be invisible, not recognised or would be attributed to the contract post-holder.

Another relevant dimension forming part of the context here was that the coordination and project planning were behind schedule and more funding was desired than was available, so a further funding bid was being put together. It was an expectation of the post-holders preparing this that an evaluation strategy be included to add clout to the bid. They were also hoping to use discussions about a desirable evaluation with their evaluation consultant as a way of persuading a line manager to agree to apply for further funding. The line manager was concerned about delays and, indeed, about incurring further delays if they waited for the additional appointments envisaged with enhanced funding. So, in this case, the evaluation was inextricably bound up in the politics of management of work.

Evaluation itself can also be seen as a tool for visibility. The line manager accepted the need for a distinct evaluation focus on the coordinated project but wished to carefully restrict the inclusion of other permanent post-holder activities in this area (which might legitimately be considered as relevant) due to a priority to evaluate contract-funded work.

How did the evaluation consultant respond? By agreeing that, if a work aim is to achieve more coordination in activities, then the evaluation should reflect this in its boundary/scoping, but also that it is not possible to evaluate something until its happening, and that evaluation is not responsible for determining the programme content even though it may influence its direction. So, here in this example, it appeared that the political issues related to the following:

- drawing the boundaries of evaluation;
- the use of evaluation as a tool among staff and managers negotiating work plans;
- the identification of evaluation with assessment of the post-holders not the activity; and
- the politics of profile yielded by evaluation.

The issue for the evaluation consultant was avoiding inappropriate use of their role while maintaining the relationship of openness and trust needed with all staff concerned in order to continue supporting their evaluation planning as commissioned.

An example such as the one described earlier in this chapter provides an excellent opportunity to illustrate how and where politics enter into the evaluation process. Nevertheless, what must be considered when illustrating aspects of evaluation with a case study in teaching is the difficulty of anonymising sufficiently, and the importance of doing so when discussing political issues. The presentation here has removed any reference to topic/subject area or type of organisation and by doing so its use in teaching is questionable in the absence of important context material. The necessary reduction in specific information offered, in order to achieve anonymity, makes it more difficult to illustrate either how the political context operates or how competing interests and perspectives are played out in particular evaluation settings. Political contexts are created through the detail of day-to-day practices and relationships within and between organisations and individuals.

The construction of hypothetical case studies is one way of developing this approach, enabling a more anonymised demonstration of typical or important political issues by drawing upon a series of 'real' evaluation stories. However, the provision of case studies to indicate what happened (real), or what might happen (hypothetical), in evaluation practice, while useful, is essentially a descriptive exercise which remains limited in its scope as a tool to support learning for action and reflection. They take time to introduce and discuss productively in a class context, yet need to be balanced within curriculum priorities alongside delivery using more generalised approaches to topics. They are also constrained in their capacity to deliver insights for students about their own responses as evaluators to situations they may face, what the options and choices available to them might be, and how they would actually respond to the politics of evaluation.

Alternative strategies need to be devised which can help students to distil the essence of politics within evaluation through exploration of a range of contexts while using their own practical experience as a positive learning tool. It is important, in our view, that learning and teaching about evaluation move beyond just hearing about what other evaluators do (both real and hypothetical) and one way in which we have attempted to achieve this has been through the introduction of workshop activities. These, while drawing on 'real' evaluation situations, invite students to consider their response to a specified scenario. In relation to the micro-politics of evaluation, they might be asked: what would you do on meeting a key stakeholder (with whom there had been some difficulties during an ongoing evaluation) at a social occasion? Alternatively, they are presented with a brief to develop a proposal to evaluate a safer communities initiative within an urban area likely to involve varied stakeholders including residents, the police and those perceived to make the community less safe. Both of these exercises would be based on existing projects but used in ways which do not 'give the game away' and could therefore potentially jeopardise the evaluator or others involved in the evaluation. These types of activity involve students in a dynamic and active process – facing the challenges perhaps before they are required to face them in the 'real' setting.

Aspects of politics: those we have yet to capture

The conclusion of the real evaluation story above provides illustration of the areas we do not believe we have captured yet in teaching and learning. As previously noted, we are aware that there are many ways in which it is not or may not be possible to always convey the nature of politics within evaluation through what are essentially class-based experiences. However, there are many areas to consider (Box 15.2).

Box 15.2: Aspects of politics to consider in teaching

- Defining *boundaries* of programme evaluation. What are the influences of organisational structures, and what kinds of relationships and processes need to be unpacked?
- The use of evaluation as a *political* tool in organisations, thereby appearing to enhance bids and reflect the status of work responsibilities.
- Equating evaluation with *posts* rather than *activities*, suggesting concern about cross-cutting programmes and shifting commitments.
- Perceived problems *in communication*, where expectations of evaluation may differ and individuals are required to deal with responses to evaluation as political statements.

However, it seems that this is not just a question of building in more issues for student discussion as there are a number of reasons which suggest that this may not be appropriate in all settings. The following are some examples.

Confidentiality

There is a level of descriptive detail needed to identify the subtle and sometimes complex reality which shapes perceptions of evaluation by stakeholders, but which may easily breach confidentiality of participants.

Flux

There will almost invariably be a shifting context for evaluation where internal or external changes can alter the way in which an evaluation is perceived, and some aspect of the setting or relationships can suddenly become sensitive. This may be coupled with the idea of the elusiveness of the experience of evaluation as negotiation.

Student familiarity with organisational context

To many, the organisational environment and inherent politics may be unfamiliar territory. Appreciation of the principle of stakeholder interests is fundamental to learning and teaching in evaluation, but students often bring the experience of only one of these to their learning, and perhaps none. Conveying the diversity and validity of such interests and perspectives within the evaluation context in a constructive rather than seemingly negative manner can be difficult. In some cases, there may be limited experience of organisational or service settings in general to underpin teaching-led illustration of micro- or wider political processes.

We conclude by suggesting that the 'politics of evaluation' represent more than a single and therefore tokenistic course topic. They underpin every aspect of evaluation – from commissioning, design and delivery through to dissemination – and as a result need to underpin how evaluation is introduced to those keen to become evaluators, enhancing rather than detracting from or being obscured in the evaluation process. The challenge is: how do we do so?

Overview

- Alongside the expansion of evaluation activity has been a growth in demand for the teaching and training of would-be evaluators.
- Course content should include political as well as methodological issues.
- The case study approach is one means of introducing students to political aspects. However, a potential difficulty with this is ensuring the data is adequately anonymised. There are also limitations with the use of hypothetical case studies.
- An alternative approach would be to invite students to consider their own responses to specific scenarios. This would use real projects but in such a way as to avoid jeopardising anyone involved in the evaluation.
- There are a number of political dimensions to evaluation that have not yet been captured in teaching and should be considered.

References

Alkin, M. (1990) 'Debates on evaluation', in A. Clarke with R. Dawson (eds) (1999) *Evaluation research*, London: Sage Publications, p 19.

Clarke, A. with Dawson, R. (1999) *Evaluation research*, London: Sage Publications.

Pawson, R. and Tilley, N. (1997) *Realistic evaluation*, London: Sage Publications.

Rossi, P.H. and Freeman, H.E. (1993) *Evaluation: A systematic approach*, San Francisco, CA: Sage Publications.

Scriven, M. (1991) *Evaluation thesaurus* (4th edn), London: Sage Publications.

What the politics of evaluation implies

Susan Balloch and David Taylor

Evaluation has become a routine exercise in many central government programmes and increasingly is a requirement for voluntary and community groups receiving project funding. The pragmatic monitoring that this requires has often encouraged a concentration on the techniques of audit at the expense of reflection on the significance of evaluation, its relationship to research and the theoretical concepts on which it is often shakily based. This volume has tried to redress some of this imbalance through a wide-ranging discussion of the politics of evaluation grounded in real examples.

The conference from which this volume grew expressed considerable scepticism and pessimism about the politics of evaluation. The audience was concerned at the obvious inadequacy of the rationalist model that assumed 'knowledge' acquired from evaluation could be fed neatly into strategic planning and policy implementation. Concluding the day's proceedings, Michael Hill reflected, however, that suspicion of the aims and intentions of agencies involved in neighbourhood renewal, youth justice, social services assessments and health partnerships – to name a few of the major issues discussed in this volume – should not make us apologetic about being evaluators.

Drawing on his own research (Hill and Hupe, 2003), Hill argued that recognising that evaluation and assessment procedures are themselves social constructs operating in a politically charged environment did not prevent us either from attempting a rational analysis of policy nor attempting to learn from experience. To want to ask honest questions about 'what works' and to try to 'speak truth to power' can still be defended as honourable and important activities. To be fair, as Rowe and Taylor (Chapter Thirteen of this volume) point out, New Labour's use of 'what works'-type language does suggest a clear intention to learn from evaluation in order to replicate good practice and thus improve public services. Yet to understand 'what works', we need to know so much more: why things work, for whom they work and what features of any programme have the most impact. With this in mind we are able to identify some ways forward which will take the politics of evaluation into account while supporting evaluation as a valuable and viable form of research.

Acknowledging the politics of evaluation

Involve the central actors

First, we should note that no evaluation of any worth can afford to neglect the views of the central actors, be they young people, residents of a neighbourhood renewal area, parents or others. These groups should take precedence over practitioners and the evaluators themselves. However, because dominant discourses tend to be rooted in the managerialist/consumerist model, service users often feel their contribution is tokenistic. Thus, there is increased questioning about the purpose of user involvement in evaluation – is this really to change and improve people's lives or merely to add to a body of knowledge which might even be used in an oppressive or disempowering manner?

Although there have been increasing requirements for greater user involvement in research and evaluation under New Labour, the empowering potential of user involvement depends on the nature, process, purpose and methodology of the evaluation process. The chapters in Part Two of this book in particular have shown that although participatory evaluation is difficult to achieve, creative thinking can surmount many of the immediate obstacles by using less rigorous data. Participatory evaluation can be used to build skills and knowledge in communities and ensure locally relevant questions are addressed by using less traditional and more inclusive techniques such as photography, sculpture, textiles, storytelling, social mapping and drama. Importantly, however, being participatory involves more than a technique or approach: rather, it depends on an attitude characterised by the willingness to share decision-making and power.

Challenge prescribed indicators

Second, as Squires and Measor and Ambrose (Chapters One and Two of this volume) all emphasise, it is the duty of social scientists undertaking evaluations to challenge research processes that subordinate informed local evaluation and silence issues which fall outside defined technical boundaries. Challenging prescribed indicators serves to improve power-sharing as those specified from above may not cover the concerns of service users or residents. Ideally, structure, process and outcome indicators should be separately identified and emerge from a participative process.

Although central government is committed to prescribed indicators, even in the face of severe criticism, there are some signs, at least in social services, that government is ready to modify these and include locally determined elements. However, evaluations commissioned within the restraints of a 'Best Value' culture focused on goals and outcomes can prevent an evaluator from asking why a programme works. The approach is not conducive to user involvement as it enables only the involvement of relatively empowered service users. In Platzer's opinion (Chapter Five), advocacy projects need to be distanced from the Best

Value outcome-oriented culture in order to have the opportunity to explore processes which empower service users.

Take a positive approach

Third, we need to consider the advantages of a positive approach as opposed to a cynicism that might encourage us to emphasise primarily what goes wrong or reject evaluation altogether. The appreciative inquiry technique advocated by Cousin, Cousin and Deepwell (Chapter Seven) is one example on which to draw. Rather than adopting a negative stance, their type of evaluation requires a collaborative effort to discover that which is healthy, successful and positive in organisational life. In the course of this, we are advised to explore not only outcomes, but the processes by which outcomes are achieved. In many instances these can prove more important than the end goals themselves.

Further examples of a positive approach may also be found in Part Three of this volume, where the contributions reflect on the potential contribution that evaluations may make to organisational change. Evaluations have successfully used mixed methods to establish quantitative and qualitative data on partnership activities. They have identified not just the internal and external factors impeding partnership working but also those positive factors that can support it. These include clarifying aims and objectives, establishing commitment, ensuring continuity of personnel, guaranteeing funding arrangements and creating processes for shared learning. Recognising the domination of political factors in partnerships, and the implicit political role of the evaluator, does not preclude useful reflection on what can work.

Share the learning

As Rowe and Taylor state (Chapter Thirteen of this volume), "Evaluation makes little sense unless it is understood as part of a learning process", contributing to decision-making and organisational learning and providing transferable knowledge. While the former are not so difficult to achieve, there are particular difficulties in transferring learning from one locality to another, particularly in the context of community-led regeneration initiatives where change cannot be simply attributed to a particular intervention but must be considered in its political, economic and cultural dimensions. Here, it seems that shared learning is more likely to be achieved through the use of common concepts, such as Boeck and Fleming's (Chapter Fourteen) social capital framework for evaluation, than through comparable findings.

Finally, then, we can say with some conviction that evaluation is a rewarding, worthwhile and creative activity. Conceptually, it has much to gain from understanding both the political context and the political constructs involved, recognising policy processes and political demands that drive activities. Pragmatically, it requires the evaluator to master not just quantitative and qualitative research processes but also to develop the political acumen of a skilled negotiator and the sensitivities of an experienced counsellor. It is definitely not for the faint-hearted.

References

Hill, M. and Hupe, P. (2002) *Implementing public policy*, London: Sage Publications.

Index

Page references for figures and tables are in *italics*; those for notes are followed by n

Cohen, S. 33
Coleman, J. 120, 224, 225
Commission for Health Improvement 146
Commission for Healthcare Audit and Inspection (CHAI) 70, 146
Commission for Social Care Inspection (CSCI) 58, 64, *65*, 70, 72, 146
communicative approach 191-2
community 207
Community Care 67
Community Care (Delayed Discharges) Act 2003 144-5
Community Health Councils (CHCs) 167, 168
community health work 223-35
community newsletters 121
compliance 23, 35-6
Comprehensive Performance Assessment (CPA) 63-4
Compulsory Competitive Tendering (CCT) 58
confidentiality 126, 243, 246
constructivists *see* social constructionists
consumerist approach 78-80, 84
Cooke, B. 77
Cooper, K. 148
Corbin, J. 110
councils with social services responsibilities (CSSRs) 11-12, 57, 60
Cousin, Glynis 110-11, 114
Cousin, Judith 111, 112-13
Cousins, J.B. 6
Crawley 155
Crawshaw, P. 122, 125
Creative Learning Links 104-6
creative methods 101-7, 111, 114-16
crime 32-3
Crime and Disorder Act 1998 21
Croft, S. 77
Crompton, A. 3
cross-charging 144-5
Cusick, J. 120

D

Dads and Lads project 120, 122
Daly, Mary 4
data-driven evaluation 110
David, M. 125
Dawson, R. 88-9
De Montfort University 227
Deepwell, Frances 111, 114
Delivery and Improvement Statements 61

democratic approach 79-80, 84
Department for Education and Skills (DfES) 70, 120, 129
Department for the Environment, Transport and the Regions (DETR)
Modern local government 58
Modernising local government 58
National Strategy for Neighbourhood Renewal 97
New Deal for Communities 194, 197, 199
Department of Health (DH) 70, 142
care trusts 136, 144
internal monitoring 164, 168
local accountability 140
Modernising social services 57, 59, 71
National Service Framework for Older People 161, 168
A new approach to social services performance 60, 61, 63, 71
The new NHS 59, 138
Performance Assessment Framework 60, 66, 67, 72n
performance indicators 63
winter pressures 153, 154, 158, 159
Department of Transport, Local Government and the Regions (DTLR) 63, 64
design 113
destiny 113
Devanney, C. 210, 216, 219
Devolving Decision-Making 67
Dewson, S. 109
disabled people's movement 77, 81
discourse 29-30, 80-1
discovery 113
drama 103
dream 113

E

East Brighton New Deal for Communities (eb4U) 11
additional indicators 46, 53-4
community-specified indicators 46
criteria for indicators 42, *43*
local consultations 45-6
shortcomings in indicators 42, *44-5*
Eating Disorders Association (EDA) 122
EKOS 208, 209, 210, 211, 212, 215, 216, 217
El Ansari, W. 147
emancipation 81
employment 175-85

Y

Also available from The Policy Press

What works?
Evidence-based policy and practice in public services
Edited by Huw T.O. Davies, Sandra M. Nutley and Peter C. Smith

"... excellent ... an intelligent and enjoyable state-of-the-art review of the issues involved in doing research to inform policy and practice." *Dr Gordon Marshall, Chief Executive, Economic and Social Research Council*

"... extremely valuable ... It serves as useful material for teachers of evaluation or policy analysis, and for those educating future evidence-based practitioners. Managers within statutory and non-statutory agencies will also find much of value." *New Zealand Journal of Social Policy*

"... interesting and informative ... should be widely read and prescribed in social policy classes." *Journal of Sociology and Social Welfare*

This book provides a timely and novel contribution to the debate surrounding the role of 'evidence' in specific public policy areas. It explores the creation, dissemination and use of evidence within the areas of healthcare, education, criminal justice, social care, welfare, housing, transport and urban renewal.

Paperback £18.99 US$29.95 ISBN 1 86134 191 1
Hardback £45.00 US$81.00 ISBN 1 86134 192 X
216 x 148mm 396 pages July 2000

A more equal society?
New Labour, poverty, inequality and exclusion
Edited by John Hills and Kitty Stewart

"A comprehensive and authoritative analysis of what New Labour's welfare reforms have achieved to date." *Alan Deacon, School of Sociology and Social Policy, University of Leeds*

This major new book provides, for the first time, a detailed evaluation of policies on poverty and social exclusion since 1997, and their effects. Bringing together leading experts in the field, it considers the challenges the government has faced, the policies chosen and the targets set in order to assess results. Drawing on research from the Centre for Analysis of Social Exclusion, and on external evaluations, the book:

- asks how children, older people, poor neighbourhoods, ethnic minorities and other vulnerable groups have fared under New Labour;
- seeks to assess the government both on its own terms – in meeting its own targets – and according to alternative views of social exclusion.

Paperback £19.99 US$29.95 ISBN 1 86134 577 1
Hardback £55.00 US$79.95 ISBN 1 86134 578 X
240 x 172mm 408 pages January 2005
CASE Studies on Poverty, Place and Policy Series

Partnership working
Policy and practice
Edited by Susan Balloch and Marilyn Taylor, Cities Research Centre, University of the West of England

"This is an excellent book and should be read by anyone involved or thinking of getting involved in partnership working ... one of the essential items to cover in making partnerships succeed is reading this book from cover to cover."
Journal of Interprofessional Care

"... instructive and inspiring." *Widening Participation and Lifelong Learning*

This stimulating book analyses experiences of partnerships in different policy fields, identifying the theoretical and practical impediments to making partnership work and critically evaluating the advantages and disadvantages for those involved. Going beyond the confines of statutory partnerships it addresses other important forms of collaboration between voluntary, private and statutory sectors and service users and community and minority groups.

Paperback £19.99 US$32.50 ISBN 1 86134 220 9
Hardback £50.00 US$69.95 ISBN 1 86134 347 7
216 x 148mm 304 pages July 2001

Public policy for the 21st century
Social and economic essays in memory of
Henry Neuburger
Edited by Neil Fraser and John Hills

"... a welcome volume ... a book for anyone seriously
interested in contemporary economic and social affairs."
Roger Berry MP, Tribune

"Short, concise and analytical essays that deal in different
but always interesting ways with contemporary issues of central relevance to
students of public and social policy. They stand as valuable and readable
contubutions in themsleves and considered tributes to the man to whom this
book is dedicated." *Journal of Social Policy*

Public policy for the 21st century draws together a collection of lively and
authoritative essays on the future of public policy by distinguished academics in
the field. Compiled in memory of Henry Neuburger, a leading economic analyst
and adviser whose career spanned half a dozen government departments and
included advising the Labour Party leadership during the 1980s, the essays
together form an excellent introduction to key issues in contemporary policy
making.

Paperback £19.99 US$32.50 ISBN 1 86134 267 5
Hardback £50.00 US$69.95 ISBN 1 86134 268 3
216 x 148mm 288 pages December 2000

To order further copies of this publication or any other Policy Press titles please contact:

In the UK and Europe:
Marston Book Services, PO Box 269, Abingdon,
Oxon, OX14 4YN, UK
Tel: +44 (0)1235 465500
Fax: +44 (0)1235 465556
Email: direct.orders@marston.co.uk

In the USA and Canada:
ISBS, 920 NE 58th Street, Suite 300, Portland, OR
97213-3786, USA
Tel: +1 800 944 6190 (toll free)
Fax: +1 503 280 8832
Email: info@isbs.com

In Australia and New Zealand:
DA Information Services, 648 Whitehorse Road
Mitcham, Victoria 3132, Australia
Tel: +61 (3) 9210 7777
Fax: +61 (3) 9210 7788
E-mail: service@dadirect.com.au

Further information about all of our titles can be
found on our website:

www.policypress.org.uk